MARRIAGE & FAMILY STEWARDSHIPS

MARRIAGE & FAMILY STEWARDSHIPS

Wesley R. Burr • Brenton G. Yorgason • Terry R. Baker

BOOKCRAFT • SALT LAKE CITY, UTAH

Library of Congress Catalog Card Number: 82-71670
ISBN 0-88494-460-3

First Printing, 1982

Lithographed in the United States of America
PUBLISHERS PRESS
Salt Lake City, Utah

To our wives:
Ruth, Margaret, and Patty

CONTENTS

PREFACE

In 1976 Elder Ezra Taft Benson gave several addresses in which he discussed the role of Brigham Young University and the Church Educational System. He commented:

> This university was built by the consecrated funds of the Church for the purpose that our youth could be taught the truth, both secular and spiritual. That commission places a great responsibility on both teacher and student. Of that unique commission, President Marion G. Romney has said:
>
> "The unique commission of the Brigham Young University has always been and now is threefold. First, to help you recognize that there are two sources of learning—one divine, the other human; second, to urge and inspire you students to drink deeply from both sources; and third to teach and train you to correctly distinguish between the learning of the world and revealed truth, that you may not be deceived in your search." *

Two of the authors heard these suggestions, and the third read them in the newspaper, and a seed was planted. The seed was nourished the way Alma taught in his sermon on testing ideas (Alma 32:28-32), and we learned that it was a good idea. We then began what we thought would be a few months of research and a few months of writing—to produce a textbook about marriage that integrated the truths learned from both spiritual and secular sources. The months turned into years, and the years taught us many things.

Some of the things we learned we had partially understood before, but we learned to understand them better. For example, we learned that when scientific and religious ideas fit together, like the pieces of a large puzzle, they have a certain order. The religious ideas provide the basic philosophy of life, the values, and the goals. They are the foundation of our thinking. The scientific ideas tend to complement these truths with more specific insights that help us find ways to attain the religious goals. The scientific findings help us know which ways of behaving will help us attain the religious ends most efficiently and with the least cost.

We also gained a deeper appreciation and understanding of how the Holy Spirit guides. Sometimes when we were pursuing an idea, we were impressed to read a certain journal or book, and we found information that helped complete the idea. At other times, we were overcome with a stupor of thought and felt a heavy and repressing feeling to stop and not include a particular idea or point of view. At other times, we were impressed to stop writing and seek guidance through prayer. Sometimes ideas would come to us individually or as a group, and we would have a deep feeling in the breast that the ideas should be included. We therefore believe that we have been aided in this project many times, and that the final product is better than it would have been if we had used only our own resources.

---

* "God's Hand in Our Nation's History." *Speeches of the Year,* 1975-76, Provo, Utah: Brigham Young University Press, p. 314. Similar thoughts also expressed in "The Gospel Teacher and His Message," an address to educators in the Church Educational System, September 17, 1976.

We are not suggesting that everything in this book is perfect. We have been limited by our perspectives, and the book reflects these limitations. We do, however, believe that the project has been aided in numerous places by inspiration, and we wish to testify to this and acknowledge our appreciation of it.

Some of the things we learned in this project were entirely new to us. For example:

1. We had to do a lot more pioneering than we thought would be necessary. There has been so little integration of religious and scientific thought in this area that we became modern pioneers, building bridges and crossing plains in ways that had never been done before.

2. It was easier to integrate some religious and scientific ideas than we had thought. Some of the terminology is almost identical, and at other times the only problem is that different terms are used to describe the same idea. This turned out to be a reassuring lesson.

3. It was more difficult to integrate some ideas than we thought. We know that the Lord "will yet reveal many great and important things pertaining to the kingdom of God" (Article of Faith 9), and this means that we have only a partial understanding of some religious truths. We also know that the social sciences are still young and that they have only begun to discover the truths they will eventually find. This means that in many areas we have to be tentative, and we cannot yet be sure how some truths and partial truths fit together.

4. Writing a book like this is a never-ending process. We could revise it and improve it forever. When we realized this, we decided that we would "keep to the task" until we were satisfied that the product would be useful to students, and we would then have it published. We think it is now ready. We realize, however, that the book may still have weaknesses. We hope that readers will be patient and helpful with these "mistakes of men" by calling them to our attention.

It is important for readers to know that this book is not an official statement of The Church of Jesus Christ of Latter-day Saints or of any of the organizations in the Church. The book discusses the Church's teachings and theology extensively, but the ideas in it should not be viewed as official or unofficial statements by Brigham Young University, the Church Educational System, or the Church. It is a book written by three authors who are trying to help young people in their marriages, and the authors are solely responsible for the content.

There are many who provided counsel and advice in this project. The authors are deeply grateful for their counsel and assistance, and the book is much better as a result of their suggestions. First, we are grateful to our previous students who have taught us many things and helped shape the ideas in this volume. Second, we appreciate the many colleagues who have provided guidance and support. These colleagues should not be held responsible for the book, but it would have been much less adequate without their assistance. Alphabetically, those who provided assistance are: Brent Barlow, Douglas Brinley, Carlfred Broderick, Kenneth L. Cannon, Richard C. Chidester, Larry Dahl, Henry B. Eyring, Jeffrey Holland, Thomas B. Mortensen, J. Joel Moss, Terrance D. Olson, George Pace, Spencer W. Palmer, Blaine R. Porter, Robert F. Stahmann, Darwin L. Thomas, and Robert K.

Thomas. Also, Debbie Cenatiempo and Jean Billings typed the manuscript several times, and appreciation is expressed to them.

We are also deeply grateful to our wives, who have participated in many ways in the preparation of this book. They have provided inspiration and encouragement in addition to invaluable advice and counsel. They have helped in writing some sections and in improving other parts. They have taught us many things about what it takes to create celestial marriages, and not only is the book better because of them, but more importantly, they have created more than a little joy and beauty in our marriages and lives.

THREE
BASIC
CONCEPTS

There are three concepts that you should understand before you read this text. These three terms provide a perspective, a set of lenses, that will enable you to better understand the later chapters. The concepts are

Stewardship

Systems

Principles

Let us examine what they mean, beginning with the concept of stewardship:

STEWARDSHIP

A steward is someone who is given the responsibility to take care of something. When you are given stewardship over something, you do not own it, but you are to manage and supervise it. For example, when you rent a house or a car, you temporarily have a stewardship over what you are renting. When you check a book out of a library, you have a stewardship over the book while it is entrusted to your care.

There are three main characteristics of a stewardship:

First, a stewardship involves decisions. The steward manages or controls something that belongs to someone else. The decisions are not made by the owner, but are the responsibility of the steward. The decisions are not easy or automatic, and many of them demand thought, analysis, and care. Some of them are also "dilemmas" in which choices have to be made between two or more desirable things. For example, you may have to choose between independence and dependence, or between freedom and restraint. You may have to choose whether to spend your money on an education or on clothes or on furniture—

because you don't have enough money to get all of them. Other decisions deal with time, because there are only twenty-four hours in a day and there isn't enough time to do everything you would like.

Second, a stewardship includes assuming the responsibility for what happens. The steward who makes good decisions receives the rewards or benefits of his wisdom. If he makes bad decisions, he must suffer the consequences. This process can be seen in the parable of the talents (Matthew 25:14-30). The servant who handled his talents (stewardship) wisely was given additional blessings, but the servant who did not make wise decisions lost his blessings.

Third, a stewardship includes considerable *freedom* because the owner or master is not present. The owner may occasionally visit or communicate with the steward to provide direction, and he may answer questions concerning the stewardship, but the owner does not interfere in the decisions because he has delegated them to the steward.

We can have stewardship over many different things. When the early Saints in this dispensation lived the united order, some of them were given certain amounts of land as their stewardships. Others were given stewardships over other things such as "literary concerns" (D&C 72:20).

It is helpful to think of *marriage as a stewardship.* Notice that it fits all the criteria. Each person is responsible for his marriage, but he does not own it. He has to make decisions and manage the marriage, and it offers a lot of freedom for individual decisions. Each person will be held accountable for what he does with his marriage. For the wise steward, marriage can become a celestial relationship, and it will continue in the next life. For the unwise steward, marriage will terminate at death, or even earlier in a divorce court. The idea of a "marital stewardship" will be a central idea in each of the later chapters, and we will learn some things that can help us be wise and capable stewards.

SYSTEM

What is a system? The dictionary defines it as "a set or arrangement of separate things organized into a whole." You can think of your body as a *system* of organs. You have a heart, lungs, bones, muscles, and nerves, all organized into a whole—and each part has a structure, function, and purpose. An automobile is also a system. It has tires, motor, steering wheel, seats, horn, and so forth, and all of the parts work together—sometimes. As most of us have learned, a small flaw in one part of the system can bring the whole system to a screeching halt. For example, a flat tire or empty gasoline tank stops the whole automobile system.

What about a flower garden? Is it a system? Certainly! It contains many parts that are organized into a whole. You place seeds in the ground, and a combination of rain, soil, fertilizer, cultivating, pruning, and tending produces beautiful and fragrant flowers. You put certain things into the garden system and get certain things out of it. In "systems" terminology, there are *inputs* and *outputs.* In a flower system, you put in seeds, cultivation, and watering, and nature puts in sunlight and soil. The outputs you receive from it are

Even a dating relationship is a system.

beauty, loveliness, fragrance, and an enhancement of the quality of your life. In your automobile system, you put in gasoline, oil, and money, money, money—and the outputs are transportation, fun, and work. And if you have a classy sports car, you can also get dates, recognition, attention, and acceptance by others.

What about marriage? Is it a system? It has many parts, such as two people, time, affection, love, tenderness, assistance, security, children, and more. And the parts are organized into a whole. As this book will demonstrate, marriage is a system, and it is useful to view it as such. When you look at marriage as a system, you can better understand some of the things that happen. For example, why do some marriages lose their luster and the partners become estranged from each other? In systems terminology, sometimes couples forget that a marriage needs inputs of courtesy, attention, affection, understanding, and love. Look at the flower garden: If you didn't water it, the flowers would die. In the same way, if a person doesn't nourish the love in his marriage, it, too, will die. Everyone needs to learn what types of inputs his marriage needs to produce the outputs that he wants—love, security, companionship, understanding, and closeness.

Your marriage system is different, however, from the other systems in your life. It lasts longer than most systems because it will still be with you in the next life. It is also more delicate and tender than most of your systems; some of its most important parts are love, tenderness, affection, and empathy. It is also one of your most important systems. You literally build your life around your marriage and family. They are the hub, the central system, the core of most of what you do in life.

The later chapters all build on the idea that *marriage is a system.* And as you view marriage as a complex and delicate system, you will learn some things you can do to be a wise *steward of your marital system.*

PRINCIPLES

Joseph Smith was once asked how he was able to govern his people so well. He responded that it was because he taught them correct principles and let them govern themselves. This book attempts to incorporate this approach by teaching correct principles about marriage.

Before we begin discussing principles, we must first be sure that we know what principles are. For example, do they have webbed feet? Are they green? Do they always end in a question mark? Are they the same as commandments?

What Are Principles?

Again, a definition: Principles are ideas that are stated in declarative sentences, and have the following five characteristics:
1. They are *laws* (or are at least *lawlike*).
2. They have two or more *variables.*
3. There is a *predictable relationship* between the variables.
4. They are *general.*
5. They are *universal.*

The following paragraphs explain these five characteristics in some detail:

1. *Principles are lawlike.* Ideally, principles identify laws of the universe, such as the law referred to in the scriptural comment: "There is a law, irrevocably decreed in heaven . . ." (D&C 130:20). In the social sciences, we have to be content with our principles being *lawlike* because we are not yet sure which ideas are really the true and most useful principles. Two examples of principles are these:

> The more alike a man and woman are in their beliefs and values, the higher their chances of successful marriage.

> The more spouses act in loving ways, the better the marriage.

2. *Principles have two or more variables.* Variables are things that can vary or change. Height, weight, amount of attention, amount of love, amount of skill, and socio-economic status are examples. *Middle-class* is not a variable, since it is a place or category in the variable of socio-economic status; and *six-foot-two* is not a variable, since it is a category or point on the variable of height. In the examples under number 1, the variables are amount of similarity, chances of a successful marriage, amount of loving, and the quality of a marriage.

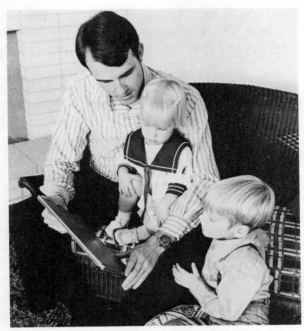

*A family with children is a complex system
with many stewardships.*

3. *There is a predictable relationship between variables.* The principles must state how the variables are normally related to each other. For example, there is a relationship between similarity and marital satisfaction. The more marriage partners are alike in their values, the better their chances of satisfaction (the-more-the-more). Thus the principle identifies a relationship. The key idea is that if the causal variable is ever changed (altered, increased, or decreased), this will create a predictable change in the effect variable.

There are also several terms that describe different types of relationships in which more of a causal factor creates more of the effect (the-greater-the-greater or the-more-the-more, and also the-less-the-less). This is called a *positive* relationship. When we have a relationship in which it is the-more-the-less, this is a *negative* or *inverse* relationship.

The word *predictable* is important because it means that we can count on the relationship occurring—unless some other factor prevents the predicted effect. That sometimes happens. For example, even with the law of gravity, which is fairly predictable, we don't always get the expected result. Try dropping a feather above a fan.

4. *Principles are general.* This means that a principle is not specific or concrete. In other words, principles are abstract laws that can be applied in many specific situations. For example, the principle about similarity can be applied in anybody's marriage. It applies to Bill and Sue as well as Greg and Mary. If we were to say that since Bill and Sue are similar

they are usually satisfied, this is not a general idea. It is a specific idea about a specific couple. Principles, such as the law of tithing and the law of the harvest (whatever we sow we shall reap), are general principles because they can be applied to many specific situations.

5. *Principles are universal.* This means that, all other things being equal, we can expect a principle to be true in all situations, in all historical periods, and in all cultures. Similarity in marriage helps Eskimos, Indians, blacks, and whites. It is true for father Abraham and will be true in the Millennium.

How Do You Use Principles?

To use a principle, you must first learn it—learn it well. Second, you decide what your goals are. This means that you decide what kind of output you want in your system. Do you want a particular effect to be high, low, or medium? Third, you find ways to manipulate some part of the system or change the input (the causal factors), so that it will produce the desired output or characteristic in the system.

How Are Principles Different from Commandments?

Principles are always hypothetical statements: *If* we do X, then Y will happen. Principles don't tell us what to do. They just tell us what will happen *if* we do something, and they always have at least two variables.

Commandments usually tell us what to do regarding the causal variable in a principle. Therefore, they usually have only one variable. For example, a principle says: If we pay tithing, we won't burn. (See D&C 64:23.) Your goal says, I don't want to burn. This yields the commandment: Pay tithing. A principle says that the more similar the man and the woman are, the greater their chances of a successful marriage. If someone's goal is to have a successful marriage, this yields a commandment: Marry someone who is similar.

SUMMARY

This book teaches some correct principles about the marriage system. And as we learn how to use the principles, we learn new ways to be wise stewards over this important and delicate system.

MARRIAGE
AND FAMILY
IN PERSPECTIVE

*The most important of the
Lord's work that you will ever do
will be the work you do
within the walls of your own home.*

— *Harold B. Lee*

When creating the earth, the Lord followed the pattern he had established in other worlds. He placed a married couple here, at the same time commanding them to "multiply, and replenish the earth" (Moses 2:28). This provided for us the oldest social institution, the *family.*

Since this beginning, we have been admonished by the prophets that the normal and best way to live is within such a family unit. Even so, there are a number of philosophers and scholars who think we would be better off if we replaced the family institution with a different system. For example, Karl Marx and Friedrich Engels suggested that the family is a destructive force and that it ought to be eliminated (Engels 1902).

This antifamily thinking prompted the communist revolutionaries in Russia, and later in China, to work toward the goal of eliminating family life (Geiger 1968). Also, when the Jewish people began their return to Palestine about a century ago, there were a large number of them who thought that the family system they had known did more harm than good, and they tried to do away with it (Spiro 1956).

Although these antifamily sentiments have been expressed in cultures other than our own, even in America there is an increasing number of scholars who are questioning the value of the family institution as an effective system of living (Casler 1974).

This leads to questions such as . . .

Are marriage and the family necessary?

What is the role of the family?

Do we know of better ways of organizing society?

Why have marriage and family life?

To fully understand the role of marriage and family life, it would be well to consider these questions from a broad perspective—to examine them from a *religious* as well as a *secular* perspective. Let us first examine what the Lord has revealed about the role of marriage and family life.

REVEALED INFORMATION ABOUT MARRIAGE AND FAMILY LIFE

Marriage and Family Are at the Heart of the Gospel

The Lord has revealed that the intelligence or spirit element of man had no beginning and will have no end (D&C 92:23-38; Smith 1938, pp. 352-54). We were, however, born in a pre-earthly life as spirit children of heavenly parents, and we lived for a time as a heavenly family. Even though our spirit bodies resembled the ones we now have (1 Nephi 11:11; Ether 3:16), these spirit bodies did not have the physical elements of flesh and bone. They were made of a "more fine or pure" matter (D&C 131:7) than are our physical bodies.

We learned many things and experienced a great deal of joy in our pre-earthly life, but we could not have a "fulness" of joy in that incomplete condition (D&C 93:33-34). Before we could obtain a fullness of joy, we needed two additional things: first, a physical body, and second, the knowledge and skills we could acquire by living in a situation where good and evil were competing with each other (2 Nephi 2:23). A plan was introduced that would allow these conditions to be met.

There are several aspects of our pre-earthly condition that help us understand the central role of marriage and family life. The parents we were born to in heaven were a married couple (D&C 131:4; 132:19), and their desire was to help their spirit children progress and grow. This was done by teaching them, creating earths for their use, and providing other necessities for the further progress of the spiritual family of which we are all a part. This understanding leads to other questions, such as:

Why did they do it?

What was the purpose of this family activity?

What gives it meaning?

These questions, too, have answers. As the scriptures teach, "men are, that they might have joy" (2 Nephi 2:25). It is this *joy* that gives meaning and purpose to life and everything in it. Our heavenly parents worked at helping us grow so that we can experience greater joy, and through this service they, in turn, experience the greatest joy. Thus we see that the most joyful or exalted experience possible is attaining godhood and helping others, and we also see that this is done only as *married couples*. Without marriage there would be no spirit children (D&C 131:4) and no opportunity for the ultimate happiness.

The plan that was introduced in heaven to allow us eternal growth and happiness was the plan of salvation. After it was introduced there, our divine parents implemented it by creating an earth and placing us on it. Consistent with the plan, evil was allowed to enter the world. As each of us was born into the world, he was given his free agency to cope

Our "work and our glory" is to help each other grow and progress.

with the forces of good and evil. Making the proper decisions while in mortality will allow us to ultimately achieve godhood. Those of us who progress to the point of godhood will procreate spirit children and provide earths for their mortal development, thereby repeating the cycle of family life.

To complete this eternal cycle of growth, each of us must not only take the preliminary steps of faith, baptism, reception of the Holy Ghost, etc., but must also be endowed with power within a holy temple, and there be sealed in celestial marriage by the proper authority. Finally, together with his mate, each must continue faithful unto the end by overcoming all things.

Thus we see that marriage is much more than a convenient social arrangement or civil contract. It is a sacred and eternal covenant that existed before the foundations of this earth were laid. It is an "order of the priesthood" (D&C 131:2) which is everlasting. It is a holy ordinance that plays a vital role in helping us gain exaltation and eternal life.

These insights help us understand why the Lord, when he was creating the earth, said, "It is not good that the man should be alone; I will make him an help meet for him" (Genesis 2:18). These insights should also help us understand why he revealed to the Prophet Joseph Smith that "whoso forbiddeth to marry is not ordained of God, for marriage is ordained of God unto man" (D&C 49:15). They should also help us understand why the Lord emphasizes marriage so much that it is performed only in special rooms in the most sacred of all places—the holy temple.

These insights should also help us understand that parenthood is a central part of our existence. This state existed before the earth was created, it exists on the earth, and will continue to exist through the eternities. There is literally no other alternative as to how we should organize our lives. Those who think that state-run nursery schools, hospitals, and paid nurses can bear and rear children and meet the long-term needs of individuals just do not understand what humans are like and what they need. They do not understand the purpose of life, the reason for existing, or the sources of meaning and beauty and happiness.

SECULAR REASONS FOR MARRIAGE AND FAMILY LIFE

Sociological Reasons

Sociologists have determined that there are a number of essential functions that must be met if a society is to continue (Parson 1951; Winch 1971). For example, a society must find some method of replacing the individuals in it, because people inevitably age and die. Also, human infants are initially unable to care for their personal needs, and so society has to find some method of providing such necessities as food, water, shelter, and nurturing for infants and children. It must also create some system for teaching the children what it means to be human—how to talk, reason, think, and how to provide the necessities for life. Some of the other needs that a society must cope with are the need for managing people so they can live in enough peace that they won't eliminate each other, and how to adapt to the changes that are necessary with new technology, climatic changes, and social innovations.

All of us recognize that we have created social institutions to perform these essential functions. We have created governments to help create order, and we have created schools to help us learn the things we need to know to survive. In addition, we have organized a complex medical institution to cope with illnesses and accidents that threaten lives and happiness.

The institutions of marriage and family life perform several of these vital functions. It is these institutions that are responsible for the orderly replacement of people through birth, and these systems are the ones that provide for the nurturing and early training of children. It is also these systems that meet a large number of the emotional and psychological needs of people by providing love and acceptance and understanding. It is in marriage and the family where people are cared for and loved and accepted, and where they create the bonds with others and commitments and service that meet the deepest and the most delicate and sensitive emotional needs.

It is interesting to speculate about whether it would be possible to create a different social institution that could effectively perform the functions performed by marriage and family life. What would the new social institution be like? How would it function?

Some have suggested that communes would be more effective than families. This view was so popular in the 1960s that thousands of young people flocked to what they thought were utopian systems to replace the "defective" family system. Research in the 1970s and 1980s suggests that these communal systems cannot effectively meet the needs of even a small segment of society. They can last for a short period of time if they have a strong, charismatic leader, or if there is a dominant ideological perspective to hold them together for a while, but a commune is too large and complex a social unit to be the basic building block of a society. People relate in a long-term, intimate manner with a very few people, and communes quickly divide into factions. Men and women pair off with their biological children in subsets that quickly recreate the basic pattern of a husband and wife (with occasional polygamous arrangements) and their biological children being the basic unit. These units then form ties with their immediate kin, such as parents and uncles and aunts.

There have been numerous other experiments where societies or cultures have tried to replace marriage and family life. One of the most publicized of these is the kibbutz pattern that was begun in the early 1900s. (Spiro 1956.) A kibbutz is an agricultural collective settlement that has common ownership of property, and communally organized production, consumption, and care of children. The children are reared in nurseries and special schools, and have quarters that are separate from those of their biological parents.

The original settlers of the kibbutz wanted to do away entirely with marriage and family life, but their dream has not worked. As new generations have been born and reared in this style of life, they want to re-adopt the family and marital institutions. The parents in the kibbutz have a unique bond with their children, and they have been gradually wanting to have more and more responsibility for the rearing and guidance of those children. Additionally, members have asked to have special ceremonies, much like weddings, when they decide they want to share their living quarters with a partner. It is likely that before the kibbutz experiment is a century old, despite the ideologically extreme views of its founders, the members will have re-created the institutions of marriage and family life.

The communist experiments in Russia and China have followed similar patterns. When the Bolshevik revolution occurred in Russia in 1917, the party that eventually gained control decided that the family system was an undesirable obstacle to social progress. They thought that the important social unit should be the state. They therefore passed laws that made marriage and divorce mere matters of registering with an office, and they adopted policies that would gradually eliminate family life. Even so, within two decades they realized that the welfare of their society depended on family units, and they could not invent institutions that could effectively replace marriage and family life. The result was that they reversed their policies and laws and have since encouraged stable marriage and family life (Geiger 1968).

Several conclusions emerge from this sociological analysis of marital and family institutions. One obvious conclusion is that societies cannot last without the social institutions of marriage and the family. They would disintegrate by not having any people after a generation or so, or they would fall into chaos or destructive wars. *The family system is absolutely essential.*

Another conclusion is that people from Plato to Marx have tried to invent social institutions to replace the family, and have tried to call their inventions something besides

More precious than rubies.

marriage and family. Even so, just like the animal that has webbed feet and a flat bill, they can call it whatever they choose, but it is still a duck. People can argue all they want that they can replace the family, or that the world is flat, or that ducks don't quack, but time and experience and scholarly analysis all argue that *they* are the real quacks.

There are many psychological reasons that marriage and family life are the best ways to organize humanity, and that the substitutes (such as orphanages, welfare, and being single) are, at best, dismal and unsatisfying alternatives.

Urie Bronfenbrenner's 1970 study of how children develop in different nations has demonstrated that there are several things that are essential if we are to raise healthy, well-adjusted children. Some of these essentials are well-understood things such as good nutrition and proper exercise and the opportunity to learn and grow. One of the others, however, is not as universally understood. It is that children need to have people who care for them in "nonrational" ways. They need adults who are so wrapped up in the child, so attached to the child, so wild about the child that the child is deeply loved—loved in a way that cannot be bought at any monetary price. The key adults in the child's life need to be so involved with the child that they truly care, and are willing to nurture and tend and help and assist and nurse and guide and encourage and watch and invest of themselves in ways they only will if their relationship is centered around noneconomic, nonrational, noncommercial, nonbusiness, and nonpaycheck types of things. It has to be an emotional commitment, one that comes from committing oneself to values and goals and beliefs that connect the child to the adults. This is called *parenthood,* and it occurs when one man and one woman come together as one in body and spirit and mind and life, and invest themselves in each other and their children. It is only when we have these ingredients that we have the optimal conditions for creating healthy humans.

When marriages are terminated through divorce, the intricate and complex and delicate conditions essential to the husband-wife relationship and the parent-child relationship are often strained. While excellent relationships develop in many second marriages, a child's ties with his two parents tend to become fragmented as he tries to move from one to the other and attempts to create new, deeply meaningful relationships with the strangers that his parents marry.

These are some of the psychological reasons

why marriage and family life are important,

and why they are the best way to live life!

INTEGRATING THEOLOGICAL AND SECULAR IDEAS

It is helpful to integrate some of the theological ideas with the sociological and psychological ideas about why marriage and family life are so essential. As we circumscribe these truths into a whole, we discover that the theological ideas provide a foundation. They provide a perspective about where we came from, why we are on the earth, where we are going, and what we ought to be doing while we are on the earth. We learn that the most important parts of life are to have joy and to help each other, especially our children, grow and develop. *That* is what life is all about. Therefore, our primary goals in life ought to center around our family life.

What happens when people don't have the basic perspective about life that is provided by these truths? They do not realize that the most important work that we will ever do is within our homes and in our marriages and with our children. They also notice that it is money that buys the visible and tangible things that are rewarded in the earthly societies. They also notice that it is power and influence that buys fame and fortune, and the natural result is that they learn to value material and economic and professional (occupational) things the most. We realize that most people in our modern society do not have the gospel's perspective. In fact, very few of the people who control what happens in the mass media, government, business, and the educational institutions have this perspective. This means that people without this perspective have determined what our society will be like, and the Church's point of view is an ignored, unappreciated set of truths that has little influence. We find ourselves a small group of people who have an island of useful beliefs in an ocean of drifting, superficial, irrelevant, temporarily exciting, artificially glamorous, but ultimately empty and shallow beliefs.

These conditions, with most people not understanding the true role of marriage and families, and a few people having a proper perspective, are illustrative of Lehi's dream about the world (1 Nephi 8). Many of the people in his dream were walking aimlessly in a mist, without a sense of direction. That is the way most people are today. Some of these masses find glamorous and luxurious styles of life in the big buildings where they park their three cars and watch their big screen TVs—and they look down on the few who are marching to a different drummer, the few who see delightful trees and are walking on a fairly narrow path to get to the trees. The few realize that the path and the trees along it provide a much deeper joy and pleasure and happiness, and they would like the confused and jeering and taunting masses in the big buildings to join them. The masses, however, don't understand the intangible and less glamorous insights that give the people on the path their sense of direction and happiness. Some of the people on the path stumble and fall off and have great unhappiness in their lives, and some of them try to make the most of their broken marriages and poor family relationships. Even so, they aren't able to experience the great joy and happiness of those who are able to create warm, helpful, understanding, lasting, loving marriages and family life.

DIFFERENT KINDS OF FAMILY SYSTEMS

We have shown that the family institution is an essential, permanent, and desirable way of organizing humanity. This then leads to new questions such as . . .

What should families be like?

How should families be organized?

Are there different types of family life?

Sometimes we have an overly simple view of families. We think that the normal family has a father, mother, and several children. But, what about our premortal family life? Was it the same? And, what about our postmortal family life? What will it be like? Fortunately, the revelations from the Lord have provided a few glimpses into the different family systems that each of us participate in in different stages of our progression and growth. To begin, let's start with what family life was like in the premortal existence.

Premortal Family Life

There is a great deal we don't know about our premortal family conditions, but the Lord has revealed enough for us to be able to put together a few pieces of the puzzle. We had parents and siblings. Our heavenly parents were exalted beings with resurrected bodies of flesh and bone. All of the people who will ever come to this earth were at some time born to heavenly parents. When we were born, our bodies were not some ephemeral or nonmatter type of body. They were composed of spiritual matter, which is "more fine or pure, and can only be discerned by purer eyes" (D&C 131:7) than we have in this life. Those bodies also had the same general shape as our earthly bodies. We learn this truth from an incident that occurred about two thousand years before the Savior was born to Mary in the meridian of time. The Lord showed his finger to the brother of Jared when he touched some special stones, and the brother of Jared "saw the finger of the Lord; and it was as the finger of a man, like unto flesh and blood" (Ether 3:6). Later, the Lord showed him his entire body, and commented: "Behold, this body, which ye now behold, is the body of my spirit; and man have I created after the body of my spirit; and even as I appear unto thee to be in the spirit will I appear unto my people in the flesh." (Ether 3:16).

We also know that Jesus Christ was the firstborn in this spirit family and that one of our brothers was the individual who rebelled and became Satan. This teaches us that it was possible for us to choose whether to follow the teachings of our parents or to rebel and disobey, so we apparently had free agency in this family. Thus, we lived in a family, but it was a different type of family than we are accustomed to in this life. We will always be members of this family, and we are interacting in this family when we pray to our Heavenly Father and when we refer to other members of the human race as our brothers and sisters.

Earthly Families

We are all familiar with our earthly families. You grew up in your parents' family, and scholars call this family system the *family of orientation*. After you're grown, you leave this family, marry, and begin your *family of procreation*. As you move through your adult years your family of procreation has its own life cycle, and the average person's cycle is depicted in figure 2:1. People spend the first twenty to thirty years raising children, and then usually experience a number of years as a couple who do not have children in the home. This middle-age stage of the family life cycle is almost a unique style of family life itself, since the relationships, the way you spend your time, and the things that are important are very different from any of the other family systems or stages of the life cycle. And, most people spend fifteen or twenty years in this stage. Many then discover, usually to their surprise, that they also spend a number of years of their lives as "singles," and this too is a unique type of family situation. They have family members who live in others' households, but they find themselves adjusting to a unique set of unforeseen circumstances. Most of us would do well to pause and think a little about how we will probably experience the life cycle depicted in figure 2:1, and we can do that with Activity 2:1 at the end of this chapter.

Post-Earthly Families

Most adults in the Church have learned that marriage can be for time and eternity, and they want to have eternal marriages; but we do not know very much about what our family life, or lives, will be like in the next life. Parents and children who are sealed together by the Holy Spirit of Promise will have a parent-child relationship in the Celestial Kingdom, but not enough has been revealed for us to know details of that life.

*Figure 2:1   Typical Family Life Cycle**

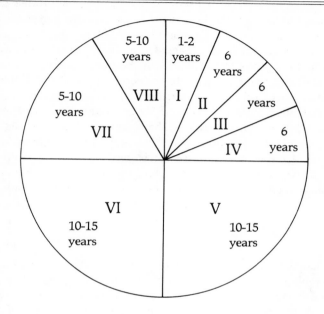

Stage I: Married and no children.
Stage II: Preschool children. Oldest children are preschoolers.
Stage III: School age. The oldest children are in elementary school.
Stage IV: Teenage. The oldest children are teenagers.
Stage V: Launching stage. Oldest children are leaving home.
Stage VI: Empty nest. Children are launched, but couple not retired.
Stage VII: Retirement. Couple retired.
Stage VIII: Single stage. One member of couple deceased.

There will also be another family system that will be created in our post-earthly existence. After couples have reached a certain level of perfection, they will be able to also have spirit children, just as our heavenly parents gave birth to us in our pre-earthly existence. These spirit children will probably be very much like we were. They will have bodies that will be spirit bodies that will be made out of spiritual matter—more fine and pure than the physical materials our earthly and our resurrected bodies will be made of. Apparently, just as our heavenly parents' work and glory was to bring to pass our progression and growth, we will teach, instruct and help our spiritual children.

* Source: U.S. Bureau of the Census and the National Center for Health Statistics.

For those who reach that exalted state, it seems that the heaven they create and people with their spirit children, though a place of great joy, will not be free from difficulties and opposition. Apparently the spirit children will be able to rebel and disobey their parents, just as the one-third of our brothers and sisters disobeyed our heavenly parents in the war in heaven that occurred before our earth was organized. The heavenly parents there will undoubtedly experience joy and happiness when their children do well and sadness and pain when they act disobediently. For those of us who achieve that state, our joy will be greater than we can now imagine, greater than anyone's earthly understanding can comprehend (D&C 76:89-90), but we will also have opposition (D&C 29).

We need to also realize that it will only be a small proportion of the individuals who will have come to the earth who will participate in an eternal marriage and who will have spirit children. Only those who are righteous will get into the celestial kingdom, and only those who attain the highest place in that kingdom will be able to have spirit children (D&C 131:1-4). The governing factor here is the sealing of husband and wife for eternity by the proper authority. No other form of marriage will suffice for this purpose, because a covenant that

> is not by me or by my word, which is my law, and is not sealed by the Holy Spirit of promise, through him whom I have anointed and appointed unto this power, then it is not valid neither of force when they are out of the world, because they are not joined by me, saith the Lord, neither by my word; when they are out of the world it cannot be received there, because the angels and the gods are appointed there, by whom they cannot pass; they cannot, therefore, inherit my glory; for my house is a house of order, saith the Lord God.
>
> Whatsoever you seal on earth shall be sealed in heaven; and whatsoever you bind on earth, in my name and by my word, saith the Lord, it shall be eternally bound in the heavens. (D&C 132:18, 46.)

The best condition possible for those who are not thus sealed is described by the Lord in two earlier verses:

> Therefore, when they are out of the world they neither marry nor are given in marriage; but are appointed angels in heaven, which angels are ministering servants, to minister for those who are worthy of a far more, and an exceeding, and an eternal weight of glory.
>
> For these angels did not abide my law; therefore, they cannot be enlarged, but remain separately and singly, without exaltation, in their saved condition, to all eternity; and from henceforth are not gods, but are angels of God forever and ever. (D&C 132:16-17.)

IMPLICATIONS OF THIS PERSPECTIVE ON MARRIAGE AND FAMILY LIFE

This perspective about marriage and family has several implications for Latter-day Saint college students. It can help them organize their lives, and help them decide what is truly important to them. It can also provide a peace of mind and security about life by helping them know more about why they are here on the earth and where they are going in the next life.

Another implication is that it can help young adults understand the developmental tasks that are unique to the young adult years. What are *developmental tasks?* They are defined by Duvall as "growth responsibility that arises at or about a certain time in the life of an individual, successful accomplishment of which leads to success in later tasks" (Duvall 1977, p. 485). When you were about a year old, you had developmental tasks of learning to walk and feed yourself. When you were about six you had a developmental task of learning how to be honest, and if you learned it then it helped you with later development. Children who do not learn honesty in those early years find it very difficult to truly learn it later. In your adolescent years you learned how to work diligently and how to interact with members of the opposite sex in friendships. If you learned these tasks well, this too helps you with later tasks, and if you didn't accomplish them then, it interfered with your later development.

*So, what does this perspective of marriage and family life
teach young adults about their developmental tasks?*

It helps them realize that they have developmental tasks about marriage and family life. For example, they need to prepare themselves so they will be ready for marriage by the time they are twenty-two to twenty-five years old. Very few people are ready for marriage at age nineteen. Oh, it is true that a lot of people get married at that age, and most of them think (at that time) that they are ready, but most of them realize a few years later that the task of the teenage years is to prepare for adulthood and marriage—not be married. This means that men and women should be preparing themselves so they can make decisions and communicate with members of the opposite sex. They need to learn how to recognize their emotions and manage them to be productive forces in their lives rather than producers of undesirable behavior. The young man needs to be preparing himself so he can provide adequately for a family—and in today's world that is no small matter. And, notice, if a young man does not meet this developmental task at this stage of his life, it will interfere with his ability to perform the different tasks that will face him when he is thirty and forty. The implication of this is—young men, get with it!

What do young women need to do to prepare themselves for marriage and family life? They need to also do many things, such as learn how to manage a home, take care of children, assist their husbands in providing the economic necessities of life, and communicate effectively about the complex and delicate and involved concerns of married life.

There are many things young people can do to meet these developmental tasks, and two of them that are immediately relevant are: (1) Study the remaining chapters of this book with great care, and learn from them new skills and ideas that can help them manage their marriage and family stewardships, and (2) complete Activity 2:2 at the end of this chapter. That activity will help you move one more rung up the ladder of getting ready for the exciting and fulfilling satisfactions that await the well-prepared person.

SUMMARY

This chapter has provided a point of view, a set of lenses to help us look at marriage and family life. The perspective that it creates uses revealed truths and truths that have been discovered in the social sciences—and it demonstrates that marriage and family life are at the heart of the plan of salvation, all earthly societies, and each of our individual lives. The chapter also discusses the different kinds of family systems that each of us have lived in and will be able to live in, and it discusses several activities that young adults can complete to help themselves become better prepared for their marital and family stewardships.

ACTIVITY 2:1
Planning Your Family Life Cycle

1. First, fill in the age you will probably be in each of the following "turning points" in your family life cycle.

	Probable Age
Get married	_____
Have your first child	_____
First child start school	_____
First child start junior high school	_____
First child leave home (mission or college)	_____
Last child leave home	_____
Retire from profession or career	_____
One member of the couple pass away	_____
Second member of the couple pass away	_____

2. Now compute how many years you will probably spend in each of the following stages of your "family life cycle."

		Years in Stage
Stage I:	*Pre-Children* Married and no children	_____
Stage II:	*Preschool* Oldest children preschoolers	_____
Stage III:	*School-Age* Oldest child in elementary school	_____
Stage IV:	*Teenage* Oldest child teenager	_____
Stage V:	*Launching* Children are leaving home	_____
Stage VI:	*Middle-Age* Children gone, not retired	_____
Stage VII:	*Retired Couple* Retired, neither deceased	_____
Stage VIII:	*Single* One member of the couple deceased	_____

3. Describe the biggest surprise you had in trying to estimate what your family life cycle will probably be.

4. Describe what you are going to do differently *now* to prepare yourself for your entire life cycle.

ACTIVITY 2:2

Discovering Your Developmental Tasks *

1. First, examine the following list of developmental tasks that face young husbands and wives.

Developmental Tasks of Husbands and Wives

Developmental tasks of the young husband	*Developmental tasks of the young wife*	*Complementary Possibilities*
Becoming established in an occupation	Making a home and managing the household	☐ Complementary: Sharing responsibility in homemaking.
☐ Being trained for a career. ☐ Assuming responsibility for getting and holding a job. ☐ Working toward security and advancement in his work.	☐ Getting settled in her home. ☐ Establishing and maintaining household routines. ☐ Learning the many skills of homemaking and housework.	
Assuming responsibility for the support of the family	Becoming a financial helpmate in establishing the home	☐ Complementary: Being economic partners.
☐ Earning the family income. ☐ Planning for the long pull of family support through the years.	☐ Working until her husband is established if necessary. ☐ Seeing her work as secondary and possibly intermittent. ☐ Having a "back-up" economic plan if something happens to husband's earning power.	

---

* Adapted from Evelyn Duvall, *Family Development,* Philadelphia: J. B. Lippincott Co., 1977, p. 194.

Establishing mutually
satisfying sex relationships

☐ Being able to interact with
wife sexually.
☐ Developing competency
as a husband.
☐ Promoting mutual
enjoyment.

Becoming "domesticated" as
a married man

☐ Sharing leisure time with
his wife.
☐ Developing mutual
interests.
☐ Cultivating joint activities.
☐ Getting into the young-
married set.

Becoming a satisfactory
sex partner

☐ Learning her sex role as
wife.
☐ Being able to interact
effectively with husband.
☐ Promoting mutual
fulfillment.

Assuming hostess and
companionship roles as
a married woman

☐ Planning for recreational
activities as a couple.
☐ Accepting and refusing
social invitations.
☐ Entertaining friends,
associates, and families.

☐ Complementary:
Being able to communi-
cate intimately with the
other.

☐ Complementary:
Both husband and wife
learn to move in tandem
in their social life as a
couple.

---

2. Mark those that you are ready and able to accomplish with an "R," and those you still
need to work on with a "W."

3. Develop and implement a realistic plan for working on the tasks that you have marked
with a "W."

SUPPLEMENTARY READINGS

Bennett, Archibald F. *Family Exaltation.* Salt Lake City: Deseret Book Co., 1957.
Brown, Hugh B. *You and Your Marriage.* Salt Lake City: Bookcraft, Inc., 1960.
Duvall, Evelyn. *Family Development.* Philadelphia: J. B. Lippincott, 1977.
Kimball, Spencer W. *Marriage.* Salt Lake City: Deseret Book Co., 1978.
Petersen, Mark E. *Marriage: Covenants and Conflicts.* Salt Lake City: Bookcraft, Inc., 1977.
Skidmore, Rex A. *Marriage: Much More Than a Dream.* Salt Lake City: Deseret Book Co., 1979.
Smith, Joseph Fielding. "Marriage: The Covenant of Exaltation," pp. 58-79 in *Doctrines of Salvation.* Salt Lake City: Bookcraft, Inc., 1955.
Winch, Robert F. *The Modern Family.* New York: Holt, Rinehart and Winston, Inc., 1971.
Yorgason, Brenton G., Terry R. Baker, and Wesley R. Burr. *From This Day Forth.* Salt Lake City: Bookcraft, Inc., 1982.

LOVE
ONE
ANOTHER

*The Lord God hath given a commandment
that all men should have charity,
which charity is love.
And except they should have charity
they were nothing.*

—2 Nephi 26:30

When the Lord was asked which commandment was the greatest, he replied, "Thou shalt love the Lord thy God with all thy heart, and with all thy soul, and with all thy mind. This is the first and great commandment. And the second is like unto it. Thou shalt love thy neighbour as thyself. On these two commandments hang all the law and the prophets." (Matthew 22:37-40.)

If loving is that important in interacting with neighbors, it must be even more important in marriage. Thus the first and probably most important principle for marriage is:

1. The Love Principle: The more spouses act in loving ways, the better the marriage and family life.

What is meant by *love*? Does it mean that spouses hold hands, embrace each other often, kiss, sit close to each other, and show their affection in other ways? Yes, these behaviors can be a part of love, but they are a very small part. What, then, are the important parts, the essential ingredients, the indispensable parts? Paul and Mormon describe in detail what love is, and they teach that love—or in their terms, charity:

suffereth long
is kind
envieth not
vaunteth not itself
is not puffed up
doth not behave itself unseemly
seeketh not her own
is not easily provoked
thinketh no evil
rejoiceth in truth

Concern for others can be shown in many ways.

> beareth all things
> believeth all things
> hopeth all things
> endureth all things
> is the pure love of Christ
> endureth forever

(See 1 Corinthians 13; Moroni 7.)

These characteristics of love encompass three main themes. The themes are: (1) that we should be concerned about others rather than be selfish; (2) that we should be patient and enduring with ourselves and others; and (3) that we should be righteous in our hearts as well as in the way we behave. Let us examine each of these themes of love more closely:

Being Concerned About Others

Concern for others includes several separate behaviors. Five of these are: (1) seeketh not her own; (2) vaunteth not itself; (3) is not puffed up; (4) envieth not; and (5) is kind.

In modern terminology, such phrases as "caring about others," "becoming involved," "worrying about the welfare of others," and "losing ourselves in the service of others" describes this beautiful process. The opposites are selfishness, conceit, egotism, uninvolvement, and being concerned only about ourselves.

Modern prophets have added new insights regarding this part of love. President Spencer W. Kimball has taught:

> The marriage that is based upon selfishness is almost certain to fail. The one who marries for wealth or the one who marries for prestige or social plane is certain to be disappointed. The one who marries to satisfy vanity or pride or who marries to spite or to show up another person is fooling only himself. But the one who marries to give happiness as well as to receive it, to give service as well as to receive it, and looks after the interests of the two and then the family as it comes will have a good chance that the marriage will be a happy one. . . .
>
> Total unselfishness is sure to accomplish another factor in successful marriage. If each spouse is forever seeking the interests, comforts, and happiness of the other, the love found in courtship and cemented in marriage will grow into mighty proportions. (1976, pp. 22-23.)

Being concerned about others is not a black-or-white condition in which you are either concerned or not concerned. It is a continuum that varies in degree or amount as shown below:

0	1	2	3	4	5
No Concern	Slight Concern	Considerable Concern	High Concern	Very High Concern	Excessive Concern

It is possible to change the amount of concern we show a little or a great deal, and we can change it in short periods of time. For example, when a person encounters stressful situations such as final examinations, a broken engagement, or health problems, he may temporarily decrease the amount of concern he shows for others. At other times, such as during a relaxing vacation, when he becomes engaged, or at a holiday such as Christmas, a person may increase the concern he shows for others.

It is important to realize that concern is not a value in which more is always better. Just as it is undesirable to have too little concern, it is also undesirable to have too much concern. It would be unwise for a person to be so concerned about other people that he neglected other important parts of life. For example, he could be so concerned about others that he would not get enough rest, would worship too little, or would fail to provide the economic necessities he should. This means that there is an optimum level of concern. It helps to have quite a bit, but having too much hurts. If a person is between 2 and 4 on the above continuum, he's probably all right. If he is below 2 or above 4, he may want to make some changes in his life. He may be too selfish, or so worried about others that he's neglecting other things.

When you look at your marriage as a system that you manage, you realize that concern should be one of the characteristics of the marital system—a characteristic that you ought to continually monitor. Everyone needs to be alert as to how much concern he has, to see whether or not it is within the level that he thinks is wise. Too little or too much concern

The Art of Marriage

Happiness in marriage is not something that just happens. A good marriage must be created. In the art of marriage, the "little things" are the big things. . . .

It is never being too old to hold hands.
It is remembering to say, "I love you," at least once each day.
It is never going to sleep angry.
It is forming a circle of love that gathers in the whole family.
It is at no time taking the other for granted; the courtship shouldn't end with the honeymoon, it should continue through all the years.
It is doing things for each other, not in the attitude of duty or sacrifice, but in the spirit of joy.
It is speaking words of appreciation and demonstrating gratitude in thoughtful ways.
It is not expecting the husband to wear a halo, or the wife to have wings of an angel. It is not looking for perfection in each other, it is cultivating flexibility, patience, understanding, and a sense of humor.
It is having the capacity to forgive and forget.
It is giving each other an atmosphere in which each can grow.
It is not only marrying the right partner—it is being the right partner.
It is discovering what marriage can be, at its best, as expressed in the words of Mark Twain used in a tribute to his wife: "Wherever she was, there was Eden."

—Author unidentified

will disrupt some of the other parts of the marital system. When one's concern is within the desirable limits, he should continue with his current style of life. When he realizes that his concern for others is lacking or excessive, he needs to admit he has a problem, talk about it with those close to him, and then make some changes.

People also need to be wise in making sure that they are more concerned about the things that make a difference in marriage, and less concerned about the things that are less important. If you were in a manufacturing plant that produced dynamite or nitroglycerin, you would need to be very concerned about the physical safety of others. In marriage, since there is less danger of being blown up, you don't have to be as concerned about physical safety. But there are other areas that need continual attention.

What are they?

Should you be highly concerned about providing a luxurious house or expensive car for your spouse? Should you be concerned about correcting your spouse when he or she makes a mistake? Should you always be straightening the other person out in arguments? Should you be highly concerned that the other person doesn't laugh too loudly or dress in too relaxed a manner while you are in public? The answer to these questions is a resounding *no!*

What, then, should you be concerned about?

Each person should be concerned about his partner's feelings or emotions. When a person disagrees with his partner, he needs to be concerned about how he makes the other person feel. He can ask himself: Have I said things unfairly? Have I been inconsiderate of my partner's opinions in a way that will make him or her justifiably upset? Am I so worried about being right that I step on the other person? If the other person has to give in, how will he or she feel, and what am I going to do to help the feelings? And at other times, if my partner wants me to stay home for the evening, read, go out, pray, go to the temple, or just talk, am I concerned with how my partner will feel if I agree or disagree? *Your feelings are an important part of marriage, and you need to always be very concerned about them.*

In addition to feelings, you should concern yourself with how much you are helping your partner accomplish the things that he or she wants to accomplish. When you try to help your partner, does he or she think you are pressuring or cajoling? Are you trying to get your partner to accomplish the things *you* want him to accomplish, or the things *he* wants to accomplish? There is considerable scientific research (discussed in chapter 11) suggesting that the former is a disruptive type of concern, while the latter is a helpful type of concern.

One final aspect of concern is that we also need to be concerned about ourselves. Some people teach that we should forget about ourselves and not be concerned about ourselves or love ourselves. These are unfortunate and pernicious teachings that distort the true meaning of love. The Savior taught that we should love our neighbors "as ourselves." Not more. Not less. *As ourselves!* This means that we should be as worried about our own rights and wishes and desires as we are about the wishes and needs of others. It means that we should feel good about ourselves and pay attention to ourselves. It means that there is a sensitive balance where, in President Kimball's words below, we should "give happiness as well as receive it."

Many are aware of this sensitive balance, and they are concerned about others and themselves in healthy ways. A small minority of people are not concerned enough about themselves, and they need to stick up for their rights and needs more. But the large majority of people are in the other condition, the one that President Kimball calls "selfish." They are too concerned about themselves and not concerned enough about the people around them. They would find that their marriages would be much better if they removed this tendency from their lives. Their selfishness destroys their marriages, their friendships, their peace of mind—and unless they change, it will prevent their exaltation. They would be much better off if they could move to level 3 or 4 on the continuum.

Let us continue with the second theme of love identified by Paul and Moroni:

Lord, make me an instrument of thy peace.
Where there is hatred, let me sow love.
Where there is injury, pardon;
Where there is doubt, faith;
Where there is despair, hope;
Where there is darkness, light; and
Where there is sadness, joy.
O divine Master,
Grant that I may not so much
Seek to be consoled as to console;
To be understood as to understand;
To be loved as to love;
For it is in giving that we receive;
It is in pardoning that we are pardoned and
It is in dying that we are born to Eternal Life.

—St. Francis of Assisi

Being Patient with Others

Mormon and Paul identified four parts of this dimension of charity. It (1) suffereth long; (2) is not easily provoked; (3) beareth all things; and (4) endureth all things.

In considering a Christlike relationship, we can gain many insights by taking a positive view of these four concepts. As we do, let us think of patience not as a passive quality, but as an active one. Patience is not simply "putting up with" or "tolerating." It is concentrated strength. It is the ability to be counted on by your partner as well as others, as a constant rather than an unknown. Mohammed once said that patience is the key to contentment. That is, when you love someone you are not easily brought to anger, but rather you overlook weaknesses or differences by feeling safe, secure, and content in the depth of this relationship.

One of the mistakes couples often make in marriage is to lose the spirit of love (and of patience) and begin to emotionally attack their partners rather than discuss a problem or situation that has arisen. Not only does this make partners defensive, but it also whittles away at the very core of their self-esteem. When a person exercises patience in an awkward or unpleasant moment, this very act allows time to assess the situation, and he can then act toward the situation, rather than react and attack his partner.

As you consider the other aspects of patience, you should keep in mind that all great marriages are the result of patient working and adjusting together. When you "suffer long," you are assuming the role of the steward who has the responsibility for a complex and not easily understood system. To suffer does not merely mean to endure pain and anguish, but, as Webster states, "to undergo or experience any process that results in change, to allow; permit; tolerate." Growth takes some suffering. Progress and improvement in and out of marriage demand some suffering. Surely, then, we ought to invest and endure, to create beauty and joy and growth.

Sometimes it is necessary to bear things in marriage. None of us is perfect, and a person gets to know his spouse's faults well in a marriage relationship. This makes it necessary at times to share and bear together things both partners would rather avoid. Those who can help each other bear their burdens will build each other, and build relationships that will be beautiful. When a marriage is stumbling, chances are that one or both partners are not accepting certain responsibilities in that marriage unit. Rather, they are passing those responsibilities on to their spouse or discarding them altogether. Marriage partners should be willing and ready to bear the weight of many unknowns, and then reap the rewards that come from bearing up well.

If we look at only these four ingredients of patience, we may think of marriage as an endurance marathon, something that is endlessly ongoing, with much suffering—holy deadlock rather than wedlock. Fortunately, this is only one part of the total picture, which picture includes joy and happiness. It is, however, a part—and it is a part that makes a difference. When you "endure all things" or "endure forever," you are weaving a tapestry of love, and the attribute of patience weaves ever so tightly into the fabric of your personality.

Becoming Truly Righteous

President Spencer W. Kimball has shown that to be a loving person, one must also be a righteous person:

> To be really happy in marriage, there must be a continued faithful observance of the commandments of the Lord. No one, single or married, was ever sublimely happy unless he was righteous. There are temporary satisfactions and camouflaged situations for the moment, but permanent, total happiness can come only through cleanliness and worthiness. One who has a pattern of religious life with deep religious convictions can never be happy in an inactive life. The conscience will continue to afflict unless it has been seared, in which case the marriage is already in jeopardy. A stinging conscience can make life most unbearable. Inactivity is destructive . . . in varying degrees. (1976, pp. 23-24.)

Paul and Mormon described this part of charity with five different terms. Charity (1) thinketh no evil; (2) rejoiceth not in iniquity; (3) rejoiceth in truth; (4) doth not behave itself unseemly; (5) believeth all things. Thinking no evil means that a person looks for the good in himself and his spouse. He thinks of good ways to behave, and he has a pure mind. An evil person is morally corrupt and wicked. He neither edifies nor enlightens others, but instead chooses darkness and secrecy to cover his disobedient behaviors. He is destructive to faith, good morals, and godly virtues.

Paul and Mormon proclaim that a charitable person "thinketh no evil," which presumes that if one has no evil thought, he will commit no evil deeds, for "As [a man] thinketh in his heart, so is he" (Proverbs 23:7). Thus, thinking no evil helps us act in good ways.

Rejoicing not in iniquity, but rejoicing in truth can help a marriage, adding beauty and depth. It will help us add noble qualities to our lives and develop trust and unity. It helps us avoid iniquity and maintain a posture of obedience to God's commandments.

Believing all good things can also help a marriage. Belief is a synonym for faith throughout the scriptures, and it can be defined in the same manner (see Matthew 9:27-31). Just as belief and faith are necessary for our salvation (Hebrews 10:39; D&C 20:29), belief and faith in others are necessary for one to be a loving person. "Faith is not to have a perfect knowledge of things; therefore if ye have faith ye hope for things which are not seen, which are true" (Alma 32:21). It takes this type of faith in others to create the trust that is needed in marriage. Having confidence in each other helps a couple through life's difficulties and binds them to each other.

Some of us fear rejection by those we love, and we are afraid to reveal who we really are. We hide our true feelings and retreat into ourselves. This lack of faith or belief in ourselves and others can stop us as fast as anything in the development of significant relationships. Unless we learn to *believe in* others, we can never learn to be charitable or loving persons.

This part of love, like concern and patience, can also be placed on a continuum, as shown below. On one end of the continuum, at 0, is no righteousness, which would characterize an evil person, devoid of light and goodness and totally disobedient to the laws of God. Numbers 1, 2, and 3 represent increases in the righteous dimension, and 4 represents a very righteous person. One difference between righteousness and concern is that too much concern for others can hinder a marriage. There is an optimal amount, and too little or too much is bad. Righteousness is different: The more righteousness we have, the better.

0	1	2	3	4
No righteousness	Slight righteousness	Considerable righteousness	High righteousness	Very high righteousness

The Sermon on the Mount

This beautiful sermon also helps us understand what the Savior means by *love,* and many of its teachings help us know how to love in marriage. In the Beatitudes, the Savior taught us to be meek, merciful, pure, and peacemaking. Those who love as he teaches will use these ways of behaving. When you are tired, or unhappy, or when things are not going well, meekness, mercy, peacemaking, and a pure heart are like oil on troubled waters. And when one displays the opposites—arrogance, cruelty, troublemaking, and deception—things are always worse.

The greatest paradox in all human interaction is also in the Sermon on the Mount, and it is a key ingredient in the Savior's view of love. The natural pattern is for us to like those who like us and dislike those who don't like us. We do nice things to those who do nice things to us and get even when they abuse us. We return good for good and evil for evil.

This, however, is a lesser kingdom law, not a celestial law. The celestial law is to return good for good *and* good for evil. As the Savior taught,

> And behold, it is written, an eye for an eye, and a tooth for a tooth; But I say unto you, that ye shall not resist evil, but whosoever shall smite thee on thy right cheek, turn to him the other also; And if any man will sue thee at the law and take away thy coat, let him have thy cloak also; And whosoever shall compel thee to go a mile, go with him twain. . . .
> Love your enemies, bless them that curse you, do good to them that hate you, and pray for them who despitefully use you and persecute you. (3 Nephi 12:38-41, 44.)

How does this apply in marriage? None of us have perfect spouses, and so at times our spouses act in "less-than-desirable" ways. To be more clear, they are sometimes tired and ornery, and they say things that hurt us. They are not always fair and polite and considerate. They also have disagreements and arguments. They clam up, tell us off, get mad, get even, get lost, and get our goat. When these unfortunate moments occur, what do we do? Do we use the telestial or terrestrial laws and do unto them as they have done unto us—or worse? Or do we return good for the bad, pleasant for the unpleasant, kind for the unkind, soft for the hard, and patient for the impatient? Most of us are still in a fairly "fallen" state, and so we aren't able to live the Lord's law all of the time. Sometimes we are able to return good for evil, but few, if any, of us can do it all of the time. The law, however, is still there. The more a person can be loving, *especially when it is hard to do,* the better his marriage. The importance of being loving when it is hard is illustrated by the following lines:

> It is easy enough to be pleasant
> When life flows by like a song,
> But the man worthwhile is one who will smile,
> When everything goes dead wrong.
>
> For the test of the heart is trouble,
> And it always comes with the years,
> And the smile that is worth the praises of earth
> Is the smile that shines through the tears.
>
> —Author unidentified

Another important teaching in the Sermon on the Mount is that we are to be forgiving (3 Nephi 13:11-15). We need to be quick to forgive when we are wronged and always be ready to give each other another chance. Everyone does things that are unwise, inefficient, and thoughtless, and a forgiving spouse can help boost his partner's morale and motivate him or her to try to do better. The inability to forgive is always worse than the original wrong. As the Lord has said, "For he that forgiveth not his brother his trespasses standeth condemned before the Lord; for there remaineth in him the greater sin" (D&C 64:9).

In summary, it can be seen that love (charity) is a complex set of behaviors. It includes such different things as a concern for others, patience, a seeking for righteousness, mercy, a returning of good for evil, and a willingness to forgive. It is an absolutely essential ingredient if a marriage is to be successful. Without it, a person will very soon have nothing in his marriage. With it, he will be able to build a beautiful relationship that will do more than merely endure; it will create great joy and happiness and peace. Loving behaviors, therefore, ought to be the foundation upon which you build your marriage.

REASONS WHY LOVING IS IMPORTANT IN MARRIAGE

The social sciences help us understand why the love principle is so very important in marriage. A psychologist named Morton Deutsch has summarized a great deal of research and come up with an idea that he calls a "law" of human behavior. He has named it Deutsch's law (Deutsch 1973)*; in simple terms it is this:

2. Deutsch's Law: The more you act in a certain way, the more others around you also tend to act in that same way.

This law can be seen in such simple acts of life as smiling. If you smile at someone, he also tends to smile. The law operates in many other situations. If you start raising your voice and arguing, what do the others around you do? Calm down and speak softly? Almost never. Usually, the voices get louder and louder, and the argument gets more heated. If you compete with someone else for power or fame, what does he do? He competes too. If you help someone else get power or fame, what does he usually do? He helps you. If you are kind, considerate, and cooperative, what does this promote? It tends to create the same behavior in those around you.

What does Deutsch's law have to do with the love principle? It helps us realize why the love principle works. As the law suggests, when one person is loving, others tend to also act in loving ways—and the love spreads and spreads. Intimate relationships such as marriage thrive on the kindly, pleasant interaction that occurs when partners are loving, and they choke or die of apathy when the loving stops. Therefore, if a person wants a good cornerstone or foundation for a marital relationship, he ought to decide early in his relationship that he will always try to be as charitable as possible, *and he will try the hardest when it is the hardest to do.*

Deutsch's law is useful for more than just the love principle. It also helps you understand several other scriptural teachings and scientific findings. It helps you realize the significance of the scriptural saying: "A soft answer turneth away wrath: but grievous words stir up anger" (Proverbs 15:1). It helps you realize why the Lord taught the Golden Rule. When you act the way you'd like others to act, it promotes desirable types of interaction among everyone around you. The law also helps you understand why the Savior taught that you

* This idea is also expressed in a large amount of other scholarly literature. It is, for example, a central theme in the work of Jourard (1971) and Guerney (1978).

Children Learn What They Live

If a child lives with criticism,
    He learns to condemn.
If a child lives with hostility,
    He learns to fight.
If a child lives with ridicule,
    He learns to be shy.
If a child lives with shame,
    He learns to feel guilty.
If a child lives with tolerance,
    He learns to be patient.
If a child lives with encouragement,
    He learns confidence.
If a child lives with fairness,
    He learns justice.
If a child lives with security,
    He learns to have faith.
If a child lives with approval,
    He learns to like himself.
If a child lives with acceptance and friendship,
    He learns to find love in the world.

—Dorothy Law Nolte

should turn the other cheek, go the second mile, and give your cloak too when you are sued for your coat. When you return good for evil, you tend to spread goodness and extinguish evil. The ones who do evil to you will be more inclined to do good in the future because of the good you return to them.

It is important to realize that Deutsch's law has two different parts. One part is that your actions tend to be spread out around you. When you do something nice to someone else, that person tends to act nicely to the others he meets, and your act is multiplied many times. If you are kind and cheerful to your mate in the mornings, it will be easier for your mate to be kind and cheerful to the others he or she meets that day. This is the "ripple effect." You see it when you throw a pebble in a calm pond; the ripples spread out in all directions. This is shown in the top drawing in Figure 3:1.

The second part of Deutsch's law can be called the "restoration effect." This part states that the actions that spread out from you also tend to come back to you. If you are patient and understanding with faults of your spouse, the spouse will probably be more tolerant

Figure 3:1   The Two Parts of Deutsch's Law

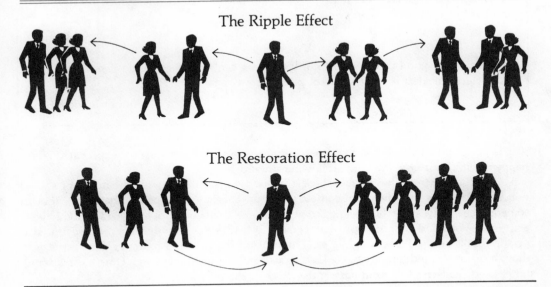

The Ripple Effect

The Restoration Effect

and understanding of your limitations and weaknesses. If you do something nice for your spouse, the chances are fairly good that your spouse will then do something nice for you. If you are considerate, your spouse will be considerate.

> If you are angry . . .
> If you are untrustworthy . . .
> If you are deceitful . . .
> If you listen . . .
> If you are tender and thoughtful . . .

This second part of Deutsch's law is diagrammed in the bottom part of Figure 3:1. This part is also described by Alma in his blessing to his son Corianton. He teaches what restoration is, and he illustrates Deutsch's law by explaining that whatever a person sends out shall be returned to him again.

> And now behold, is the meaning of the word restoration to take a thing of a natural state and place it in an unnatural state, or to place it in a state opposite to its nature?
>
> O, my son, this is not the case; but the meaning of the word restoration is to bring back again evil for evil, or carnal for carnal, or devilish for devilish—good for that which is good; righteous for that which is righteous; just for that which is just; merciful for that which is merciful.
>
> Therefore, my son, see that you are merciful unto your brethren; deal justly, judge righteously, and do good continually; and if ye do all these things then shall ye receive your reward; yea, ye shall have mercy restored unto you again; ye shall have justice restored unto you again; ye shall have a righteous judgment restored unto you again; and ye shall have good rewarded unto you again.
>
> For that which ye do send out shall return unto you again, and be restored. (Alma 41:12-15.)

A kind word is never lost. It keeps going on and on, from one person to another, until at last it comes back to you.

—Anonymous

If there is any good deed I can do, a kindness I can show, let me do it now. Let me not defer or neglect it, for I shall not pass this way again.

—Author unidentified

It is possible to have a law that does not always operate the way we expect it to. This happens with Deutsch's law in the following situations:

1. *Norms.* When we have strong beliefs or social norms that say we should do or should not do something, we tend to conform to our beliefs. This means that even though someone else may share his feelings, if you believe that you should not talk about your emotions, you tend to not copy that person, but to keep your feelings bottled up. If a person thinks he should be tough, strong, and bossy, he will tend to act in these ways even though others around him are being kind, considerate, and cooperative. Thus, norms sometimes keep Deutsch's law from having the effects it should.

2. *Power struggles.* If a person is trying to get more power in a relationship, Deutsch's law doesn't operate very well in creating good or pleasant results. If either person starts being kind or soft or cooperative, the other one will probably take advantage of the situation to get more power rather than copy the behavior. This is one reason that it is wise for couples to work out a power relationship that is agreeable to both of them.

3. *Scarce resources.* Whenever something is valuable and scarce, we hold on to it. If we think that compliments or praise are scarce, and that we will "use them up" if we pass them out, we'll hold on to them—even when others pass them out. If someone starts passing out scarce things, like money, others seldom reciprocate.

4. *Habits.* When we have deeply ingrained habits, we tend to stay with them rather than change. Therefore, if someone has a habit of being impatient or cross, he usually does not change very quickly just because others around him start being patient and pleasant. As we break these habits, we begin to see the law operating.

A different avenue of thought also supports the love principle. Erich Fromm has suggested that the "art of loving" is the key to fulfillment and happiness in everything that is precious in life. His view of love is summarized as follows:

Love is not primarily a relationship to a specific person; it is an *attitude,* an *orientation* of *character* which determines the relatedness of a person to the world as a whole, not toward one "object" of love. If a person loves only one fellow man, his love is not love but a symbiotic attachment, or an enlarged egotism. Yet, most people believe that love is constituted by the object, not by the faculty. In fact, they even believe that it is a proof of the intensity of their love when they do not love anybody except the "loved" person. This is the same fallacy which we have already mentioned above. Because one does not see that love is an activity, a power of the

Love Begets Love;
Courtesy Begets Courtesy

One day in western Canada a dinner guest in a home noticed that before taking his own seat at the dinner table, the husband walked over to his wife's place and held her chair for her while she sat down.

The guest, half in jest but half in seriousness, asked if that were the usual custom in the home, or if it were "company manners."

The husband smiled, and suggested that the question be directed to his wife. She in turn said, "Ever since we were married he has shown me this, and every other courtesy."

Then she laughed softly and added, "But you should watch the scramble when the boys are home to see who will help mother with her chair."

And where did those boys learn to honor and respect their mother in this way? From the husband and father who set the example.

Some years afterward, the same dinner guest was with another group in another city. When he was introduced to those present he discovered one couple by the same name as the family in Canada, and he asked if there was a relationship. The young man was a son of the couple in Canada.

The guest then told the story of his experience in the Canadian home. The wife of the son from the Canadian family then said, "I'd like to tell you a sequel to that story. You should see my boys scramble to help me with my chair."

Love begets love. Respect and courtesy bring response in kind. And where father respects wife, children respect mother and show her the same kind of courtesy they see manifested by the father. (Mark E. Petersen, *Marriage and Common Sense* [Salt Lake City: Bookcraft, 1972], pp. 98-99.)

soul, one believes that all that is necessary to find is the right object—and that every thing goes by itself afterward. This attitude can be compared to that of a man who wants to paint but who, instead of learning the art, claims that he has just to wait for the right object, and that he will paint beautifully when he finds it. If I truly love one person I love all persons, I love the world, I love life. (1956, pp. 38-39.)

Fromm also has some insights into why so many of us pay little attention to love. After pointing out that love demands a great deal of effort and concern, he comments:

And, maybe, here lies the answer to the question of why people in our culture try so rarely to learn this art, in spite of the deep-seated craving for love, almost everything else is considered to be more important than love: success, prestige, money, power—almost all of our energy is used for learning of how to achieve these aims, and almost none to learn the art of loving.

Could it be that only those things are considered worthy of being learned with which one can earn money or prestige, and that love, which "only" profits the soul, but is profitless in the modern sense, is a luxury we have no right to spend much energy on? (1956, p. 5.)

Without Love, We Have Nothing

The scriptures give us another reason why the love principle is vital in marriage. Paul and Mormon use a unique terminology in talking about charity, and none of the prophets ever use the same terminology about any other aspect of the gospel. Phrases like the following illustrate their point:

> "and have not charity, I am nothing."
> "for if he have not charity he is nothing."
> "and have not charity, it profiteth me nothing."
> "if ye have not charity, ye are nothing."
> "the greatest of these is charity."
> "wherefore he must needs have charity."

Apparently, one can have great virtue and many admirable characteristics, and do unbelievably good works, but none of these things matter at all if he does not have charity. As Paul said:

> And though I have the gift of prophecy, and understand all mysteries, and all knowledge; and though I have all faith, so that I could remove mountains, and have not charity, I am nothing.
> And though I bestow all my goods to feed the poor, and though I give my body to be burned, and have not charity, it profiteth me nothing. (1 Corinthians 13:2-3.)

Apparently a Christlike love is the one thing that is *absolutely necessary* in life. Other things such as faith, good works, tithing, providing a good income, rearing children properly, being generous to your spouse, being a good manager of money, coming home on time, giving your spouse attention and affection, and being a good citizen all help—but they are qualitatively different. You would never say that if you don't come home on time, you are nothing; or if you don't pay tithing, your other good traits are of no value; or if you are not generous to your spouse your marriage is a failure; or if you can't cook your marriage is of no value at all. These things help a marriage, but not one of them is absolutely necessary. Thus, if you have charitable love, the other things add to the quality of your marriage. If you don't have charitable love, you cannot have a successful marriage.

It is no accident that this chapter discusses charity. This is the first of many chapters discussing things you can do to have a successful marriage, and the first chapter ought to discuss the most important dimension: charitable love. Each of the following chapters, in a different way, builds on this foundation. *All of the later chapters tie back to this chapter. All of them show how charity is important to them. Thus, charity is a unifying theme or thread throughout this entire volume.*

To carry the analogy further, it is possible to build a marriage in different places. You can build on rock or on sand. Those who build on and around charitable love build on rock, where marriage can endure forever. Those who build mostly on a concern for themselves build on sand, and when the inevitable rains and winds of life come, such marriages will fall—and great is the fall of each marriage that does not last. This chapter deals with the foundation, the bedrock—charity. The later chapters help you know how to sow and cultivate on this foundation. They help you know when you are sowing by the wayside, and when you are sowing among thorns, and when you are sowing among stony places. Many marriages start out on the bedrock of charity, and they have a rich topsoil that will yield joy forever. Some marriages start out on the bedrock, but the seeds that are to yield fruit later are sown in stony places where there is little soil. The marriage starts out with promising shoots in a glorious and exciting way, but unwise planting causes the marriage to wither away.

The conclusion?

We can conclude that charity is absolutely necessary, *but by itself it is not enough.* We also need to learn how to do such things as wisely communicate, solve problems, manage money, and make good decisions in the daily struggles of life. We need to learn how to prepare ourselves to give and receive affection and cope with crises.

BECOMING MORE LOVING

How Loving Are You?

You can easily be concerned about others in a loving way when things are going well for you. You can love those who love you, do nice things for those who are nice to you, and be patient with those who are patient with you. But having real love means that you will respond in a loving way when things are not going well. As the Savior taught: "Ye have heard that it hath been said, Thou shalt love thy neighbour, and hate thine enemy. But I say unto you, Love your enemies, bless them that curse you, do good to them that hate you, and pray for them which despitefully use you, and persecute you. . . . For if ye love them which love you, what reward have ye? do not even the publicans the same? And if ye salute your brethren only, what do ye more than others? do not even the publicans so?" (Matthew 5:43-47.)

As Deutsch's law teaches, man's natural inclination is to return evil for evil, anger for anger, and wrong for wrong. Doing this, however, perpetuates these undesirable experiences. The truly loving person will try to break the cycle by doing the unnatural: returning good for evil, love for hate, and kindness for anger. It is difficult and challenging to do this, but it is especially important in marriage. In those moments when you think you have been wronged, you are much further ahead when you dig into your resources and find positive, kindly ways to respond. One reason this is useful in marriage is that many of the situations in which a person feels he has been wronged are misunderstandings or unintentional acts by those who love him. By turning the cycle around, you create peace and love and positive feelings.

A loving style of life also demands considerable maturity. Children naturally exhibit loving behaviors, but they can also be very unloving. Sometimes they are kind, gentle, loving, suffering, modest, and concerned about others. At other times, they are egotistical, selfish, concerned only about themselves, arrogant, impolite, and boorish. It is only when

To love takes time, patience, interest, attention. . . .

children are virtually grown that they are able to eliminate the unloving ways of behaving and become truly loving people. Paul was aware of this maturational aspect of love. He commented at the conclusion of his discussion on love: "When I was a child, I spake as a child, I understood as a child, I thought as a child: but when I became a man, I put away childish things." (1 Corinthians 13:11.)

Thus the loving style that the Savior taught is a difficult style of life to learn, and it can only be fully learned when one has reached a high level of maturity. Many do not master it in this life. Most of us are still in the process of trying to improve this part of our lives. The better a person becomes at it, the better his marriage will be.

What do we do in the meantime?

Each person ought to evaluate himself to determine where he is in the process of perfecting this part of his life. Are you fairly loving in some ways and not loving in others? If so, where do you do well, and where do you need the most improvement? It is only when you have insights like these that you can work effectively to improve yourself. Activity 3:1 at the end of this chapter is designed to help you evaluate yourself, to determine how loving you tend to be. Each of us ought to complete that exercise, to make an honest evaluation of himself.

Developing an Action Plan

Some of us learn a great deal from evaluating our loving (Activity 3:1), and others of us learn little, but all of us can use this exercise to help determine in which areas we need the most improvement. Some learn that they are more loving than they thought, and others learn that they love less effectively. Some are surprised at the differences between the way they see themselves and the way others see them; others are surprised at how similar the two views are. Whatever you learn, the exercise sets the stage for the next question:

*Since we all have room for improvement,
what should we do to improve?*

Several scholars (Scoresby, Apolonio, and Hatch 1974) have developed a method of making self-improvements that is effective and easy to use. They call it an "action plan." You can make action plans for many different things, and you will do so many times in the later chapters. The idea is introduced here so that you can use it to develop a personal plan that will help you improve your loving behavior. The outline for action plans is Activity 3:2 at the end of this chapter.

Improve Yourself Gradually

As you evaluate your tendency to be loving or unloving, and attempt to improve yourself, you need to keep several other things in mind. The Savior has given us some very lofty goals in this area, but he knows that we are living in a mortal condition where we have weaknesses and difficulty attaining his high goals. In his words, we are in a "fallen" condition. While we are in this less-than-ideal condition, we need to be wise in selecting strategies that will help us eventually attain the lofty goals he has given us. Some of us are wise, but others of us do not choose wise strategies. Let's briefly review several wise and unwise strategies.

One unwise approach is to think that the Lord expects us to become perfect immediately. We can call those who believe this the "overwhelmed." We overwhelmed Saints are intolerant of ourselves and others because we think that any failing or sin in ourselves or anyone else is damnable. We do not feel very good about ourselves because we know we are unacceptable, and we look down on others, too, when we see their imperfections. Some of us think that the Church is for the righteous; therefore, when people are dishonest in their business dealings or break the Word of Wisdom, we think they are being hypocritical when they come to church. Unfortunately, our strategy of becoming perfect (living all of the commandments *right now* and being intolerant of any failing) gets in our way; we are becoming perfect at a slower rate than we could if we were to find a better strategy. Our belief actually slows down our speed in becoming perfect. We would show more wisdom if we were to realize that we all need a great deal of time to perfect ourselves and that, while we are working at perfection, we may make many mistakes. As we (and others) make mistakes, we need forgiveness, encouragement, and acceptance. We don't need nagging, and we don't need to be continually reminded of our faults. We need understanding, patient spouses who will give us the time we need to perfect ourselves at our own speed.

Another unwise strategy can be called the "permissive" approach. We permissives do not realize that we need to continually work at the process of perfecting ourselves. We think that it will be an easy task that we can accomplish at a later time, and so we put it off. Unfortunately, we can't put it off. Our procrastination will build habits and beliefs that prevent us from learning how to be loving. In other words, we are building a different lifestyle that will get in the way of becoming Christlike—and the longer we behave this way, the harder it will be to begin the long process of unlearning our undesirable habits and learning to behave in loving ways. We permissives are the ones Nephi spoke of when he said: "And there shall also be many which shall say: Eat, drink and be merry; neverthe-less, fear God—he will justify in committing a little sin; yea, lie a little, take the advantage of one because of his words, dig a pit for thy neighbor; there is no harm in this; and do all these things, for tomorrow we die; and if it so be that we are guilty, God will beat us with a few stripes, and at last we shall be saved in the kingdom of God." (2 Nephi 28:8.)

One of the wise strategies we could adopt would be to set two types of goals, long-term and short-term. Each of us should have the long-term goal of becoming perfect in every way, but we should also realize that it is impossible to attain it immediately. Therefore, we must set a number of short-term goals and work on them, realizing that we are temporarily falling short of perfection. This approach permits us to concentrate on a few things at one time and improve them, while focusing on other things at a later time. This strategy demands some tolerance of imperfections and some acceptance of ourselves and others in our growing condition. Ironically, this acceptance of ourselves as we are helps us grow faster than the overwhelmed or permissive strategies.

As we adopt this strategy, we need to concentrate first on the most basic and funda-mental parts of the gospel—patience, kindness, concern for others, endurance, honesty, forgiveness, humility, and so on. Then, as we become fairly proficient in these areas, we can move on to higher laws such as purifying our minds and inclinations, avoiding pride, and being forgiving. As you make your action plan to help you become more loving, you need to set realistic short-term goals so that you can progress line upon line, precept upon precept. If you set goals that are too high, you are ignoring the scriptural advice that you should not "run faster or labor more than you have strength" (D&C 10:4). When you set realistic goals and work at them, you can gradually learn how to be better, and you will reap ever-increasing joy and peace.

SUMMARY

This chapter suggests that the one thing that makes the most difference in marriage is charitable love. If you are unselfishly concerned about the welfare of those around you, are patient in dealing with differences and problems, and try to do what is right, you make an immeasurable contribution to success in marriage. This chapter also identifies different aspects of charity, and includes an exercise to help you determine when and where you are loving and unloving. Both religious and scientific literature are discussed, and both show that love is important. Deutsch's law is discussed; it helps us understand why loving behaviors are so vitally important in marital relationships.

ACTIVITY 3:1
Evaluating Your Loving

Goal: To determine how loving you are by identifying where you are most and least loving.

1. Get a sheet of paper and write the answers to the following questions.

2. Use the following scale to evaluate yourself on the following twenty-two behaviors. Wait until you are alone and in a place where you have privacy and can think deeply and honestly.

0 = Rarely
1 = Occasionally
2 = Most of the time

When things are going well for me	When things aren't going well for me

1. I am as concerned with others as myself.
2. I am more concerned with others than myself.
3. I am patient.
4. I do the righteous thing.
5. I am long-suffering.
6. I act kindly toward others.
7. I am hopeful and optimistic.
8. I endure things well.
9. I am gentle.
10. I am meek and humble.
11. I am helpful to others.
12. I am considerate of others.
13. I envy others.
14. I boast.
15. I act in a "puffed-up" manner.
16. I am easily provoked.

17. I think about evil things.
18. I am glad about unfortunate or evil things.
19. I fail in my responsibilities toward others.
20. I hurt others' feelings.
21. I say things I don't mean and later regret.
22. I force my opinions on others.

3. Now, have two people who know you fairly well evaluate you the same way.

4. Compare the evaluations and determine the areas where:

   a. I am the most loving.
   b. I am the least loving.
   c. I am the most similar when things are going well and poorly.
   d. I am the most different when things are going well and poorly.
   e. I agree the most with the others that evaluated me.
   f. I agree the least with the others that evaluated me.
   g. I feel I would like to make improvements in the next weeks.

ACTIVITY 3:2
An Action Plan·

1. What do I want to change?

   Is it to stop doing something?
   Is it to start doing something?
   Is it to do something more often?
   Is it to do something less often?
   What it is I want to do: _____

   _____

   _____

2. How much commitment do I have to make the change?

   Will I be honest about my actions in regard to the action plan?
   Will I be responsible for what I do? (no shifting of the responsibility to another person
      or to situational circumstances)
   Do I really want to make the change?
   What will be the reward for changing?
   How committed am I to change? _____

   _____

   _____

3. What exactly is my plan?

Is it a small unit of observable behavior? (This may be part of a larger unit you are interested in changing, but keep it small and manageable.)
How often do I plan to do it?
When do I plan to do it?
State it in behavioral terms; include who will do *what* for *whom* and *when* I will finish it.

4. Follow-up.

Keep a record of the result in my action plan. Remember that approximations are successes, not failures. Perseverance may bring total success.
Here are the results of my action plan after completing it: _____
_____
_____

SUPPLEMENTARY READINGS

Covey, Stephen R. *Spiritual Roots of Human Relations.* Salt Lake City: Deseret Book Co., 1972.

Deutsch, Morton. *The Resolution of Conflict.* New Haven: Yale University Press. 1973.

Fromm, Erich. *The Art of Loving.* New York: Harper & Row, 1956.

Lee, J. A. "The Styles of Loving," *Psychology Today,* October 1974, pp. 43-51.

Madsen, Truman G. *Four Essays on Love.* Salt Lake City: Bookcraft, Inc., 1971.

Skidmore, Rex A. *Marriage: Much More Than a Dream.* Salt Lake City: Deseret Book Co., 1979.

4

CREATING
SELF-WORTH

*For as he thinketh
in his heart, so is he.*
—Proverbs 23:7

Self-esteem is a term that defines how well you like yourself. If you like who you are, you have high esteem, and if you do not like yourself, you have low esteem. Self-esteem is different from *self-concept*. The self-concept is the view or picture one has of himself—what he thinks he is. In other words, a person's self-concept is the image he has of himself, and his esteem is the evaluative judgment that he makes of this conception. Notice how the following statements differ in indicating self-concept and self-esteem:

I have curly hair (self-concept).
I'm better looking with my hair curly (self-esteem).
I can hit a golf ball 230 yards (self-concept).
Ah, I'm good enough now that I can hit it 230 yards (self-esteem).
I can't do anything right (self-esteem).
I'm no good anyway (self-esteem).
I'm a B-average student at the university (self-concept).
Being a student at the university gives me a feeling of accomplishment (self-esteem).

Our self-esteem usually goes up when we act the way we should. It goes down when we do things we believe we shouldn't. Also, when others treat us as friends we feel good about ourselves and have high esteem. When others ignore us or indicate we aren't acceptable to them, our esteem drops.

A GENERAL PRINCIPLE ABOUT SELF-ESTEEM

Modern social science has discovered that changes in our self-esteem have some very important effects on our behavior. As our esteem increases, we have confidence in our abilities, and we work harder at doing the things that we want to accomplish. Social

> I must conquer my loneliness
> alone.
> I must be happy with myself
> or I have
> nothing
> to offer you.
> Two halves have
> little choice
> but to join;
> And yes, they
> do make a whole,
> but two wholes
> when they coincide . . .
> that is
> beauty,
> that is
> love.
>
> —Peter McWilliams

psychologists call this an increase in our "striving behaviors." We strive harder to do the things that we want to do, and as a result we do a better job. We accomplish more and we feel better about it. This has a cyclic effect as our esteem prompts us to work better and accomplish more, and this in turn further enhances our esteem, which prompts us to work harder, and so on. The result is that a person who has high esteem is apt to be highly effective.

Decreases in our esteem have the opposite effect. As our esteem decreases, our striving behaviors decrease, and we do things less well. This sets the opposite cycle into effect. As we do things less well our esteem drops, which further decreases our performance. If this cycle is not stopped, it can have a devastating effect on our lives.

Decreases in our self-esteem also have several other effects. Each of us has a point on his self-esteem continuum at which he becomes threatened. If his self-esteem drops below that point, it troubles him; he becomes anxious and upset. That point is probably found at different places for different people, and different things threaten different people, but we all get threatened when our esteem drops below that point.

The first thing most of us do when our esteem is threatened is resort to some defense mechanism to ward against the threat. Some of the common defense mechanisms that we use are listed on page 46. Threats also make us concerned about ourselves and so our

---

Common Defense Mechanisms

Projection: Inappropriately placing the blame for problems or difficulties on others, or attributing one's own unethical desires to others.

Compensation: Covering up a weakness by emphasizing or concentrating on traits that are acceptable, or making up for frustration in one area by turning to another area.

Regression: Retreating to behaviors that were appropriate at an earlier stage of development (such as childhood). Usually this involves less mature behavior, such as having temper tantrums, throwing things, and crying.

Putting others down: Trying to depreciate the value, contributions, or traits of other persons so that one will be more adequate as compared with them.

Denial: Refusing to perceive or face something by being preoccupied with other things, getting sick, selectively perceiving, etc.

Aggression: Attacking persons or things to get even, divert attention, "show" them, or defeat them. Aggression can be physical or verbal and is frequently covert rather than overt.

Reaction-formation: Coping with dangerous or unacceptable feelings or desires by expressing exaggerated opposing attitudes and types of behavior.

Emotional insulation: Withdrawing emotional involvement by becoming passive, apathetic, or uninterested.

Repression: Preventing uncomfortable, dangerous, or threatening thoughts from entering one's consciousness.

Acting out: Reducing anxiety that is aroused by forbidden or uncomfortable thoughts or wishes by permitting their expression.

Diverting attention: Focusing on different issues so that one's inadequacies will be less visible.

Escape: Departing either physically or mentally from a situation that is too hurtful.

---

attention turns inward. We worry and fret about ourselves. We get depressed and angry. We worry less about the welfare of others because we're so concerned about ourselves, and this means that we are less loving people. Our anxiety, worry, defensiveness, and self-concern also interfere with our ability to communicate and solve problems. The net result is that substantial decreases in self-esteem undermine our ability to manage our lives effectively. Our marital stewardships usually suffer and so can other aspects of our lives.

These processes can be summarized in a general principle* that is worth remembering. It is:

* There is a great deal of scientific evidence for this principle. Reviews of some of the research are in Wilie (1979) and Coopersmith (1967).

Figure 4:3   Effects of Self-Esteem on Other Things

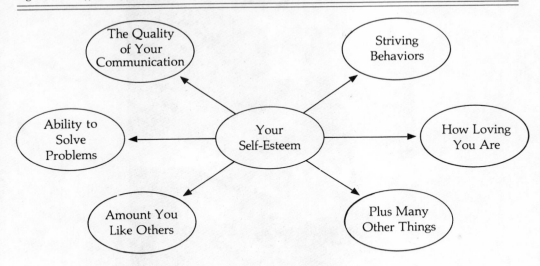

3. The Self-Esteem Principle: Changes in your self-esteem influence many aspects of your lives, including your ability to be a loving person, the quality of your communication, the quality of your problem solving, your striving behaviors, and your feelings of liking or disliking those who influence your esteem.

The relationships in this rather complex principle can be seen in Figure 4:3. They can also be summarized in a different way, as shown here:

Decreases in Esteem	*Increases in Esteem*
decrease striving behavior	increase striving behavior
decrease quality of communication	increase quality of communication
decrease quality of problem solving	increase quality of problem solving
decrease loving behavior (charity)	increase loving behavior (charity)
decrease the amount you like the person who prompts the decrease	increase the amount you like the person who assists in the increase

HOW CAN YOU USE THE SELF-ESTEEM PRINCIPLE TO BUILD RELATIONSHIPS?

The self-esteem principle teaches that the way you feel about yourself is an important part of life. It also shows several things you can do to help build good relationships with those around you. If each of us can maintain a positive self-image and help others enhance their esteem, a number of things will improve. We will like each other more and want to be around each other. We will also be able to communicate and solve problems better. Most importantly, we will act in more loving ways toward each other.

Showing an interest in someone creates
self-esteem . . . in both.

The payoffs are tremendous!

This principle is also taught in the scriptures. The Savior said that the most important commandment we have is to love God. The second most important commandment "is like unto it, Thou shalt love thy neighbour as thyself" (Matthew 22:39). This is a commandment that we often keep perfectly—we love others the same as we love ourselves. If a person believes he is of no worth, others have no worth to him, and he feels inadequate in expressing love to them. To show love either to God or to his other children, our brothers and sisters, we must first feel good about ourselves.

This leads to the question: "What can you do to enhance esteem?" The following six skills or behaviors can help you enhance your own esteem or the esteem of others—or both.

Getting and Keeping a Perspective as to Who You Really Are

Your view of who you are influences your esteem. If you think of yourself and others as the culmination of an evolutionary spiral in which you are just a bit more advanced than the chimpanzee, you will easily become discouraged. Or if you view yourself the way a few

---

True Greatness

A man is as great as the dreams he dreams,
As great as the love he bears;
As great as the values he redeems,
And the happiness he shares.
A man is as great as the thoughts he thinks,
As the worth he has attained;
As the fountains at which his spirit drinks
And the insight he has gained.
A man is as great as the truth he speaks,
As great as the help he gives,
As great as the destiny he seeks,
As great as the life he lives.

—C. E. Flynn

---

psychologists do, as a bundle of conditioned responses and nervous synapses, you'll never have much esteem. Or you can put together a combination of pseudoinsights of scholars of the past few centuries and really get discouraged.

What is the truth as to who we are?

Each of us is an important individual in a vast and beautiful scheme. Part of us, our intelligence, has existed forever and will continue to exist forever. We are the children of Deity. We were given spiritual bodies by heavenly parents who cared for us and loved us enough to build an earth where we could come to get the benefits of physical bodies and grow through earthly experiences. Our potential is majestic. We can become gods. We can learn how to create worlds and give life and beauty to new spirits, new people who need us. Each man is a potential prince and king, a leader of millions, a creator and ruler. Each woman is a potential princess and queen.

One cause of low self-esteem is a failure to recognize the potential worth of man, which in turn can create difficulties in a marriage. It is difficult, in fact it is impossible to realize who we really are—offspring of Deity and gods in embryo—and at the same time have low self-esteem. It is only when we forget who we are that our esteem can drop. It is easy and proper and good to ponder these things for a while, to embrace them in our hearts in quiet moments and develop a proper pride, a wholesome confidence, a dignity and majesty that swells and grows. Even though in our mortal condition we may fall and stumble, lose our way, make mistakes, and do many things that require repentance, we ought to have an underlying feeling that we have a divine destiny, a noble heritage, a supreme importance.

Supportive friendship creates feelings of self-worth.

Treating Others with the Respect This View Creates

Once we have a proper view of who we are in an eternal scheme, we can easily treat ourselves and others with respect. Each person is a child of God and can grow to become a god—even if he is presently behaving in very ungodly and immoral ways. For example, how many Sauls are there among us who are behaving wrongly but will repent and become great people? How many of those around us are like the sons of Mosiah, delinquents of their day, who will eventually turn around and become saints? If we treat everyone with respect and consideration, if we love our enemies (Matthew 5:43-44) and do good to those who revile and oppose, it will enhance their esteem and our own, and help improve our world.

When you disagree with someone, do you still treat him as an important person? When you take someone out for a date, or are taken out, do you treat that person with the dignity he or she deserves? When you do, it enhances their esteem and your own, and all reap the benefits.

Learning to Recognize Levels of Esteem

One useful skill inherent in the self-esteem principle is being able to tell when someone else has high or low feelings of esteem. Knowing how others feel about themselves can help

Years ago, a young man in London aspired to be a writer. But everything seemed to be against him. He had not been able to attend school more than four years. His father had been flung into jail because he couldn't pay his debts, and this young man often knew the pangs of hunger. As a boy, he got a job pasting labels on bottles of blacking in a rat-infested warehouse; and he slept at night in a dismal attic room with two other boys, guttersnipes from the slums of London. He had so little confidence in his ability to write that he sneaked out and mailed his manuscript in the dead of night so that nobody would laugh at him. Story after story was refused. Finally the great day came when one was accepted. True, he wasn't paid a shilling for it, but one editor had praised him. One editor had given him recognition. He was so thrilled that he wandered aimlessly around the streets with tears rolling down his cheeks.

The praise, the recognition that he received by getting one story in print changed his whole career, for if it hadn't been for the encouragement, he might have spent the rest of his life working in rat-infested factories. You may of heard of that boy, too. *His name was Charles Dickens.*

—Author unidentified

you know how to respond to them. On the other hand, if you are not sensitive to changes in others' esteem, you may behave in harmful ways. The following account from a former student is an illustration.

> Now that I understand about self-esteem and what it does I can see what I was doing in a relationship with a girl. We developed a pattern of cutting each other down in our jokes and humor. At first it was fun, but then it wasn't. She would cry a lot and we'd get into fights until we broke up. I bet that things would have been different if we'd lifted each other up rather than cut each other down.

Most of the time we have to rely on nonverbal behaviors for clues as to how others are feeling about themselves, since most of us do not verbalize these feelings. It might help if we were more verbal, but in the meantime we need to be sensitive to the many subtle indicators of high or low esteem.

You may want to find new ways to tell what is happening to your self-esteem, and find new ways to enhance it. Or you may want to find new ways to enhance the esteem of others around you. The three activities at the end of this chapter can help you grow in these areas. Activity 4:1 is the most elementary one because it deals simply with ability to recognize changes in self-esteem. Activity 4:2 can help you increase your feelings of self-worth, and Activity 4:3 can help you understand and cope with defensiveness.

SUMMARY

This chapter first explains the difference between self-concept and self-esteem. Self-concept is what a person thinks he is, and self-esteem is how much he likes or dislikes what he thinks he is. The self-esteem principle explains that increases and decreases in self-esteem influence many things in a person's life, such as his ability to be loving, the quality of his communication, his ability to solve problems, the amount he likes others, and how hard he strives to get good things done. It is therefore a very important part of life, and each person would do well to adjust his expectations and behavior so he can feel good about himself.

ACTIVITY 4:1
Recognizing Changes in Self-Esteem

Goal: To improve your ability to recognize changes, especially negative changes, in self-esteem.

1. With another person (spouse, fiance(e), roommate, friend), make a list of verbal and nonverbal signals that indicate a lowering of self-esteem in yourself and others around you.

2. Put the list in a place where you can refer to it often until you know it fairly well.

3. After being conscious of these factors for a week, evaluate the effect this awareness has on you and your relationships.

ACTIVITY 4:2
Understanding and Improving Your Own Self-Esteem

Goal: To better understand what influences your feelings of self-esteem.

1. List on a piece of paper five actions that enhance your self-esteem and that you do on a regular basis to convince yourself you are an adequate, acceptable person. (Some can do this easily, but others have difficulty. If you have difficulty doing it, discuss the problem with someone you are close to and see if he or she can help you.)

2. List on the same piece of paper five actions that tend to decrease your self-esteem periodically (or continually)—situations or events that contribute to uneasy, guilty, or uncomfortable feelings.

3. Think about the items on the two lists and try to determine what your "net" feelings about yourself tend to be.

4. Identify two or three things you could do to create a more positive image of yourself, and implement them for one week.

5. How did this activity change you?

ACTIVITY 4:3
Recognizing Defensiveness

Goal: To increase your ability to recognize defensive behavior.

1. Get someone you live with to help you with this exercise. It will involve having an initial discussion of fifteen to thirty minutes and then being alert to several things for a week.

2. Review the list of defense mechanisms on page 46 together with the other person so that you both understand what they are.

3. During the next week each of you point it out to the other whenever you think he is acting defensively. It may be wise to identify what kinds of statements would be acceptable ways to point this out, as moments when we are defensive also tend to be moments when we are less open-minded about having others tell us we are defensive.

4. Whenever possible in these defensive situations, try to identify the reasons for the defensiveness. This type of analysis will probably also help you increase your ability (a) to see what influences self-esteem and feelings of anxiety, and (b) to see what effects changes in self-esteem and anxiety have on defensiveness.

5. At the end of the week, evaluate the experience to determine what effect this exercise has had on (a) your ability to communicate, (b) your feelings toward yourself, and (c) your feelings toward the other person.

5

COMMUNICATING
IN
MARRIAGE

*. . . and with all thy getting
get understanding.*

—Proverbs 4:7

The following situation indicates the importance of communication in marriage:

I was more than a little relieved as we finally pulled out of the driveway and headed for my chaplain interview with one of the brethren in Salt Lake City. Living in southern Utah had its advantages, among which was the opportunity for our children to grow up with responsibilities on the farm. This was a moment, however, when I was glad to know that these daily chores would soon be in our past.

Even though Jenifer and I had both grown up in this community, I was now ready for a change, and I felt that being away from our families would be good for our relationship. After all, she did have a tendency to run to her mother whenever we had a conflict. As a matter of fact, it was because of this that I had decided to leave the seminary classroom and enter the military as a chaplain. Thank goodness, I thought, Jenifer always goes along with my decisions.

The miles passed in silence, with Jenifer and me both in deep thought. It was just four hours later that we arrived in the parking lot east of the Church Office Building. Both of us were anxious and nervous as we were introduced to the general authority who was to provide the final stamp of approval for our new life.

"Please come in and sit down," he said with a comforting calmness. We had scarcely done so when he leaned back in his chair, looked me straight in the eye, and said, "So your sights are set on a life of travel, Brother Durrance. Please tell me how you feel."

I looked at Jenifer, who seemed even more nervous than myself. Swallowing hard, I took a deep breath and exclaimed, "More than anything in the world I want to expand my horizons and represent the Church well in the chaplaincy."

I had hardly finished speaking when I realized that he was not looking at me, but was looking thoughtfully at Jenifer. Sensing something was wrong, he asked, "Please tell me how you feel about this change, Sister Durrance."

For a moment there was silence as tears began to well up in her eyes, and then the dam burst. Jenifer just cried and cried, and there I was, not knowing what to do. At last she regained her composure and whispered, "I feel like a total failure. I know that I should be supportive of James, but I just can't stand the thoughts of leaving our home, our families, and all of the roots we have established. I have never lived any place else, and I will just die if we go into the military."

I was stunned! I couldn't believe what I was hearing. The rest of the interview was meaningless, as I knew my dreams had been shattered.

It was a long ride home.

This couple had come so far, but they had communicated so little. Communication is the lifeblood of a growing and meaningful relationship. It is therefore crucial that you learn to communicate effectively. This chapter and the two that follow identify several principles and skills that can help you improve your communication. The later chapters then build on this foundation.

A GENERAL PRINCIPLE

The main principle of communication in marriage is as follows:

4. The Communication Principle: The more effective the communication, the better the marriage and family life.*

Effective communication is not simply a matter of speaking clearly or listening well. It is much more complex and subtle than this. There are millions of little things in a marital system, such as the time of day, the color of the room, moods, and biorhythms, that all influence communication.

There are some parts of communication that are necessary and other parts that are helpful but not necessary. Being able to express yourself and listening to others are essential parts because communication breaks down when you don't do them. Being alert to the feedback that you get from others also helps, but it isn't absolutely necessary. This is similar to the functioning of a car. There are some parts that are absolutely essential if the car is to run effectively: wheels and gasoline, for instance. When you run out of gas, the whole car comes to a stop, and when you have a flat tire or no tire at all, the car can't move. A nice wax job, soft seats, a stereo, and tinted windshield make the car better, but you can get by without them.

The following pages identify some skills that can help you communicate effectively. Some of these skills are absolutely necessary, but others are helpful but less crucial. As you study the skills, you ought to identify the ones that you are pretty good at and those in

---

* Common sense argues that this generalization is valid. In addition, there is considerable scientific evidence for it. Navran's (1967) comparison of happily and unhappily married groups found a correlation of .82 between quality of communication and marital adjustment. He concluded that "communication and marital adjustment are so highly correlated that anything having an effect on one will have a similar effect on the other" (p. 183). Bienvenu (1970) and Murphy and Mendelson (1973) made similar studies later, and found essentially the same relationships. Slightly different methods were used by Kahn (1970) and Corrales (1975), but they too found significant relationships between the quality of communication and marital satisfaction. More recently, Holman (1980) studied a group of Latter-day Saint couples, and he found that communication was correlated higher than any of his other factors.

which you have room for improvement. You can then develop your own plan to grow and improve.

COMMUNICATION SKILLS

Listening

Listening is one of the essential parts of communication. Most people know it is important to listen, but many who have this intellectual awareness do not have good listening habits. For example, how often are you thinking so much about what you are going to say that you don't really listen to what the other person is saying? How often are you so sure of yourself that your mind slams shut while someone else is trying to explain something? And how often do people say something that is important to them—only to have the next comment completely ignore what was said? Oh, that we could be like the wise old owl:

> A wise old owl sat on an oak.
> The more he saw, the less he spoke.
> The less he spoke, the more he heard.
> Why can't we all be like that bird?
>
> —Author unidentified

It may help your listening if you think about how important it is to our Father in Heaven. As he introduced his Son to Joseph Smith, he commented, "This is My Beloved Son. Hear Him!" (Joseph Smith—History 1:17). The Savior also taught that as we get "ears to hear" and "eyes to see," we should hear and see as much as we can, listen and look as much as we can, to try to understand. Later, as he gave revelations to Joseph Smith, he would frequently begin by saying things like "Listen to the voice of . . . Jesus Christ," and "Hearken and hear, O ye my people" (D&C 39 and 41). To hearken means to give careful attention. The prophets have also given more than a little attention to listening. Paul pleaded with King Agrippa, "Wherefore I beseech thee to hear me patiently" (Acts 26:3), and John commented, "Blessed [are] . . . they that hear the words of this prophecy" (Revelation 1:3).

Real listening is one of the highest forms of human influence. When we listen, it becomes Heavenly Father's most prominent method of influencing us. It is an art that is learned and that requires an emotional and spiritual sensitivity that goes beyond words alone to the feelings and real meanings of what is said. By truly listening you are saying to another, "You're a person of worth; I love you, respect you, and want to understand you." Marion D. Hanks once said, "Every human being is trying to say something to others, trying to cry out, 'I am alive. Notice me; speak to me; listen to me; confirm for me that I am important, that I matter!'"

Listening involves many different things:

1. The physical aspects of listening are to: (a) lean toward my partner to show involvement and concern; (b) look at my partner, because emotions are often communicated

Listening is an art.

through the eyes and I can better understand my partner's feelings by watching his/her eyes; (c) give my partner feedback by nodding my head or vocalizing a few responses from time to time.

2. The attitude and spirit I adopt is the most important aspect of listening. I can go through the outward motions of listening but not really be hearing anything if I don't have the proper attitude and spirit.

3. I can best help my partner by being completely understanding and setting aside my own perception, reactions, and feelings as I listen.

4. I must put myself in my partner's shoes and try with all of the energy of my heart to see the world through his or her eyes.

5. I must try by my tone and manner to convey that I accept unconditionally my partner's right to express honestly his or her own unique feelings and views of the world.

6. I cannot ask interrogating or side-tracking questions or present my own opinions, perceptions, or viewpoints about what my partner is saying. If I do need to ask questions in order to understand better, I ask them in a tentative way and in a tone of voice that communicates acceptance—i.e., "What do you mean by . . . ?" or "Do you mean . . . ?" or "Tell me more about your feelings."

7. While I am trying to understand, I should not interpret things for my partner; I should not make suggestions about how to alter the situation. My goal is to simply hear, understand, and accept my partner's feelings and views. Achieving acceptance and understanding may also involve feeding back an understanding of what my partner is saying for verification. (i.e., "It sounds like you feel . . .") Real acceptance and understanding take active listening and communicating to my partner what I hear him/her saying without opinions and judgment. I must also communicate what I need from him in order to understand him more completely.*

It is almost impossible to train a person to speak openly, honestly, and constructively of his innermost feelings, wishes, and needs unless he has acquired the faith that such expression will meet with acceptance rather than with coolness or rejection.

Activity 5:1 at the end of this chapter can help you evaluate your listening habits, and even those of us who are sure we are good listeners may benefit from completing it. You may find that there is a difference between your view of your listening habits and the opinions others have about how well you listen. When this is the case, you may want to find some ways to improve your listening skills.

Checking Out

Many times you will find yourself in situations in which
—You think you understand the person, but you aren't sure.
—You are finally getting a glimpse of what is going on.
—You are pretty sure you understand, but the other person doesn't think you do.
—You think you understand what is happening inside the other person, but the other person doesn't seem to understand yet.

In these situations, the skill of *checking out* can be useful. Checking out is the process of asking a question or saying something to find out if you are understanding correctly. In some situations it is simple: For example, you may hear someone ask for something at the dinner table and not be sure whether he said the water or the butter. A simple statement like, "You wanted the butter?" may be enough checking out. In other situations, such as when you are trying to understand complex and deeply felt emotions, checking things out takes more time—and also more tact, delicacy, patience, and understanding.

There are three main ways to check out one's understanding (Miller, Nunnally, and Wackman 1975, 105-9). They are: (1) ask a simple question; (2) make a summary statement; and (3) reflect or paraphrase. There are some do's and don'ts for each of these.

Asking a simple question. Questions that ask *who, what, when,* or *how* are usually the best type. For example:

1. Who did you say did it?
2. What did you mean when you said . . . ?
3. Where did you say you were?

---

* Some of this material is adapted from Bernard G. Guerney, Jr., *Relationship Enhancement,* 1978.

4. When do you think I should . . . ?
5. How often did you say?

These questions are open-ended, and you usually get quite a bit of information. If you want some more specific information, you can ask more specific questions, such as:

1. Did you say Harry should do that?
2. Was it five or six?
3. What did you think was the cause of . . . ?

When you are checking out, it is usually wise to avoid questions that ask "Why?" A *why* question usually leads to new issues, new information, or exploration of something that hasn't been covered before. It seldom helps you verify what was just said.

Summarizing. Here you try to pull a number of things together and check them all out at once. You do this with a statement rather than a question, but you often imply that you'd like the other person to let you know if you've summarized it all correctly. Sometimes you may even make a summary statement and then add something like, "Have I got it straight?"

Summarizing places more responsibility on the person who is checking out, because that person is then restating the point or idea in his or her own words. It takes more time and energy, but it is sometimes more useful than a simple question, because a misunderstanding in the summary can be pinpointed and corrected. Also, if the summary is correct, the other person has more assurance that he or she has been understood.

It is usually wise to state the conclusion or summary in a tentative manner rather than state it as a firm conclusion. This makes it easier for the other person to either confirm it or to correct it. Some examples of summary statements are these:

"Then what is at the bottom of it is that I haven't shown as much consideration as I should, and this has gradually made you feel like I don't care about our relationship?"

"So you'd prefer bucket seats, and you want the green car if we can get the stripe down the side, but you'd rather have the blue one if we can't get the one with the stripe?"

"I gather that you wouldn't be too happy about having my mother stay with us all summer, but two weeks would be okay."

"When we add it all up, it looks like it would be better not to buy it. Is that where you are?"

Paraphrasing. This is the process of restating or reflecting what the other person has said. Sometimes this is done naturally. For example, if someone tells you his telephone number, you will often repeat it back to see if you have it right. In other situations it is not as natural, but it can be very helpful. When someone is expressing his reasons for doing something, sharing his feelings or opinions or wishes, you can learn a lot by paraphrasing what you think he has said. When someone is trying to understand a problem he is having or just getting something off his chest, you can be very helpful to him if you listen a lot and paraphrase a little.

Occasionally the other person's exact words can be used, but it is generally more helpful to use different words. It is also useful if the paraphrasing can get closer to the heart of the issue, the feeling, or problem rather than repeat the ideas exactly. This has the advantage of helping move the conversation along, as well as checking out. The following example illustrates this process:

"I feel like Mother is always watching me when she's here, and that inside she's shaking her head about how I do things. I've tried to not get stirred up inside, but there are times when I can just feel her eagle eye on me, and when she says something about how I ought to be doing things, I just get all tied up inside."

"You resent it when she criticizes you."

"That's right, and it's more than just a little too. Sometimes . . ."

Many nonverbal messages are communicated when you paraphrase. If these messages have a connotation of condemnation or wrongness, the reflection will tend to make your spouse stop exploring feelings. If the nonverbalized messages convey an empathetic understanding and a warm concern, the reflection tends to increase the exploration of feelings.

As with all of the skills and techniques discussed in this chapter, reflection or paraphrasing is not a cure-all for communication problems. It does, however, seem to be a method of communicating that you can use effectively at certain times to create certain processes in your marital system. Gordon* (1970, pp. 57-59) has identified some further effects of paraphrasing beyond the getting of information. He suggests that it:

—helps individuals free themselves of troublesome feelings.

—helps individuals become less afraid of negative feelings.

—promotes a relationship of warmth between two individuals who are communicating.

—facilitates problem solving by the individual to whom the reflection is directed.

—creates a greater tendency to be willing to listen to the reflector's thoughts and ideas.

—leaves the initiative in the conversation with the individual to whom the reflection is directed.

—replaces other ways of interacting that have harmful effects.

Gordon has also identified several situations in which paraphrasing is useful, and several situations in which it is inappropriate. He suggests that it is the most useful when a person has a problem (in Gordon's terms, "owns" a problem). It is helpful for one to get the problem out in the open or talk about it in such a way that he can better define what the problem is. He can explore its implications or search for ways to cope with it without having someone else actively make suggestions, propose solutions, or evaluate or judge him or the problem.

Gordon then suggests that reflection is useless and inopportune, for example, when persons explore their own feelings, when there is too little time to "open up" feelings and work them out, when a situation is resolved, when people are tired of exploring their own

---

* Gordon uses the term "active listening" to describe paraphrasing. Others, such as Carl Rogers, have used the term "reflecting" to describe this process.

feelings, and when another person needs assistance or help. The following examples illustrate situations in which reflection is inappropriate. A straight answer is all that is wanted.

Husband: Can you give me a ride to the office this morning? My car is still in the garage.
Wife: You'd like a ride to the office.

Wife: How much would it cost to re-cover the living room couch?
Husband: You're worried about the cost of re-covering it.

Sometimes we think that paraphrasing is merely putting the other person's ideas in another way, trying to say the same thing with different words. Such word-swapping may merely result in the illusion of mutual understanding as in the following example:*

Sarah: Jim should never have become a teacher.
Fred: You mean teaching isn't the right job for him?
Sarah: Exactly! Teaching is not the right job for Jim.

Instead of trying to reword Sarah's statement, Fred might have asked himself, "What does Sarah's statement mean to me?" In that case the interchange might have been more useful:

Sarah: Jim should never have become a teacher.
Fred: You mean he is too harsh with the children? Maybe even cruel?
Sarah: Oh, no. I meant that he has such expensive tastes that he can't ever earn enough as a teacher.
Fred: Oh, I see. You think he should have gone into a field that would have ensured him a higher standard of living.
Sarah: Exactly! Teaching is not the right job for Jim.

Some people have difficulty learning to paraphrase because they think it is phony or that it is a kind of mind-reading. They think that they are expected to say what the other person is thinking. Of course, you'd feel inadequate to such a task. However, the task is a simple one if you remember that your paraphrase is not an attempt to prove you can read the other's thoughts; it is an attempt to let him know the meaning *you* get from his statements.

Although most people paraphrase far too little, it is possible to do it too much. If you paraphrase almost everything someone says, he may become annoyed at your unwillingness to assume that you understand even simple, obvious points. Or he may begin to suspect that you are trying to put words in his mouth, or that you are avoiding expressing your own opinions.

Frequent paraphrasing seems especially appropriate in two general conditions: (1) When mistakes might be costly, accuracy of communication becomes more important. To assume understanding rather than checking it out under such a condition is to risk grave conse-

---

* The rest of the section on paraphrasing is adapted from Wallen (1968).

quences. (2) Strong feelings in the sender and/or the receiver increase the possibility that comments will be misunderstood. Strong feelings have the effect on human communication that static does on electronic communication: They distort or obscure parts of the message. In such cases, paraphrasing becomes crucial as a way of insuring that the message comes through as intended. The next time someone is angry with you or you are angry with him, try paraphrasing what he says until he agrees that you understand what he is trying to convey. Then note the effect this has on the other person's feelings and also on your own. You can also use Activity 5:2 at the end of this chapter to improve your ability to paraphrase effectively.

Reversing places. Sometimes when you are communicating you are not sure that the messages you want to send are being correctly understood by the other person. At other times, you think that you correctly understand what someone else is trying to communicate, but the other person doesn't think that you understand him or her. The technique of reversing roles can be used in such situations to determine how well the receiver of the message is understanding the sender. When you reverse places, you agree to change positions temporarily so that the one who was trying to communicate the information becomes the listener. The person who is temporarily assuming the role of the "sender" of the message then tries to explain the information to the person who was previously trying to help him or her understand that same message.

Sometimes you understand the information others are trying to explain more correctly than they think, and when you reverse roles, the others are surprised to hear you accurately tell them what they have been trying to communicate. At other times, you may think you are accurately understanding, but you are not. When this occurs, the reversal can help the others explain their ideas because your attempt to communicate the information can give them some clues about which parts you do and do not understand. The opposite, of course, also works, for at times you are better understood than you think you are, and at other times other individuals will not understand you as well as they thought they did. When they misunderstand you, role reversal can help, as you can carefully observe which parts of your messages the other persons have not correctly understood and can then restate those parts.

There are several different ways you can bring up the suggestion to reverse places. You can say such things as, "Let me explain," or "Let me see if I understand you. Is this what you are saying?" Reversing places is a fairly time-consuming device, and it would be awkward to use it very often. The device can, however, be useful in demonstrating that a person hasn't been understood. It also frequently has a useful side effect when a conversation is becoming heated or the individuals are becoming angry. In such cases, role reversal may be enough of a break in the exchange to disrupt the sequence of events. Also, what happens in reversing places is so unpredictable that it usually slows down the pace of the conversation and occasionally provides some useful humor. It takes time and patience, however, to reverse places, and so there are many situations in which it isn't appropriate.

Activity 5:3 at the end of this chapter can help you increase your ability to reverse roles. You may want to try it.

Issue Versus Personality

Scholars who study communication (Magoun 1956; Blood 1969) believe that it is helpful to separate an issue that is being discussed from the personalities of the individuals. It is not always possible to do this, but when issues can be depersonalized, it is usually easier to communicate. This point can be illustrated with several examples:

Separating Issue from Personality	*Mixing Issue with Personality*
"I'd like to have a discussion about the things we have been having for dinner lately."	"I think that your cooking is a problem."
"I think we have a problem with some of the things we have been eating."	"You're not buying the right food."
"Our being late all of the time is frustrating to me."	"You're always making us late."
"Are you satisfied with that painting job?"	"You're a sloppy painter."
"I'd like to get my way more."	"I think you're too bossy."
"I don't think my feelings and opinions are considered enough."	"You're inconsiderate."

It is easier to separate issues from personalities when the problems being discussed are fairly impersonal, such as deciding which color to paint a living room, where to take a vacation, or whether to subscribe to a magazine. Unfortunately, many of the issues in marital relationships are personal issues, and when such concerns are addressed it is more challenging and difficult to isolate the issue from the person.

It is most difficult to depersonalize an issue when the problem is part of an individual's personality. Even when this is the case, however, the problem will seldom involve his or her total personality, and it may be wise in such instances to separate from the individual as a whole the one aspect that is being discussed. Such problems must be dealt with delicately and sensitively if they are to be handled constructively. They are probably among the most difficult marital problems to solve, largely because of their personal nature.

Touching

You may have learned early in childhood that a large part of your communication with others is nonverbal. You learned that you need to pay attention to the way people say things, and that such behaviors as a long sigh or a facial expression can help convey to you an understanding of what others *really* mean. You have also learned an elaborate set of gestures with your hands and faces. These nonverbal skills become so important that you probably feel stifled and uncomfortable when you cannot see the other person or cannot use your hands to help express yourself. Those who don't believe this can try Activity 5:4 at the end of the chapter. It is fun and takes only a minute or two. Try it as part of a family home evening lesson.

Touching is one method of communicating nonverbally. Even the relatively habitual process of shaking hands communicates messages of acceptance, friendship, and congeniality. There are a number of other ways that touch can be used as a means of communicating in dating and marital relationships. These methods include such relatively simple physical contacts as placing one's hand on the other person's forearm while saying something important to him or her. This type of physical contact can be used to add emphasis, to communicate personal closeness, to help communicate how intensely the verbal message is emotionally experienced, or to alleviate feelings of rejection and aloneness. More complex forms of physical contact, such as kissing and embracing, communicate large amounts of information and feeling. Many of these messages are difficult to communicate verbally, and it may be impossible to communicate some of them effectively without physical contact.

In dating and courtship, touch can be an effective ally or, if not used wisely, it can ruin relationships very quickly. One girl, known to the authors, illustrates how valuable the skilled use of touch can be:

> *A group of unusual senior boys in a high school had formed an unofficial club. Among other things, one of the tasks the boys had accomplished in their club was to rate the girls in the high school on their dating desirability. They rated them on several factors, including looks, spirituality, and personality, and came up with an overall evaluation. The girl who was rated number one was rated a little above average on looks, high on spirituality, and off the scale on personality. In observing this girl interact with others it became obvious that one of the traits that the boys had classified under* personality *was her selective and effective use of touch. When speaking to others she would occasionally touch them on the forearm or shoulder, and when being spoken to she would listen with great intensity and 100 percent attention. Nonverbally, and by the correct use of touch, she was able to tell everyone she interacted with: "I care for you a great deal; you're very special to me and more than anything else in the world I want to talk and listen to you."*

Touching almost always has meaning attached to it, and much of the time this meaning is universally understood. Sometimes, however, the meaning is unique to a particular subcultural group, a family, or a couple. You began developing a language of touch early in your life, and this language became very complex. Then as you began dating, you brought your habits of touching and not touching with you. In each relationship you gradually acquired an agreement about what different forms of touch would mean. A touch on the back of the hand in one situation may mean, "I love you—as a person you are very precious to me." In another situation it may mean, "Let me have your attention."

Sometimes it is useful to discuss your language of touch. This is especially true in situations where certain types of physical touch seem to mean one thing to one of you and

Touch communicates . . . many things . . . in many ways.

something different to the other. In these situations, a discussion of these differences in "meaning" might mean the difference between understanding and misunderstanding. A discussion of the language of touch would be useful in dating relationships when one person interprets such behavior as embracing and kissing to mean that he or she likes the other person, but does not want exclusivity or commitment in the relationship, while the other interprets the same touching experiences as connoting commitment and an exclusive relationship.

An example of a girl who could have benefited in her dating life from such knowledge is illustrated by the following situation:

Judy was a beautiful nineteen-year-old student who had a strong testimony of the gospel and believed in the Church's teaching about virtue and chastity. She fully intended to go to her marriage in the temple morally clean. To her, this meant not having sexual intercourse before marriage and also not engaging in any type of heavy necking or petting. She had been faithful to her commitments all through high school and her first year of college, even though as a popular girl she had been tempted many times.

For the last month she had been dating a returned missionary with whom she felt she was beginning to fall in love, and she was wondering if he might be the one she would develop an eternal relationship with. Doug came over one night to watch TV while her parents were gone and, after about an hour, they began kissing and embracing. Judy responded warmly as a means of communicating to him that she liked him and felt he was someone special. She had never in her dating experiences allowed just anyone to kiss her simply for the recreation of it. To her a kiss was something very special, and it meant he was a special person.

Meanwhile, Doug was interpreting her warm response quite differently. To Doug her response meant that she was encouraging him to go farther. Although he didn't believe in petting either, and had not intended to do so that night, he responded to her warmth and nonverbal encouragement by making more intimate advances. As he did, Judy froze as though she were a stone statue. This nonverbal communication was not as hard for Doug to interpret, and he sat up and asked a rather inappropriate question, "Is something wrong?" Judy couldn't believe her ears. "Is something wrong?!" she exclaimed. Angrily she explained her feeling about her body and how she felt about premarital petting and how a returned missionary also ought to feel. Doug was embarrassed beyond words; when Judy observed this she cooled down, and they talked about what had happened. It had been an embarrassing and frustrating experience for both of them, and had not been helpful to the development of their relationship. Discussion of the language of touch as their relationship began to develop could have saved the couple a great deal of embarrassment.

Sometimes when you communicate through touch, the message you send is the one you intend to send. At other times, you send messages that are quite different from the ones you want to send. Also, the messages you receive may or may not be the ones your partner wants to send. The best way to make sure that the messages you want to send are the same as the ones that are received is to talk about this part of your communication. Activity 5:5 at the end of the chapter can help you do this as it examines the meaning of some of your language of touch.

Body Positions

Differences in body position communicate many things. For example, when people sit back in chairs they are usually less interested in what is being said than when they are leaning forward. This is not always the case, but it happens so often that it has given rise to the expression about people being "on the edge of their seats" when they are interested. There is also research showing that such behaviors as folding the arms or crossing the legs at the knee are more frequent when people are withdrawing from a conversation or trying to close off information coming to them. You are probably also aware that your eyes reveal how interested you are in what is being said. When a person's eyes are roving about a room, looking at the ceiling, or continually looking down, this usually indicates that the person is less interested in what is being said than if his eyes tend to focus on or near the person doing the talking.

There are a number of ways in which knowledge about body positions in communication can promote effective communication. One way is to be aware that body positions can give

Eye contact doesn't hurt.

you clues about such things as the level of defensiveness, amount of interest, fatigue, shyness, eagerness, and concentration. When you get clues that others are listening or not listening, are open or closed to new ideas, are interested or uninterested, you can use your skills in checking out to verify your hunches. You can check out your suspicions verbally or use nonverbal messages. You can use silence, questions, gestures, summary statements, or reflection, and then respond accordingly.

Another way you can use this information is to observe your own body movements and positions. You may learn how you are responding by noting that your attention is on the ceiling rather than on what is being said—or that you are closing off information that someone is trying to give to you. Understanding your own feelings in this manner can also help you understand the feelings of others. If you're getting angry or feeling bored, there is a good chance the other person is feeling the same way. When you learn these types of things about yourself you can use that information to do such things as point out to the other person what you have learned about yourself, change your behavior if you want to, or continue doing what you have been doing. Another way you can use these insights in your marital relationship is to discuss them with your spouse to see whether he or she is aware of them. If the spouse were to learn the same things, this might increase his or her ability to send and receive information more efficiently.

Activity 5:6 at the end of the chapter can help you increase your awareness of the information that can be gleaned from observing body positions.

The Subjective Part of Right and Wrong

Disagreements are inevitable in dating and marital relationships. The two individuals are raised in different families, and they will have a number of differences as a result of the styles of their families. As President Spencer W. Kimball has observed:

> Two people coming from different backgrounds soon learn after the ceremony is performed that stark reality must be faced. There is no longer a life of fantasy or of make-believe; we must come out of the clouds and put our feet firmly on the earth. Responsibility must be assumed and new duties must be accepted. Some personal freedoms must be relinquished and many adjustments, unselfish adjustments, must be made.
> One comes to realize very soon after marriage that the spouse has weaknesses not previously revealed or discovered. The virtues that were so constantly magnified during courtship now grow relatively smaller, and the weaknesses that seemed so small and insignificant during courtship now grow to sizeable proportions. (Kimball 1976, p. 12.)

Some of these differences are so irrelevant to the relationship that they can be ignored. Others are so important that they *must* be resolved if the relationship is to continue. When you encounter differences, there is one aspect of these problems that is usually not verbalized, but it influences what happens when you try to manage them. This is whether or not you appreciate the *subjective* aspect of right and wrong.

The subjective part of right and wrong is the part that is inside each person. A person may be wrong in an absolute sense; that is, his opinion would be indefensible if it were contested, or it would be unworkable if it were tried. It is therefore absolutely wrong. However, when a person believes that the opinion is correct, the opinion is correct *to that person.* In other words, the opinion is *subjectively* right, even though in an objective or absolute sense it may be wrong.

This distinction is not trivial.

It is very important in long-term personal relationships such as dating and marriage.

It would be possible to try to resolve your differences by being highly concerned about the absolute correctness of your opinions and not being concerned about the subjective correctness—and some couples use this unwise approach. It is better to be sensitive to both the objective and the subjective correctness of the views whenever you try to resolve your differences or cope with problems. Why?

First, many differences in marital relationships are based on opinions, value judgments, or subjective interpretations. In these situations it is impossible to determine which of two conflicting opinions is really, in an absolute sense, correct. When differences of this type occur, both individuals are right in a subjective sense—even though they disagree. A concern for the ultimate, objective, or absolute right or wrong usually leads to frustration and confusion in the short run, and difficulty in communicating and solving the problem in the long run. It is more wise to recognize that, subjectively, both individuals are "right."

Then you can attempt to determine what to do—given the fact that there are two different "right" opinions. This subjective view of right and wrong can help you find a plan of action, a compromise, or an accommodation that is satisfactory to both individuals.

Second, there seems to be something about human nature that makes many persons defensive and closed-minded when others ignore the fact that *they think they are right.* If you recognize and respect subjective correctness, even though in an absolute sense you may turn out to be wrong, it generates more open-mindedness and less defensiveness. One way to approach this matter is to recognize that the world is perceived from the mind. You see and understand and believe according to the information you have, your values, and your experiences. Your views are sensible and personal and precious. If you would recognize this, it would give your communication a certain degree of integrity, respectability, and dignity that is subtly and almost imperceptibly taken away when subjective rightness is ignored.

One reason people react defensively when others don't appreciate the subjective rightness of their opinions is that their self-esteem is at least partly dependent on their beliefs. When self-esteem is intricately tied to a belief, people tend to cling to the belief rather than realize it is a subjective opinion. When this occurs, it becomes difficult for them to modify the belief. If this occurs in marriage, one of the marital partners might find it difficult to change an opinion—because of the emotional and unconscious tie to self-esteem. For example, a husband's view of his masculinity or his view of himself as an acceptable person might be jeopardized by certain behaviors that are very common in some subcultural groups. He might have grown up in a family situation in which the mark of the husband's manhood was that he handled the money or that he was the breadwinner, and these functions are therefore of symbolic importance to him. The self-esteem of most women is linked to their ideas of how their children should be raised and to the importance of their role as mothers. Most Latter-day Saint women recognize that motherhood is their most valued role, and when others discuss the possibility of their not having children, they are threatened. In other segments of contemporary society women are socialized to believe that they should be equal with males in every sense, and the self-esteem of these women may be threatened when this view is questioned. If we would recognize the subjective rightness of these opinions, it would be much easier for people to understand each other, discuss alternatives, and explore each other's ideas.

A *third* advantage of recognizing subjective rightness is that it puts the person who is trying to change someone else's mind in a helpful rather than an authoritarian role. This can facilitate communication, because people generally respond much more openly to someone who seeks to play a helpful role than to someone who tries to establish an "I'm informed and you're not" or an "I'm right and you're wrong" kind of relationship.

There is a *fourth* reason couples may find it useful to pay attention to the subjective aspect of right and wrong. When you appreciate the subjective rightness of an opinion, nobody is backed into a corner. Neither person has been completely right or completely wrong when a solution is found. Instead, each person is right in his own eyes. Each is trying to get the other to understand how he or she views the situation, and then they are working together to try to identify a solution that will be acceptable to both. Each spouse can try to communicate to the other that there might be a different way of looking at the situation rather than try to prove the other one wrong.

Thus, when you appreciate subjective rightness, your communication will probably be less *defensive.* You will also tend to be more *adaptable* and *willing to listen* to the point of view of others. You will be more *open* to suggestions. Frequently the communication will be more *relaxed,* and the issues can be discussed in an atmosphere of respect for one another's opinions and for one another as people.

Establishing Rapport

It is sometimes useful to establish an appropriate setting or atmosphere before you begin a conversation. You can do this by trying to set up an appropriate emotional climate, or tone. Sometimes this may involve just a quick check to make sure that it is a good time to talk about a certain topic. This process of preparing for a conversation can be called *establishing rapport.*

Rapport can sometimes be established very quickly; for instance, you may get a message in response to inquiry that communicates that the situation is all right. The affirmation can be a nonverbal assent, such as a nod, shrug, or glance. Pay attention to the nonverbal part of a verbal response, because a verbal yes may contain a nonverbal message that says no. At other times establishing rapport is a difficult and time-consuming process. A Coronet Films instructional film titled "Marriage Is a Partnership" has a scene in which a couple is trying to cope with a marital problem. The spouses go through a fairly elaborate conversation before their defensivensss is overcome and they are both ready to talk about the problem. The rapport-establishing conversation is repeated below with some analytical comments about some of the history and nonverbal messages.

Dialogue from the Film	*Comments*
Pete: Dotty, I . . . I got a surprise in today's mail, an offer of another job. A wonderful job, but it's way in Central City. Let's talk it over.	It is after dinner, and the couple are reading in front of a fire in a fireplace, so there seem to be few obstacles to having a conversation. This comment seems to communicate that the husband wants to talk.
It's time to get away . . . do something really decisive about the influence of your parents on our marriage.	He makes this statement cautiously rather than aggressively, but it is an emotionally packed statement, and it is put bluntly. His wife has been having problems with his mother and hasn't been aware of his problems with her parents, so she comes back with an understandably defensive comment. . . .

Dotty:	*My* parents!	So far nothing has been said to establish rapport, and the wife's shocked, defensive reaction indicates that she is probably more inclined to retaliate, argue, and defend than to discuss.
Pete:	Listen to me all the way, honey, before you get mad.	The husband could have chosen to pursue the discussion about the in-law problem, but instead he leaves the problem and actively tries to create rapport. The nonverbal messages in his comment are concern, pleading, caring, and not wanting to hurt his wife.
Pete:	It's time we . . . well . . . we have got to talk this thing out. You don't know what it's like working in the same plant as your father.	Again, he tries to bring up the problem, and indirectly communicates that part of his problem has to do with working with her father.
Dotty:	Dad likes you, Pete. He's done so much for you.	This remark communicates to the husband that his wife is still defending more than she is openly listening to his point of view.
Pete:	Sure he has, Dear. I know your Dad's been swell. Try to understand me. It means so much to have you understand.	Rather than pursue the in-law problem he wants to get to, the husband again focuses on establishing an emotional climate in which they can share information. He goes over to his wife and puts both his hands on her arm and looks at her intently as he makes these comments, and these acts also communicate concern, love, patience, and his deeply felt emotions about what he is saying.
Dotty:	Golly, if you feel that way, Pete, and you must, there must be reasons.	This statement communicates that the inclination to defend rather than listen is gone.
Pete:	Only they might not seem very important to you.	This is a final rapport-establishing comment, and the husband seems to be ready to get to the problem.
Dotty:	Tell me, Pete.	A second comment without defensive-

Pete: Things like, well, when I got that promotion in December, well you said how grand it was of your dad to help. I mean, praising me to the boss and all. I felt as though I earned that raise myself, and stories of influence like that don't help any with the other fellows. And when you appreciated your dad's efforts . . . (pause and awkwardness) I wanted you to appreciate mine.

ness. The last two comments are both uttered with warmth and tenderness.

This comment indicates a number of things. One is that the couple have enough of a sense of safety that they can talk about extremely delicate and sensitive feelings. Another is that the husband's feelings about himself are substantially influenced by his wife's feelings about him, and still another is that they have enough rapport to talk freely now.

There are numerous ways to establish rapport, and all couples have to discover which ways work best for them. Some couples rarely need to consciously concern themselves with the rapport in their relationships, and others have to spend more time getting ready to talk than they spend talking.

Create a Feeling of Being Understanding

There is an important difference between understanding someone else and the other person having a "feeling" that you are being understanding. These two usually go together, but sometimes they don't. For example, a husband may understand that his wife wants to get out of the house at the end of the day after being confined with several young children. He may even realize that it is important to her. But if he has a strong desire to stay home and resists her request to go out, she will probably think that he doesn't understand her. In this situation, he actually does understand her, but she doesn't have a feeling that he is understanding. With another couple, the situation may be reversed. Consider the following example in which each is talking to himself:

Tom (to himself): With the merger coming up, I'll probably lose my job, and we used up most of our year's supply last time I was laid off. That operation put us so far in debt that I don't know what we'll do. There's no point in talking about it with Sally; she'll just say as she always does, "I'm sure you'll work things out." She just doesn't realize how bad off we are.

Sally (to herself: I heard about the merger, and I'll bet Tom is just worried sick about it. And all the bills we have don't make it any easier. He's so conscientious that I know it's just eating away at him inside. I'll bet that the best way for me to help him is to be supportive and encouraging, and let him know that I have confidence in him.

Sally understands Tom, but he doesn't realize that she does. He doesn't have a feeling of being understood.

These two skills are very different. The ability to understand, called *empathy*, is a mental process that occurs in your head. You don't have to say anything or do anything except listen, observe, and occasionally check out your insights. The other skill is to be able to create a feeling in others that you understand them. It is much more complex because it involves interpersonal communication. You have to send the type of messages that will show you understand.

It is important to empathize correctly in dating and marital relationships, and most people realize this and are skillful empathizers. Many, however, fail to recognize that the other process is also important in these intimate relationships. In impersonal relationships, such as boss-employee, policeman-pedestrian, and doctor-patient, being an understanding person is not very important. However, in intimate relationships such as dating and marriage, where most of the important things center around such things as emotions, personal beliefs, and the person as a whole, the ability to help the other person feel that you understand is extremely important. *Sometimes in marriage a feeling of being understood is more important than the understanding itself.* Consider, for example, the following situation:

Bill: Ramona is so understanding. When things aren't going well she takes the time to help me work things out and get back on the track. When I was having problems with Jeff, I brought it up one night and she stayed home from her meeting so we could talk it through. She understood the situation really well for only getting it secondhand, and had several ideas that really helped.

Ramona: Bill and I talked the other night about a problem he was having on the job. Bill was really upset. I don't know the guy that made the mess, and I'm not sure what Bill is going to do about it. He may have to pay a fine or might even lose his job; I don't know. I tried to get the whole thing straight, but I don't think I ever did. About all I could do was listen and try to understand.

In this marriage, Ramona didn't understand very much of what was going on inside Bill, but the way she behaved created a *feeling* that she was an understanding person, and this helped a great deal. The following list of behaviors identifies some things you may want to do and not do to create a feeling that you are "understanding."

Do	*Don't*
Take the time to let the other person know you understand when you do.	Put the other person down for feelings he or she has that you don't understand. (They are genuine experiences for that person.)
Take the time to listen to your spouse, especially whenever he or she is emotionally upset about something.	
Try hard to see things from the other person's point of view rather than your own.	Criticize the person's feelings. Some feelings are irrational, but they are nevertheless real.

Try to get all the facts about something before making up your mind.

Realize that your spouse lives in a different world and may see things differently.

Check out how well you understand by repeating things back or questioning.

Do something else (like reading, or doing housework) while listening to the other person.

Jump to conclusions. Assume the other person knows you understand him.

Feedback

In feedback, the sender of a message receives some information about the messages he or she has communicated. Often this is a simple process, such as the sender asking whether the receiver understood what was said, and the receiver responding with an affirmative glance or comment. At other times the process is more complicated and time-consuming. For example, discussing the receiver's impressions of the sender's intentions can turn into a fairly complex conversation.

Feedback can include more than a verbal discussion about whether your messages are received accurately. You can get feedback by being alert to how others are responding to your messages. For example, someone may get so carried away with his own concerns that he ignores your messages, and he keeps trying to send his own messages. This behavior provides feedback about how he is responding to what you are trying to say, and it can help you know how to act. This feedback may lead you to deal with the issues he is trying to raise before attempting to further communicate your own ideas. Or, you may want to confront him with the fact that he is dealing with different issues than you want to.

Other types of behavior that provide useful feedback are: enthusiastically listening and responding, shaking the head affirmatively or in disagreement, or becoming uninterested in a conversation. The nonverbal messages that others send are among the most useful forms of feedback, and you will be a more effective communicator if you are alert to these forms of feedback. The process of role reversal discussed earlier can also be viewed as a feedback-providing situation, since the payoff of role reversal is finding out what has and has not been understood.

Pay Attention to Environment

Another skill that is essential in effective communication is being able to know how your environment influences what is going on, and then adjusting yourself to it. The following eight items are some of the things that you need to consider.

Time of day. Many people are better communicators at some times of the day than at other times. Most people find that it is difficult to be congenial communicators just before the evening meal (Bossard and Boll 1956). In the typical home, dinner time is a period of fairly hectic activity. One or both parents are arriving home from the job, and people are hungry and tired. Also, after having to perform on the job all day, it is not uncommon for a person to be tense and to need to unwind and rest. The net effect is that this is often a difficult time to communicate about something that is problematic, irritating, or serious.

The time of day also influences communication because some people wake up more slowly than others. Some people are not really fully awake until ten or eleven in the morning, and they find it difficult to communicate about serious situations before then. Others wake up early and quickly, and the morning is the best time for them to tackle their problems. Some people are the most proficient in discussing things after ten or eleven at night, and others are so exhausted by that time that they can't even keep their heads up, let alone communicate.

One conclusion that emerges from these differences is that each couple has to discover which time of day is the best and worst for them. They can then try to resolve issues or make decisions at the good times and avoid the bad times. This isn't suggesting that couples should not talk to each other at certain times of the day. A calm, humorous, or relaxed conversation just before dinner can be one of the best ways to make a day pleasant. The point is that when you pay attention to your unique daily cycles and rhythms, you can talk about some things at certain times of the day and about other things at different times of the day, improving your communication. Activity 5:7 at the end of this chapter can help you discover the times that seem to be your best and worst for serious conversations.

Nonfamily pressures. All couples experience outside pressures that interfere with the kind of communication that is necessary when major decisions have to be made, differences have to be resolved, or problems have to be coped with. Married couples who are still finishing their education will recognize that things are more hectic and pressured when finals roll around, and it is usually more difficult to solve problems then. At later stages of life, unusual pressures are brought into the home by such things as the husband being ready to close a big deal, a company merger, a legal case that is coming to a head, the architect needing the drawings in a hurry, or the Christmas rush.

It may be that the wise way to deal with external pressures is to be sensitive to them when they occur and to try to temporarily avoid facing issues that could be put off for a few days or a couple of weeks. This suggestion is, of course, contrary to the advice heard occasionally that married couples should "never let the sun set on a problem." It is therefore proposed here that occasionally the most effective thing a couple can do is let several days pass before dealing with certain problems. This is not arguing that couples should avoid facing problems indefinitely.

Physical setting. Architects and designers have long recognized that physical setting influences the way people behave. Bright colors, such as reds, oranges, and purples, excite and arouse people. Beiges, greens, and blues relax people. Hard surfaces, such as tile, brick, ceramic, and marble create different moods than soft surfaces, such as carpeting, draperies, and pillows. These effects can be used in homes to create different types of moods in different places or situations. Soft light, low, calm music, and a fireplace are common things that create an atmosphere of calmness and peace.

In addition to these obvious examples, other things such as relaxing evening wear, slippers, reading material, and soft furniture also promote relaxation, calmness, and serenity. It is, of course, not always desirable to have a calm setting for discussions about important, sensitive, or problematic issues, but many times it is desirable to do what can be done to create a pleasant setting for serious discussions. For many people, trying to resolve an important issue while driving in downtown traffic in a compact car could create obstacles to effective communication, and such situations can usually be avoided if we are sensitive to the role of physical factors.

Menstrual cycle. Most married couples eventually learn that the woman experiences systematic emotional and physical changes in the different stages of the monthly menstrual cycle. These changes sometimes influence communication. Women differ considerably in the nature of these trends (Hartman 1962, Pincus 1965), but one common pattern is for women to be more cheerful, patient, warm, and congenial during the second and third weeks after the start of the menstrual period. They experience such emotional responses as irritability, depression, and being easily frustrated just prior to the menstrual period. Many women vary from this typical emotional cycle, and a large number of women experience no discernable emotional changes throughout their menstrual cycle.

An awareness that these changes occur can be valuable in marital communication. You will know why things do not go well when you try to address problems or major decisions at "the wrong time of the month." Thus, most couples would probably be wise to observe the woman's cycles for several months to determine whether she experiences systematic emotional changes. Then, if she does, they should take this information into account in determining when to face up to and when to temporarily avoid those problems that can be postponed.

Time involved. One of the many surprises that many newly married couples have is that it takes a tremendous amount of time to solve some of the problems, issues, or difficulties that come up in marriage. This is illustrated by the remarks of a newly married wife:

> *I thought that when things would come up we'd be able to sit down for a minute or so and decide what to do. That's what I've been able to do all my life, and that's the way most things were when we were going together. But we've had so many things come up that I never even thought about, and they get so involved and complicated that . . . we just take hours and hours talking about them. It's fun sometimes because we don't have any money to go anyplace anyway, but I never had any idea that we'd spend as much of our time working things out as we do.*

Different types of discussions take different amounts of time. When couples are initially discovering such things as how they like their eggs done, who is going to do what in the morning so they can get to work on time, and what type of entertainment they ought to have on a weekend, the discussions are rarely complex or time-consuming. However, when they talk about such things as how they feel when the other is gone or near, what they want out of life, and the inadequacies they have in building bonds between them, the conversations are very time-consuming. Also, after couples have been married for a number of years they may require vast amounts of time for conversations about new ambitions that are becoming important to them, personal frustrations they are experiencing in their careers, or ways their love has changed. Couples who do not allow adequate time for such conversations pay a price. They don't develop the understanding and bonds enjoyed by other couples who do take the time.

Psychic sets. Another factor to consider when communicating in a marital relationship is that both individuals have numerous preconceptions that influence communication. Such preconceptions have come to be known in the psychological literature as *sets*. Some of these sets are systematically different for men and woman, and knowing this fact can help people communicate better. The woman's comment as she looks into her bulging closet that "I don't have a thing to wear" makes sense within a female subculture, but most males find such comments mystifying, if not inappropriate and aggravating. An example of the same type of situation reversed is the male's puzzled comment, "Do I have to *tell* her all the time how much I love her? She ought to be able to see that I do from the way I act. Why, I . . ." Many husbands agree that this is a reasonable point of view, but many wives find it mystifying, if not annoying.

The list of systematic differences between men and women that contribute to the difficulties of communication in marriage could be very long. Several examples of "traditional" differences are: emotionality in many women and a comparative lack of emotionality in men, the higher importance many males attach to sports, the wife wanting her husband to help pick out fabric for sewing, the importance to a father that his son be successful in athletics, and the importance of new clothes to a wife. The changes in modern sex roles are eliminating some of these traditional differences, but new differences will also undoubtedly appear.

Part of a relationship. Another factor that is sometimes useful to think about is that some problems in marital relationships deal with only small parts of the total relationship, while others deal with the relationship as a whole. Frequently, when couples are going together and just beginning to establish a more permanent relationship, many issues that they have to cope with genuinely jeopardize that relationship. If an issue is resolved one way, the couple will break up, but if it is resolved another way, the couple will continue to see each other. However, after two people have gone together for some time, their relationship becomes so complex, important, and secure that most of the problems confronting them deal with only a small part of the total relationship, and don't genuinely jeopardize the relationship. This is especially true after two people have developed a deeply felt love and acquired numerous bonds.

An awareness of whether an issue concerns only a small part of a relationship or the entire relationship can be useful in improving communication. If a person who is interested in maintaining a relationship believes erroneously that a problem jeopardizes the entire relationship, he experiences such emotions as fear, anxiety, or depression. He would not experience these emotions if he realized that the issue did not endanger the entire relationship. Conversely, a person who fails to realize that a problem does jeopardize an entire relationship may not give that problem the attention and concern that he or she would otherwise give it. It doesn't seem useful to identify the exact ramifications of every problem that arises, but, on the other hand, insufficient attention to the implications of problems may interfere with communication and problem solving.

Unconscious motivation. Another factor that is probably useful to keep in mind is that at least some of the reasons humans do what they do are unconscious to them. Some schools of thought, such as psychoanalysis, argue that the human mind is like an iceberg, with only a small part of what goes on in it being "visible" to consciousness, while the rest is unconscious. Other schools of thought, such as Rogers's (1951) self theory, argue that unless an individual is emotionally or mentally upset, most of what goes on in the mind is conscious. But modern scholars are virtually unanimous in believing that at least some of the reasons people behave the way they do are unconscious.

When couples are sensitive to the fact that some human motivation is unconscious, this can influence what occurs in their communication. For one thing, such couples will realize that searching for the reasons persons do or do not do some things may be a futile exercise, because the individuals themselves may not be and cannot become aware of the real reasons. Frequently this realization will lead couples wisely to shift their concentration to deciding what they can do about a situation, rather than trying to discover why the situation occurs.

SUMMARY

This chapter begins with a general principle about communication: The better your communication, the better your marriage. The rest of the chapter discusses skills you can use to have effective communication. Some of the skills deal with verbal communication and some with nonverbal communication. A few of them deal with both verbal and nonverbal ways of communicating. So many different topics are discussed in these three sections that the best way to summarize them is to list them. They are:

1. Listening
2. Checking out
   a. Questions
   b. Summary statements
   c. Paraphrasing
3. Reversing places
4. Issue versus personality
5. Touching
6. Body positions
7. The subjective part of right and wrong
8. Establishing rapport
9. Creating a feeling of being understanding
10. Feedback
11. Paying attention to your environment
    a. Time of day
    b. Nonfamily pressures

   c. Physical setting
   d. Menstrual cycle
   e. Time involved
   f. Psychic sets
   g. Part of a relationship
   h. Unconscious motivation

ACTIVITY 5:1
Am I Listening?

Goal: To get some new data about listening habits, and use it to evaluate this skill.

1. Mark on a separate sheet of paper how often you do the following sixteen things.

2. Then give the list to three other people who know you well—a spouse, fiance(e), dating partner, roommate, or sibling—and have him or her rate you.

3. Compare the evaluations and determine how you seem to be doing. If your evaluations are considerably better than the others, you may want to (a) swallow your pride and (b) turn to pages 42-43 and develop an action plan to help your listening skills.

Use the following categories for responding:

   0 = Never
   1 = Rarely
   2 = Occasionally
   3 = Frequently
   4 = Almost all the time/all the time

_____ 1. I let others finish speaking before I talk.
_____ 2. I look at the one who is speaking.
_____ 3. I'm more concerned about understanding others than convincing them I'm right.
_____ 4. I ask questions to clarify my understanding when I'm not sure.
_____ 5. I pay attention to the *way* things are said to help me understand.
_____ 6. I wait until I get all the instructions before I start leaving to do something.
_____ 7. I am open to new ideas.
_____ 8. Others think I am a good listener.
_____ 9. I pay attention to nonverbal messages too.
_____ 10. I try to listen while doing something else that also takes my attention.
_____ 11. I'm more concerned about my point of view than the other person's.
_____ 12. I change the subject when someone is in the middle of saying something.

_____ 13. I ignore what others are saying.
_____ 14. I'm too busy to listen carefully.
_____ 15. I use subtle or nonverbal cues to let people know I really don't want to listen anymore.
_____ 16. I make sure that others know I understand them.

ACTIVITY 5:2
Paraphrasing

Goal: To increase your ability to paraphrase by practicing and evaluating its consequences.

1. For a week be alert for a certain type of social situation. The situation you are looking for is one in which someone with whom you are fairly close (spouse, roommate, sibling) begins identifying a problem that she or he has that is important enough to give rise to uncomfortable emotions.

2. When this situation occurs, try to minimize as much as possible statements that: (a) identify solutions to the problem (ordering, directing, commanding, advising, lecturing, warning, admonishing, threatening, exhorting, moralizing, preaching, suggesting, or giving logical arguments); (b) put the other person down (name-calling, shaming, ridiculing, judging, disagreeing, blaming, and especially criticizing); (c) are openly supportive of the other person (praising, agreeing, reassuring, sympathizing, consoling, or encouraging). Try, whenever it is comfortable and appropriate, to repeat back to the other person *in your own words* the meaning of the message that you think he or she is trying to communicate to you.

3. At the end of the week evaluate how those conversations tended to be different from what they would probably have been if you had used more solution-providing, put-down, or supportive statements and fewer reflecting statements. How did these conversations make you feel? (This exercise is doubly valuable if several try it and then later discuss and evaluate their experiences.)

ACTIVITY 5:3
Reversing Places

Goal: To increase your ability to use role reversal effectively.

1. The next time you are having a discussion in which either you or the other person has tried to explain something but believes that it has not been really understood, try role reversal.

   a. First, ask whether it is acceptable to the other person to reverse positions to determine how accurately the information is understood.

b. When you reverse roles, do more than just use the other person's words. Try to actually "be" the other person by using the same tone of voice, inflections, gestures, and points of emphasis. Be fair—don't mimic or make fun of the other person.

2. Evaluate this experience to determine how valuable it has been in helping you to communicate effectively.

ACTIVITY 5:4
The Importance of Nonverbal Communication

Goal: To better realize how important the nonverbal part of communication is.

1. Sit on your hands and try to explain something that is complex, such as an important emotional experience or how to drive to your house.

or

Have two people sit back-to-back (so their backs touch) and then talk about something that is important to both of them.

2. Then talk about how this disrupted the "natural" communication processes.

ACTIVITY 5:5
Interpreting the Meaning of Touch

Goal: To identify the messages that are sent and received through physical contact.

1. Choose someone with whom you have a close relationship and ask that person to help you with this exercise.

2. List about five situations in which you have had some type of physical contact with this other person, or in which you wanted to have a certain type of physical contact and didn't.

3. Discuss what was communicated in each of these situations by identifying whether either person sent or received any messages through the physical contact. If either did, identify (a) what the person was trying to "say" and (b) what the other person "heard" in the messages.

4. If you cannot identify any messages in the physical contact, you may benefit from asking others (such as members of a discussion group in class) to help you discover the nonverbal messages. After you can identify these messages, you may want to discuss whether there are ways you can improve this type of communication.

ACTIVITY 5:6
Interpreting Body Positions

Goal: To increase your ability to accurately receive messages that are "sent" by body positions.

1. For one week try to be unusually alert to what body positions are "saying" to you. Keep a piece of paper with you so you can list the instances in which you received information by observing different aspects of body positions.

2. When it is feasible, try to check the accuracy of these messages by seeing whether the individual sending the message intended to send the message you received.

3. Some body positions that *may* have information in them are:
   a. leaning forward or back in one's seat
   b. shading eyes with one's hand, as if deep in thought
   c. a set jaw
   d. turning one's back
   e. no body movement at all—as if the whole body were intent on listening
   f. walking fast or slow.

ACTIVITY 5:7
Daily Rhythms Exercise

Goal: To identify which times of the day are the best and worst for serious conversations.

With someone who knows you quite well, try to identify whether there are systematic differences in your ability to communicate effectively at different times of the day. If there are, try to determine which are the most and least effective times. You may then want to try to change your patterns, or you may decide that it would not be worth the effort.

SUPPLEMENTARY READINGS

Allred, G. Hugh. *How to Strengthen Your Marriage and Family.* Provo, Utah: Brigham Young University Press, 1976.

Anastasi, Thomas E. *Face-to-Face Communication.* Cambridge, Massachusetts: Management of Cambridge, 1967.

Bauby, Cathrina. *OK, Let's Talk About It.* New York: Van Nostrand, Reinhold, 1972.

Foote, Nelson, and L. B. Cottrell. *Identity and Interpersonal Competence.* Chicago: University of Chicago Press.

Gordon, Thomas. *Parent Effectiveness Training.* New York: Wyden, 1970.

Kimball, Spencer W. *Marriage and Divorce.* Salt Lake City: Deseret Book Co. 1976.

Osborne, Cecil. *The Art of Understanding Your Mate.* Grand Rapids, Michigan: Zonderban Publishing House, 1970.

Stir, Virginia. *Peoplemaking.* Palo Alto, California: Science and Behavior Books, 1972.

6

COMMUNICATING EMOTIONS

By starving emotions we become
humorless, rigid and stereotyped;
by repressing them we become
literal, reformatory and holier-than-thou;
when encouraged, they perfume life;
discouraged, they poison it.
—Joseph Collins

To live without emotion, particularly in marriage, would be to live with only enough visual capacity to see black and white rather than colors. Emotions are not only desirable, they are invaluable as they provide life and intensity and new dimensions in our relationships. They are the rounding-out ingredients that allow us to evaluate and respond, to truly live and have joy.

WHY LEARN TO COMMUNICATE ABOUT EMOTIONS?

There are many reasons you should learn to communicate about emotions. Three of these reasons are: (1) emotions are a very important part of mortality and eternal life; (2) marriage is primarily an emotional system; and (3) when you don't communicate about your emotions, they can become very disruptive in the marriage system. You need to learn how to manage the emotional part of the system—or it will manage you.

Emotions Are an Important Part of Life

Our modern society emphasizes the rational part of living. We run our businesses efficiently, emphasize rationality in our schools, and evaluate people on the basis of how sensible they are. This emphasis on rationality increased during the Renaissance and the Industrial Revolution, and our society takes great pride in it. It has given us the highest standard of living ever known. It has sent men to the moon, and has created more technological inventions in the last hundred years than in the entire previous history of mankind.

Unfortunately, our overemphasis on the rational part of man has also created a distorted and perverted society, a society in which other aspects of man are pushed aside—at great cost. Society's image of the "true" man, a man who is *really* a man, is of an individual who is very rational and sensible, who governs himself with his mind so that he makes cost-effective decisions enabling him to get ahead in the occupational world. It is interesting to contrast this view of man with the view that is presented in the scriptures. The scriptural view places much more emphasis on spirituality *and much more emphasis on emotionality.* Most of us are aware of the spiritual part, but our society has so blinded us to the emotionality of mankind that the emotional part is a surprise.

Is it true that emotion is that important?

The scriptures teach that the purpose of life is for man to have joy (2 Nephi 2:25). And what is joy? Is it something that occurs in your minds? Is it a rational part of you? Is it something that you get by emphasizing your intellect, to the exclusion of emotions? *Emphatically no!* It is an emotion. Joy is a feeling that you get in your bosom. It is a sensation of the heart—of the soul. *Therefore, the emotional part of marriage is very important.*

What about experiencing feelings? Do the men of scripture experience feelings freely, extensively, and often? And do they talk about their feelings and emotions? It can be an eye-opener to read the scriptures looking for expressions of emotion; you may be amazed at the amount of emotion that is described. Modern society teaches that men are supposed to be tough and strong, and are not supposed to show emotion around others except in unusual or deeply moving situations such as a funeral or a reunion after a long separation. This is in strong contrast to the frequent expressions of many different types of emotion by the people that are discussed in the scriptures. The following examples from the scriptures illustrate the range of emotions that are readily identified therein—and many of these are mentioned hundreds of times.

2 Nephi 32:8	it *grieveth* me
Jacob 2:9	*burdeneth* my soul
Jacob 2:27	for I, the Lord God, *delight* in
Romans 12:15	do *rejoice,* and *weep* with them that weep
Enos 1:4	and my soul *hungered*
Enos 1:9	I began to feel a *desire* for the welfare of my brethren
Mark 1:41	and Jesus, *moved* with *compassion,* put forth his hand
Deuteronomy 28:47	with *gladness* of heart
Psalm 19:8	*rejoicing* the heart
Proverbs 17:22	a *merry* heart doeth good like a medicine
2 Corinthians 9:7	for God loveth a *cheerful* giver
Mosiah 4:3	having *peace of conscience*
Alma 42:18	brought *remorse of conscience* unto men
John 14:27	my *peace* I give unto you
Galatians 5:22	fruit of the spirit is *love, joy, peace*
Enos 1:27	then shall I see his face with *pleasure*
Luke 3:14	and be *content* with your wages
2 Nephi 4:32	my heart is broken and my spirit is *contrite*

Alma 15:4	his heart began to take *courage*
Jacob 2:7	whose feelings are exceedingly *tender*
1 Corinthians 12:31	covet *earnestly* the best gifts
1 Nephi 3:25	did *lust* after it
Deuteronomy 11:18	lay up these words *in your heart* and *in your soul*
Luke 24:32	did not our heart *burn* within us
Alma 5:14	mighty change in your *hearts*
Alma 32:28	*swell within your breasts;* and when you feel these *swelling motions . . . enlarge* my soul . . . *delicious* to me
1 Corinthians 13:4	charity *suffereth* long
Alma 14:11	the Spirit *constraineth* me
1 Nephi 16:2	the guilty taketh the truth to be *hard,* for it *cutteth* them to the very center
Proverbs 10:1	a wise son maketh a *glad* father
Ecclesiastes 11:9	Let thy *heart cheer* thee in the days of thy youth
Alma 3:26	to reap eternal *happiness* or eternal *misery*
D&C 59:18	all things made to *gladden the heart*
D&C 59:23	*peace* in this world
2 Corinthians 11:2	I am *jealous* over you with godly jealousy
2 Nephi 2:25	men are that they might have *joy*
John 3:16	for God so *loved* the world
Leviticus 19:18	not *bear* any *grudge*

This list is just a sample of the emotions in the scriptures.

Latter-day Saints should learn that this is another area in which they should be in the world, but not of the world. We ought to be much more open to our emotions than our worldly culture teaches us. We ought to be much more willing to recognize emotions, talk about them, share them, and enjoy them, than we traditionally have been. We ought to use the emotional parts of ourselves to provide a richness, a depth, and a fullness to our lives that does not exist in the contemporary, industrialized world. And we ought to start by being more emotional in our relationships with our husbands, wives, and children.

Marriage Is Primarily an Emotional System

A second reason we should learn how to deal with the emotional part of our lives is that the marital relationship is primarily an emotional one. Everyone belongs to many different social systems—neighborhood, occupation, service clubs, schools, medical community, and governments. If you were to rank these various systems according to how much they should and do emphasize rational and emotional processes, you would find that your marital system is usually the most emotional of all of your systems. Thus, in a world that should be much more emotional than it is, marriage is or should be one of the *most* emotional places.

> Unconscious feelings
> manage to
> find their own way out.
>
> Telling a person
> not to feel what he feels
> does not
> take the feelings
> away.
>
> —Thoughts by Dorothy W. Baruch
> *How to Live with Your Teenagers*

This means that if you are to be a wise steward in managing your marriage, you need to learn how to cope with the emotional part of your life. You need to learn how to recognize your emotions and share them, and to recognize and accept the emotions of others. Each of us should also learn ways to manage emotions wisely when they become disruptive.

Emotions Are Sometimes Very Disruptive

There is a general principle that helps us understand one of the ways that emotions become disruptive. It is:

5. The Emotionality Principle: When emotions become intense, they decrease self-control.

Most people can get a little upset or angry and still be kind and charitable in the way they act. But as these emotions get more and more intense, a person gradually has less and less control over them, and they take over. People start trying to get even with others; they push people around and put others down. They stop listening to the point of view of others, and they are less kind. In scriptural terms, they begin exercising unrighteous dominion, and the Spirit of the Lord leaves them. They become selfish and uncharitable, and often say things that they are sorry for later.

But the emotionality principle even operates for positive emotions such as happiness and joy. When a person is highly excited or thrilled about something, he often gets swept away and loses a bit of his self-control. He makes promises that he may later not keep, and he may forget about important appointments and commitments. One of the authors remembers some very pleasant emotions after a date which were so intense that he drove all the way home with his car in second gear. Some people get so carried away with emotions of love and rapture when they become engaged that those around them wonder how they keep from walking into trees.

THE DIFFERENCE BETWEEN THOUGHTS AND EMOTIONS

What are emotions? Webster defines them as strong, generalized feelings of psychological excitement. You don't think them; you feel them. You *experience* them. They happen inside.

There are some important differences between feeling and thinking. Thinking occurs in your head. You think thoughts; you don't feel them. Thoughts are rational, intellectual processes. They involve reasoning, and they occur in your brain. Emotions do not occur in your head. You experience some of them in your breast, or, as it is sometimes said, in your heart. Other feelings are sometimes total body experiences.

But even though thoughts and feelings are separate from each other, they are related. For example, you can have thoughts about your feelings. This occurs when an emotion becomes conscious—when you become aware of it. You then think about the feeling, and you give it a name and can talk about it with others. When you describe your feelings, you use "I" statements such as: "I feel . . ." "I'm happy that . . ." "I'm hurting . . . ," and so on. Thus, emotions can create thoughts.

Thoughts can also create emotions. For example, you may recall an event, and your memory may then influence how you feel. You can re-create feelings of happiness, joy, and satisfaction; you can also create negative feelings by remembering frustrations, disappointments, and problems.

The following awareness wheel (Miller, Nunnally, and Wackman 1975) can help you understand the difference between thoughts and feelings. It shows five parts of human

experience that are different from each other. Two of these five parts, thinking and wanting, are intellectual processes that occur in the mind. The doing part involves overt behavior such as walking, reading, or driving. The sensing part comes into play when you experience something with one of your five senses, i.e., seeing, smelling, hearing, tasting, or touching. The fifth part, feeling, is different from all of the others.

The Lord is, of course, aware of the differences between thoughts and feelings, and both are important to him. For example, he said to Oliver Cowdery, "Yea, behold I will tell you in your mind *and* in your heart, by the Holy Ghost, which shall come upon you and which shall dwell in your heart" (D&C 8:2; italics added).

Many people confuse these different parts of themselves. They think they are feeling when they are thinking. They think they are feeling when they are having sensory experience, or when they are intending (wanting) to do something. Activity 6:1 at the end of this chapter can help you see how accurate or inaccurate you are in keeping these different parts of your experience straight.

FIVE DIFFERENT ASPECTS OF EMOTION

Understanding the difference between thoughts and emotions just scratches the surface in terms of understanding emotions and how they relate to the communication process. Let us now deepen our understanding by looking at five different aspects of emotion. These are intensity, source, effects, consciousness, and decreasing intensity.*

Intensity of Emotion

The *intensity* of an emotion refers to the level of the strength or the degree of the emotion. The intensity can be illustrated by the emotion of excitement: At certain times you feel only slightly excited, while at other times you are highly excited. This range from no emotion at all to extremely high intensity of emotion is illustrated by the continuum below:

Intensity of Emotion

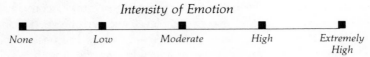

| None | Low | Moderate | High | Extremely High |

If a co-ed were annoyed (which is a feeling) with her roommate for continually leaving her nylons on the sink, the degree or amount of annoyance she felt could be described as the intensity of the annoyance feeling. She could be extremely annoyed or only slightly annoyed.

---

* This discussion is very dependent on the work of Reymert (1950), Arnold (1960), Shibutani (1961), Allport (1961), Davitz (1969), and Dittman (1972).

Source of Emotion

The *source* of an emotion refers to the situation, event, or process that leads to, creates, or gives rise to an emotion. In the preceding example, the probable source of the feeling of annoyance was the nylons being left on the sink, or possibly it was what the nylons represented—an inconsiderate roommate.

There are a great many events that can create emotional experiences. For example, things someone else does or says can create an emotional response. The decor of a room, and sounds such as soft or loud music also influence emotions, and architects and interior decorators usually pay much attention to these effects. Other stimuli, such as odors, body stimulation, and thought processes, also influence emotions. Clearly, however, the intensity of an emotion is different from its source, because the source is not the emotion itself, but that which gives rise to the emotion. Interestingly, one emotion can also be the source of a different emotion. For example, an individual who has a quick temper may show anger in a socially inappropriate situation, and this can create other feelings, such as sorrow, sadness, or guilt.

Effects of Emotion

The effect of an emotion is something other than the feeling that is produced by the affective experience. This effect can be quite direct, such as the co-ed screaming at her roommate and throwing the nylons at her. Other direct effects of other emotions may be jumping up and down or embracing someone. Or effects can be indirect, as when the roommate vents her anger on her boyfriend and he, as a result of his feelings, yells at his sister, who scolds the child who kicks the dog who chases the cat. . . . Indirectly the co-ed's emotion had an effect on the dog's behavior.

Consciousness of Emotions

A fourth aspect of emotion is the *consciousness* or awareness of emotion. Psychiatrists have distinguished between the conscious, preconscious, and unconscious levels of this variable.* When something is on the conscious level, the person experiencing it is aware of it. Consciousness means that you know what you are feeling. Preconsciousness lies between consciousness and unconsciousness. You are not fully aware of the things that are in your preconscious mind, but you can become aware of some of them by such processes as intro-spection or hearing someone make a related comment.

---

* Sigmund Freud (1893), the father of psychoanalysis, is usually credited with the discovery of the un-conscious, and since that time Freud and others such as Cameron and Margaret (1951) and Allport (1961, chapter 7) have refined the conscious-unconscious dimension by pointing out that it is a continuum rather than a dichotomy. It is of course possible to accept the existence of the unconscious without accepting other ideas in psychoanalysis. Experiments such as Kolers's (1957) have so conclusively demonstrated the role of unconscious processes in behavior that their existence is almost beyond question.

When something is on the unconscious level, it exists in your mind, but you are not aware of it. You do not know about it, and cannot recognize or perceive it. Unconscious emotions are emotions that you experience without being aware that they are there. The above example of the co-ed getting after the boyfriend would be an example of this, if the boyfriend were not aware of the emotions that were created in him by the co-ed. He could experience such feelings as hurt or anger, but be so concerned with other things that the existence of these emotions never comes into his consciousness.

Thus several conclusions can be drawn about the consciousness of emotions. One is that emotions can exist and yet remain on the unconscious level. Another is that consciousness is a different aspect of emotions than their existence, intensity, source, or effect. Also, as is pointed out later in this chapter, emotions frequently have a very disruptive influence on communication when they are unconscious.

Venting Emotions

The fifth characteristic of emotion is the process of decreasing the intensity of the feeling. After the co-ed screamed and threw the nylons, she might have felt better. If she did, she was decreasing the emotion. If, however, she felt more and more angry, she wasn't decreasing the emotion. If emotions are positive ones such as joy, happiness, or excitement, we seldom want to consciously decrease their intensity. However, if they are negative ones such as anger, resentment, frustration, sadness, and jealousy, most of us want to decrease their intensity.

Sometimes you push an emotion out of your awareness and think you have eliminated it, while later finding that it is still there. This is not decreasing it. It is *suppression,* since the emotion is still there. Decreasing an emotion actually changes its intensity, rather than just your perception of how intense it is.

SKILLS YOU CAN USE IN MANAGING YOUR EMOTIONS

The emotionality principle and the other ideas about emotions can help you manage your marital stewardship wisely, but you need a number of *skills* to be able to use them. Therefore, the rest of this chapter discusses ways you can develop the following nine skills. Later chapters then build on these nine.

I.   Expressor Skills:

1. Ability to recognize emotions in yourself and others.
2. Ability to label your emotions when you recognize them.
3. Ability to express your feelings and share them with others.
4. Ability to express negative emotions in helpful ways.

II. Receiver Skills:

5. Ability to listen with your heart as well as your head.

6. Ability to accept rather than reject expressions of others.
7. Ability to recognize nonverbal and verbal messages.

III. Managing Skills:

8. Ability to keep intense emotions from interfering.
9. Ability to decrease intensity of emotions.

Expressor Skills

Communication is the process of sending and receiving messages in a way that creates understanding. Half of this process is being able to *express* yourself in such a way that the messages you want to send are the ones that are received. When you do this, you are the expressor, or as Guerney (1978) prefers, you are in the *expressor role.* The following four skills can help you be skillful in this role:

Skill no. 1: Ability to recognize your own emotions. You probably learned in your childhood that you should deny, ignore, or suppress emotions. How many young boys are told, "You should not feel that way"; "You're a big boy now and big boys don't cry"; or "Just forget about it (the feeling). It's not important." Unfortunately, society systematically teaches people to be dishonest with their emotions. Many learn these lessons so well that they become insensitive to their emotions, and don't know what they are really feeling. Magoun (1956) feels this sensitivity is a part of honesty, and he suggests that most of us would be better off if we had more *emotional honesty.*

How can you become more aware of your emotions? First, you need to be able to tell the difference between the parts of the awareness wheel discussed on page 88. You need to be able to tell the difference between a feeling and a thought, an intention and an action. Activity 6:1 at the end of the chapter can help you develop this skill.

You can also look at your behavior to find clues about your emotions. If you are skipping along, whistling, or humming, and have an extra spring in your step, this can tell you something about how you are feeling. If you find yourself being a little more critical, negative, or disagreeable than usual, this too can give you some clues as to how you are feeling. Some people would do well to become more sensitive to these behaviors. They go through life acting pleasant in one situation and disagreeable in another, quite unaware of how they are acting and what these actions can tell them about their feelings.

Another thing you can do to become more aware of your emotions is pause and think about what is happening to you emotionally. This is the process of listening to yourself, to what is going on inside. The purpose of life is to have joy (2 Nephi 2:25), and you need to take the time to "tune in" to the experience of joy, to be alert to the response of joy inside you. Again, some people go through life without experiencing joy because they don't take the time to feel, to experience, to truly love. The Savior talked of people having "ears to hear" and "eyes to see" spiritual truths. He knew that some people could tune into spiritual experiences and some people could not. It is the same with feelings. Some of us have the ears to hear what is going on inside of us, and some of us do not. Some of us have the eyes to see our feelings and some of us . . . need glasses.

How can you learn to hear and see?

By practicing! If you want to learn to recognize your emotions, you need to spend a few minutes listening and watching. You should pause to look inside and see what you can. At first you may only rarely get a glimpse of an emotion, and you may recognize a feeling only when it is extremely intense. Later, as you tune your antennae inward, you will find that your eyes become sharper and your ears can hear more and more. You will first recognize one or two emotions, then another and another, gradually awakening yourself to an important part of your experience. Activities 6:2 and 6:3 at the end of this chapter can help you develop these skills.

Skill no. 2: Labeling your emotions. When you first get a glimpse of an emotion, you cannot give it a name. You are vaguely aware of a sensation, an experience, a feeling that you are living. Then, gradually, much like watching a sunrise become more clear and bright, you get a more clear picture of what is happening inside. As your awareness becomes clearer, you are able to tell what the emotion is and find words that describe it. This is the process of *labeling* your feelings.

Some feelings, such as anger and happiness, are easy to label. Others are much more complex and subtle, and it is more difficult to label them. Sometimes you may find yourself saying things like, "I'm not sure how to describe what I'm feeling," or "I just can't find words that express it," or "words just aren't adequate."

The process of labeling emotions is important, because having names for feelings can help you communicate about your emotions. Davitz (1969) and Powell (1974, p. 158) have identified a list of hundreds of different emotions, and a modified version of their list is reproduced below. This list wouldn't be much fun to read. (It would be like reading a dictionary.) But a review of the list can increase your *vocabulary of emotions.*

Labels for Emotions

1. accepted	17. beaten	33. confused
2. accepting	18. beautiful	34. connected
3. active	19. bewildered	35. contemptuous
4. admiring	20. bored	36. contented
5. feeling affection	21. brave	37. cowardly
6. afraid	22. calm	38. creative
7. alarmed	23. cheated	39. cruel
8. alienated	24. cheerful	40. curious
9. amused	25. close	41. cut off from others
10. angry	26. closed	42. defeated
11. anxious	27. comfortable	43. dejected
12. apathetic	28. committed	44. delighted
13. appreciated	29. compassionate	45. dependent
14. attractive	30. competent	46. depressed
15. awe-inspired	31. concerned for others	47. deprived
16. awkward	32. confident	48. deserving punishment

49. desperate
50. determined
51. disappointed in myself
52. disappointed with others
53. discomforted
54. disliked
55. dominated
56. domineering
57. eager to impress others
58. eager to please others
59. easily manipulated
60. easygoing
61. elated
62. embarrassed
63. enjoyable
64. envious
65. evasive
66. evil
67. excited
68. exhilarated
69. failing
70. fatalistic
71. fearful
72. feminine
73. flirtatious
74. friendless
75. friendly
76. frigid
77. frustrated
78. gay
79. generous
80. genuine
81. giddy
82. grateful
83. gratified
84. grief-stricken
85. grudge-bearing
86. guilty
87. gutless
88. happy
89. hateable
90. hateful
91. harmonious
92. hopeful
93. hopeless
94. hostile
95. humorous
96. hurt
97. hurt by criticism
98. hyperactive
99. hypocritical
100. ignored
101. immobilized
102. impatient
103. inadequate
104. incompetent
105. inconsistent
106. in control
107. indecisive
108. independent
109. inferior
110. inhibited
111. insecure
112. insincere
113. inspired
114. involved
115. irritated
116. isolated
117. jealous
118. judgmental
119. lonely
120. losing
121. lovable
122. loved
123. loving
124. loyal
125. manipulated
126. manipulative
127. masculine
128. masked
129. melancholy
130. misunderstood
131. moody
132. needy
133. nervous
134. old beyond years
135. optimistic
136. out of contact
137. out of control
138. overcontrolled
139. overlooked
140. odd
141. panicked
142. paranoid
143. passionate
144. peaceful
145. persecuted
146. pessimistic
147. phony
148. piteous
149. pitiful
150. played out
151. pleased
152. possessive
153. pouting
154. prejudiced
155. preoccupied
156. pressured
157. protective
158. proud
159. quiet
160. rejected
161. relaxed
162. relieved
163. religious
164. remorseful
165. repelled
166. repulsive
167. resentful
168. restrained
169. reverent
170. rewarded
171. sad
172. satisfied
173. scared
174. secure

175. self-complacent
176. self-reliant
177. serene
178. shallow
179. shamed
180. shameful
181. shy
182. silly
183. sincere
184. sinful
185. sluggish
186. soft
187. solemn
188. sorry for self
189. strong
190. stubborn
191. stupid
192. sunshiny

193. super
194. superior
195. supported
196. supportive
197. surprised
198. suspicious
199. sympathetic
200. tender
201. terrified
202. threatened
203. tired
204. tolerant
205. torn
206. touchy
207. triumphant
208. two-faced
209. ugly
210. unable to communicate

211. unappreciated
212. uncertain
213. ungifted
214. unresponsive
215. unrestrained
216. uptight
217. used
218. useless
219. victimized
220. vindictive
221. violent
222. warm
223. weary
224. weedy
225. wishy-washy
226. youthful

You might try at this time to stop and identify feelings you are experiencing right now, and see if the list can help you further identify or clarify your description of these emotions.

Skill no. 3: Sharing your feelings. Once you have learned to recognize your emotions, to label them, and to pinpoint what is going on inside of you, you can then disclose these feelings to others. Becvar (1974) has identified several different ways that a person can express feelings. First you can express them indirectly or *nonverbally* through your actions. If a person is excited he tends to do such things as jump up and down, squeal, laugh, and gesture with his hands. Each of these behaviors sends nonverbal messages to those who are watching. When a person is sad or depressed, he tends to move slowly, talk little, sigh, cup his forehead in his palm, move away from others, and look down; thus different nonverbal messages are sent.

You can also use verbal messages to share your feelings. There are two types of these. You can use *direct* statements, such as:

"I'm angry."

"I think I feel lonely tonight."

"I feel so excited that . . ."

"It is depressing to . . ."

"I feel sad about . . ."

"Deep inside there is a feeling of . . ."

Or you can use metaphors—analogies or figures of speech that describe feelings. Some examples are:

"I feel like something that the dog dragged in."

"I feel like I'm floating on a cloud."

"I feel like I'm carrying the whole world."

"I'm tingling all over."

"I feel like I'm ten feet tall."

You can, of course, combine these various methods of sharing your feelings. In fact, you always send nonverbal messages whenever you express a feeling verbally. You say it in a certain way, and an alert observer can usually get a lot more information from the nonverbal messages than from the verbal statements.

The important thing in this skill is being able to find some way to express your emotions so that your partner can understand what you are experiencing. One effective way to do it is to use "I" statements. These are declarative sentences in which the word *I* is the subject (Gordon 1970, chapters 6-7). They are very different from "You" statements and "I-You" statements. They are especially useful when you are expressing negative feelings in which someone else is involved. Some examples of "I" statements, as contrasted with "You" statements and "I-You" statements, are:

I statement:	"I'm furious."
I-You statement:	"I'm furious and it's your fault."
You statement:	"You've made me furious."

I statement:	"I'm so mad I could tear this place apart."
I-You statement:	"I'm so mad at what you've done I could tear this place apart."
You statement:	"You've ruined the whole evening with this mess."

I statement:	"I feel like I'm useless and unimportant."
I-You statement:	"It hurts me when you don't come home on time or call."
You statement:	"You don't even care about me or how I feel."

Obviously, the "I" statement has some advantages over the others. It clearly identifies your feelings, and it creates ownership. You are communicating that the feeling exists and that it is inside of you. It is your feeling. "I" statements also show that you accept the responsibility for the feeling. It may be that other factors such as the other person's behavior helped contribute to your feeling, but at this time all you are expressing is what you are feeling. You can deal with the cause or source of the emotion later, after the other person understands what is going on inside of you. If you try to identify your emotion *and* its source in the same sentence, you are usually less effective because you are conveying too much information at once to be clearly understood. Also, if the other person is a part of the source of the emotion, the "You" part of the sentence will ring so loud in his ears that he will usually not hear the "I" part. Thus an "I-You" statement frequently turns into a "You" statement in the ears of the receiver—and that is where it counts.

"You" statements are characterized by ambiguity, multiple meaning, and blaming. Seldom can the expressor own his own feelings when using "You" statements, and seldom does the receiver of such expressions ever have his/her self-esteem increased, understand clearly what has been said, or feel good about his/her relationship with the expressor. On the other hand, "I" statements indicate that you are aware of your inner feelings and that

Sharing positive emotions builds bonds and love.

you accept these feelings. Also, when "You" statements have become a habit, it becomes difficult to stop using them. It is apparently a natural reaction to blame others for the way you are feeling rather than to accept these feelings as your own, but it is also unwise. It takes a conscious effort to break this kind of habit and learn to express yourself clearly. Activity 6:4 at the end of the chapter may prove helpful to those wishing to increase their use of "I" statements.

Another part of this skill has to do with *norms.* One reason some people do not express their emotions is that they have learned the *social norm* that says they should not express them. The term *social norm* refers to the beliefs in a culture that tell you what you should do and not do. Many norms are healthy; for example, our beliefs that we should wear clothes, say "thank you," and be considerate are desirable social norms. Other norms that we get from our culture are unwise and ineffective. The norm that dictates that people, especially men, should conceal their emotions is one of the unfortunate ones. People would be much better off in their marriages if they were to follow the ancient scriptural norms of sharing emotions extensively instead of the modern norm of men being tough, silent, John-Wayne types. Some scholars have referred to this inexpressiveness as the "John Wayne neurosis" (Manville 1969; Balswick and Peek, 1971). Some examples of this norm are that people may be convinced that they are not jealous or angry when they really are, or that a father may be deeply overjoyed to see a child after an absence but is unwilling to admit to himself or to anyone else that he has emotional responses.

Marriage counselors have noted that this norm is also very prevalent in the Latter-day Saint community. An example of this is the interpretation that some couples put on the statement, "No success can compensate for failure in the home." Some feel this means that under no circumstances are they to say anything negative to their spouses about the performance of their marital roles. They think that to do so would be to admit that there is failure in their home, and this would mean that they have committed the worst type of failure there could ever be. Rather than admit to each other that they have any negative emotions about their marriages, these couples suffer in silence, as long as they can—until they either get sick or explode in uncontrolled anger and harm their relationships.

Other couples believe that though this statement is true, it does not imply that they are failures in the home if they admit to faults and imperfections in their relationships. Rather, it identifies the need for them to focus on areas they can work on and improve. These couples are able to express their negative feelings to each other without hurting each other, and thus resolve their differences and strengthen their relationships. Since norms are not innate biological phenomena, but are beliefs acquired from the groups in which we live, we can often change our norms by talking, usually at some length, about their appropriateness. Activities 6:5 and 6:6 at the end of this chapter are designed to help you do something about these normative beliefs. The first exercise can help you gain a better understanding of what your beliefs really are. This is often useful because your normative beliefs are frequently vague feelings that you have not really articulated to yourself. They are often nebulous feelings indicating that you should or shouldn't really do something or act in certain ways. The second exercise can help you decrease normatively caused reluctance to talk about emotions.

Skill no. 4: Expressing negative emotions in a healthy way. A word of caution needs to be added at this point about couples expressing intense feelings to each other. It is not the intent of this chapter to advocate the unrestrained expression of any feeling to anybody at anytime. To express negative feelings anytime, anyplace, or anywhere, just to "get them off your chest," can be very harmful.

The art of disclosing negative emotions without hurting one's partner is seldom learned very well in our society; it is an unnatural skill. The natural thing to do when you have negative emotions is to release your emotion in an unrestrained way. It is easy to lash out at others, get even, tell others off, blow off steam, and yell or hit things. The unnatural way is to accept your emotion for what it is and then be careful and loving in the way you communicate your feelings to your partner.

It takes time and effort to express negative feelings in helpful ways. It demands self-control and compassion and a loving concern for the other person. But, in the long run, it is well worth it, because it helps you work through your emotions while preserving respect and love in the relationship. Those who share their feelings in the more natural ways will very quickly destroy the precious and delicate parts of their relationships—such as feelings of trust, openness, concern, and helpfulness. These fragile and lovely things will be replaced

When our feelings are intense . . . our self-control and ability to be loving suffer.

with suspicion, defensiveness, and resentment, and will eventually disappear from the relationship.

How can you express your negative feelings helpfully? How should you act? The following guidelines can be very useful in helping you pause and realize what you can do. Again, some people may not be at a level of perfection where they can do all of the things in the following list. If this is so, they ought to try to do a few of them, and when they have developed those abilities, they can try to do the others. Also, some will not be able to follow these guidelines all of the time. Again, following them some of the time will help them develop this ability, and if they practice, practice, and practice, they will get better at it. Those with trouble in this area may find it useful to make several copies of this list and tape them on such places as the refrigerator door, medicine cabinet mirror, and automobile dashboard.

The guidelines are these:

First: Is the "total environment" right?

Check out the time of day, distractions, noise, privacy, outside pressures in the home, etc.

Second: Are you in control of yourself?

Intense feelings will interfere—in ways you may not even recognize. There-fore, you need to find out where you are emotionally. You need to go and vent your intense feelings first if they are strong enough to get in the way.

Next: Is the other person receptive?

You need to ask yourself whether your partner is defensive, preoccupied, tired, or overworked. You can ask by saying such things as: "Where are you now?" "Can I share another feeling?"

Then: Be careful and slow.

Use tact, love, and consideration, and don't dump too much at once. If the receptiveness leaves, wait until it can be re-created.

Be sure: to include yourself in the problem.

Almost all problems that cause intense negative feelings between people are the result of interaction between them rather than a single partner's actions. To include yourself, you can use "I" statements when discussing the problem. The information on page 63 about separating the issue from the personality is also helpful in expressing negative feelings effectively.

Afterward: Show an increase in love.

Receiver Roles

Communication between a husband and wife is a two-part process. You play the expressor role when you are experiencing feelings and expressing them to your spouse. You plan the role of the receiver when you listen to the revelation of feelings from your spouse. The preceding pages have dealt with some skills that can help you be a good expressor. We will now turn our attention to the receiver role in marriage.

Skill no. 5: Listening with your head and heart. Some important skills in being able to perform this receiver role were emphasized by King Mosiah in the Book of Mormon. As he gathered his people around him to instruct them and to share his feelings with them, he prefaced his remarks with the following:

> My brethren, all ye that have assembled yourselves together, you that can hear my words which I shall speak unto you this day; for I have not commanded you to come up hither to trifle with the words which I shall speak, but that you should hearken unto me, and open your ears that ye may hear, and your hearts that ye may understand, and your minds that the mysteries of God may be unfolded to your view. (Mosiah 2:9.)

In this passage of scripture, we find two of the skills necessary to understanding another's expression of emotions: (1) an attitude of attention and interest—an "I care about what you are about to say" attitude, and (2) a desire to listen with the *ears,* the *mind,* and the *heart* so as to be able to comprehend the messages sent.

Some communication theorists have identified skills that they feel are helpful in understanding emotions. Miller, Nunnally, and Wackman (1975, p. 101) suggest the following:

1) Checking out. (This was discussed in more detail on pages 58-62.) It is a means of clarifying or discovering another's awareness.

2) Acknowledging the sender's message. This means acknowledging the message and reporting back to the sender what was observed and heard. Miller et al. (1975, p. 112) define it as simple paraphrasing and giving back the sender's original message. Typical words for this activity consist of such statements as, "Oh, now I understand," "I hear you saying that . . ." or "I'm hearing . . ."

3) Confirming. Something the original sender can do as he listens to summary statements or acknowledgments is to confirm whether the receiver's acknowledgment is accurate or not. He may say, "Yes, that's right," or "Well, that's pretty close, but here's what else I was trying to say," or "That's not quite what I was trying to say; let me try again."

In summary, receiving messages from others is one of the highest forms of human influence. It is an important part of eternal interaction between men and women, and mankind and God. The Lord was very much concerned about it; he commented often about how we should listen: "Let these sayings sink down into your ears" (Luke 9:44), and "He that hath ears to hear, let him hear" (Matthew 11:15, Revelation 2:7). Listening is a learned art, and it requires an emotional and spiritual sensitivity that goes beyond words alone to the feelings and real meanings of what is said. By so doing you are saying to another, "You're a person of worth; I love you, respect you, and I want to understand you."

Skill no. 6: Accepting rather than rejecting. When someone is expressing his feelings, it is easy for the listener to look at things only from his own point of view. People say things like: "You couldn't possibly feel that way," "That's a terrible way to feel," "That's not how you really feel," or "Ha . . . !" Again, the easy thing to do, the natural thing, is far from the wise thing to do. *The natural man is again an enemy to God* and that which is good.

You need to realize that much of the time your emotions are not rational. They are neither sensible nor predictable—but they are! They exist, and they are very real. You may not like them. You may not approve of them, but denying their existence will not make them go away and cease to exist. If you wish hard enough to push them out of your mind, you may push them out of your consciousness such that you are not aware of them. And if you are abusive enough of your spouse's emotions, the other person will stop sharing his or her feelings with you.

When these things happen, the emotions are still there, and they still influence what a person does, how he acts, how he feels, and even his physical health. He just won't know what is pushing him around. He will be oblivious to what is going on inside. Then, at a later time, he'll find himself wondering what is causing all of his difficulties: his ulcer, his skin problems, his rocky marriage, his disobedient children, and his lack of peace and contentment.

If you are wise, you will accept your emotions, whatever they are. You will recognize that you feel the way you feel, and you will recognize and accept that the feelings are real, genuine, and, above all, present. You'll recognize and accept your own emotions and the emotions of your spouse. You may say, "I wish I didn't feel that way," but you won't deny, distort, or refuse to accept what is happening inside.

How can you be accepting?

The key to being an accepting person is to recognize that whatever is happening emotionally is real, and you cannot change or alter or deny that moment. It has happened. If the emotion is a pleasant one, you can savor and enjoy it. If it is a negative feeling, you need to admit it and accept it, just as you would some physical object. We all immediately recognize what it would mean if someone looked at a tree or car or physical object and tried to convince himself that it was not there. It would be a distortion of reality that would have implications for his mental stability. The same is true for denying the existence of emotions; it has implications for emotional and mental stability.

Once you accept the existence of an emotion, you can do many things about it. If you don't like it, you can do things to help the feeling go away. If the feeling is immoral or bad, such as a feeling of jealousy, coveting, lust, or unjustified anger, you can also try to repent of the feeling. You can change your situation so that the feeling will leave. You can hope and pray and try to prevent the feeling from recurring, and you can avoid similar situations in the future. What you don't want to do is deny the feeling. That merely puts it out of your awareness, where you can't control it or its effects.

If your partner has an emotion that is unwanted or inappropriate, you ought to also accept it for what it is—because it is real. Think how inappropriate it would have been for the roommate in the example on pages 89-90 to have responded to the co-ed's expression of feelings about the nylons, "Oh, come on now, you shouldn't let a little thing like nylons upset you so. You're going to be getting ulcers soon."

At times you or your partner may have feelings that you do not correctly understand. Or you may only have a vague and uncertain understanding of how you are feeling. When this happens, it is useful to be accepting and understanding and patient in your responses to each other. This will help you further explore the feelings in an atmosphere of trust so that you can correct your misconceptions and get a more clear understanding of what is going on inside.

There are at least three specific behaviors that one ought to avoid when trying to be accepting. One of these is *denial.* This occurs when you reject your mate's revelation of feelings by discounting or refusing to accept that he or she feels that way. You pass judgment on feelings as inappropriate or unrealistic, and you refuse to accept the possibility that such feelings are real. When you do this, you are telling the sender that you know more about his feelings than he does, and that he should listen to you instead of to his stomach. The following examples are illustrative:

Wife: "I just feel devastated by what's happening lately."
Husband: "Come on, dear, you couldn't possibly feel that way."

Husband: "When dinner is late every night, I turn into a raving monster."
Wife: "A little thing like that shouldn't upset you so."

A second behavior to avoid when we are trying to be accepting is the tendency to *defend* ourselves. Examples of this follow:

Wife: "I feel terrible when you're rude to my mother like that."
Husband: "I'm only trying to help you cut the apron strings and grow up."

Husband: "I'm terribly embarrassed when we're always walking into church late. Can we do something about it?"
Wife: "Well, if I were bald like you it wouldn't take very long for me to get ready either."

A third behavior to avoid is to *ignore* expressions of feelings. Some people fall into this pattern by lack of attention, by being so preoccupied with seemingly more important interests that they just don't pay attention to the messages that are being sent by their mates.

Wife: "George, I'm so upset with you. I've decided to go to my mother's."
George: "Hmm." (Continues to read the paper.)
Wife: "Furthermore, I'm going to set the house on fire as I leave, to show you how mad I am."
George: "Hmm."

Skill no. 7: Recognizing nonverbal and verbal messages. The previous chapter discussed several types of nonverbal communication that are useful to receivers of emotional messages. That chapter discussed ways in which you can receive nonverbal messages through touching, observing body positions, and treating the other person's views as subjectively correct—even though they may be incorrect in an absolute or objective sense. There are several other ways you can receive nonverbal messages that can help you be a good receiver.

One important source of nonverbal messages is the *way* a person says something. Is he talking casually, or is he intensely emotional as he says things? Does he have to pause and get control of himself as he talks? Some of the nonverbal messages sent are so obvious that anybody can pick them up; for example, when a person is crying or speaking in a loud voice it is easy to get information from these nonverbal messages. But other messages are subtle and difficult to detect, and they take more skill. For example, small things like a curled lip, a glance out of the corner of an eye, tightly closed hands, and a slightly longer-than-usual breath can send messages, if we are alert enough to hear them.

Two parts of the body provide a lot of clues about what is happening to a person emotionally—the eyes and the upper lip. The eyes can be clear or red, fixed or moving, downcast or looking at the ceiling, dry or watery, looking at someone else's eyes too little or too much, wide open or partly closed; each of these changes can give you clues as to what is happening. The eyes, however, can be voluntarily controlled to a great extent, and so it is possible to receive incorrect messages when you try to interpret the nonverbal clues. The upper lip has fewer nerve endings and it is more difficult to control voluntarily. Therefore, it frequently is a better indicator of what is really going on inside a person. A quivering lip is a pretty good indicator that a person is upset. If the lip is straight and slightly tight, this indicates tension and stress. If it is relaxed and moves easily, this indicates that emotions are less intense.

The nonverbal messages that we send are also somewhat different for each of us. One person will sigh at a certain time, and those who know the person well know that it means a certain thing. Another person will talk quickly or slowly, or not talk at all, and those who have been around him can get a little meaning from these behaviors. Frequently, however, we misinterpret the nonverbal messages we receive, or we hear some nonverbal messages but we don't know what they mean. This is where checking-out skills (pages 58-62) are very useful. You can check out your hints or suspicions, and the additional information can help you understand the other person. Therefore, one of the most useful things you can do when you are having problems understanding nonverbal messages is to turn the nonverbal into verbal. Talk about it. Get it into the open. Discuss it.

Managing Skills

Being able to express your feelings and to understand the other person is only part of the process of managing the emotional part of your marital system. These two processes help you share information and understand each other, but there are many other skills that you need if you are to deal effectively with your emotions—if you are to use them to create positive feelings like love and joy, and keep them from creating destructive feelings like suspicion, anxiety, anger, and resentment. Thus, in addition to the communication skills, you need to be able to make wise decisions and manage the emotional part of your marital stewardship. The following two skills can help in this area.

Skill no. 8: Keeping intense emotions from interfering. Positive feelings like happiness, excitement, contentment, and joy seldom interfere with anything—unless they are extremely intense. They create pleasure and add beauty to life. Negative feelings, on the other hand, don't have to be very intense before they start interfering with the operation of your system. When you get angry, it disrupts your life. If you're depressed about yourself or about life in general, it doesn't take very long for this condition to foul up many parts of the system, such as getting your daily tasks done, being affectionate, being supportive, and enjoying sexual intimacies. You therefore need to learn some things you can do to keep the emotions from disrupting other parts of your life.

What can you do?

The first thing you need to do is be fairly good at recognizing your emotions (skill no. 1, discussed on pages 92-93). If you don't have a pretty good idea of what your emotions are, you won't be very good at keeping them from interfering with other things.

Second, you can recognize when an emotion is getting intense enough that it is causing you to behave unwisely. This seems like a simple task when you first consider it, but it is much harder to do than it seems. A person says to himself, "Oh, I recognize that I'm upset, but I can control it. Let's get this thing resolved." He thinks that his anger is under control, and he tells himself that it is not causing him to be defensive, critical, angry, or closed-minded—when it actually is.

Sometimes your spouse can see what is happening before you can, and he or she can help you realize that your emotions are getting in the way. The spouse needs to do it very gently because it is usually a time when you are distressed. Gentle comments, such as saying that he seems to be acting more upset than the situation seems to demand, or asking him if he realizes how upset he is, can sometimes help.

The main part of this skill is being able to *change what you are doing when you realize you have intense emotions.* The natural tendency is to keep working at whatever you are doing and ignore your emotions. And once again, the natural pattern is an enemy to good. You need to do the unnatural thing, which is to stop and deliberately change what you are doing. Usually the best way to do this is to stop the task—if possible—and focus on the emotions. If you are having a discussion (an argument) with your spouse, you need to stop discussing whatever you are talking about and focus on the emotion. You can say things like:

"Wait a minute. I'm so upset that I need a minute."
"Hold it! My anger is getting in the way. Can we stop for a minute?"
"Let's take five and cool off."
"I'm getting carried away too much. Let's back off for a minute."
"I'm hurting so much, I'm not being reasonable. Can we deal with the hurt?"

The "natural" thing to do is say things like:

"I'm okay; let's go on."
"I am *not* mad."
"Be reasonable, do it my way" (unrighteous dominion).
"If you'd just . . ."

These "natural" ways of behaving keep the emotion intense, and you usually just get deeper and deeper into trouble. So, what do you need to do? In a nutshell:

When emotions are intense, stop what you are doing
and deal with the emotion first.

The importance of this process is illustrated by a story and some advice shared by Elder Boyd K. Packer in an address at BYU in 1970:

Never a Cross Word

Now, I will mention some things to you, young man, about her later. But now, to both of you, as you enter the marriage covenant, never a cross word—not one. It is neither necessary nor desirable. There are many who teach that it is normal and expected for domestic difficulty and bickering and strife to be a part of that marriage relationship. That is false doctrine. It is neither necessary nor desirable. I know that it is possible to live together in love with never the first cross word ever passing between you.

The Elderly Woman

I went home-teaching years ago to an elderly little woman. I was not married at the time and occasionally without a companion. She was a shut-in and she dearly loved lemon ice cream. Occasionally I would go down to the Peach City Ice Cream Company and get a halfpint of lemon ice cream and make her house the first stop.

She appreciated very much this simple kindness, and one evening she said she wanted to give me some counsel.

She told me the story of her life—marriage in the temple to a wonderful elder, living together and beginning a family, a call to open the mission field in one of the continents of the world, a happy mission, return back to the little town, entering into life's pursuits.

Then she focused in on a Monday morning. A blue, dreary wash day, Monday morning, gray and cloudy, outside and in, cross children, little irritations, a poor meal, and finally an innocent remark by one, snapped up by the other, and soon husband and wife were speaking crossly and critically to one another.

"As he left for work," she said, "I just had to follow him to the gate and call that one, last, biting, spiteful remark after him." And then as the tears came, she told me of an accident that day and he didn't return from work.

"For fifty years," she sobbed, "I have regretted that the last word he ever heard from my lips was that one, last, biting, spiteful remark."

Then came her lecture to me. It was good counsel. You know what it was without my repeating it.

The Irritated Husband

Will Carleton, in his story "The First Settlers," pictured a husband leaving an isolated cabin after several irritating experiences of looking for a cow that would get into the woods. He made some caustic remark to his bride about whether she thought maybe this time when he was gone, at least she could tend the cow.

A violent thunderstorm arose, and he returned with great anxiety from work in the woods to find a note on the table in the cabin.

"The cow was frightened by the lightning," she had written apologetically, "but I think I can find her."

When he found his sweetheart it was too late. And the author moralized over his heartbreak with these words—good words for every couple entering marriage:

Boys flying kites haul in their white-winged birds.
You can't do that when you're flying words.
"Careful with fire" is good advice, we know;
"Careful with words" is ten times doubly so.
Thoughts, unexpressed, may sometimes fall back dead;
But God Himself can't kill them when they're said.

Elder Packer's advice sets a very high standard; in fact, it is an extremely high ideal. Can you live it? Some people can live it, but many are not able to. You can, however, use the emotionality principle (page 87) and this skill (no. 8) to help you live it. As you learn to recognize that negative emotions are getting intense, and then learn to *stop what you are doing and deal with the emotion first whenever possible,* you will find that your emotions will not lead you to use cross words, and you will also find that you can more easily live this high standard.

Skill no. 9: Decreasing intensity of emotions. The skill just discussed helps you "stop, look, and listen." It helps you interrupt what you are doing so that your emotions won't have harmful effects on your relationship. Sometimes just stopping actions is enough, because the break in conversation and the brief identification of your feelings is enough to help you manage the situation wisely. Much of the time, however, you need to do more than just stop and notice that your emotion is getting in the way. You need to consciously do something to decrease the intensity of the emotion. Then you can go back to the issue or problem you were dealing with. A few very simple actions can sometimes help:

> Have a prayer
> Count to ten
> Walk around the block
> Take a few deep breaths
> Crack a joke—think of something funny
> Pause for a minute
> Do ten push-ups

If some of these simple things do not help the emotion subside, you may want to turn to some more involved ways of decreasing emotions. Some more complex methods are these:

> Read poetry—or write it
> Play the piano
> Lift weights
> Play racquetball
> Have a cry
> Scrub floors or clean windows
> Write letters
> Listen to some music
> Get a good night's rest
> Jog several miles

Activity 6:7 at the end of this chapter can help you increase your ability to vent your emotions in socially acceptable ways.

There are two booby traps that you might get caught in when you try to use these skills to manage the emotional part of your life. One is that after you vent your intense emotions, you sometimes tell yourself you don't really have a problem after all, when you actually do have a problem that needs solving. The result is that you leave the problem unsolved. What you need to do is to go back to the problem after you have cooled off, and find a solution to whatever it was that made you upset. If you don't, you may find yourself going through the same cycle time and time again.

The second booby trap is to try to kid yourself into thinking that your intense emotions don't adversely influence the way you behave. You tell yourself, "I can control myself." You observe that you don't use physical abuse. You don't yell at your spouse. You don't throw things. Therefore, you are in control. Many people are seldom aware of the subtle ways that their emotions influence the way they behave. You may not hit your spouse when you get upset, but you may give him or her the more subtle silent treatment. You may not throw things, but you may have more acid in your comments or be more cynical or critical than is necessary. Or, you may conveniently forget to have dinner ready on time or forget your wife's birthday. We need to stop kidding ourselves. When we have intense negative emotions, they *will* influence our behavior just as surely as leaves fall in the autumn and rivers run toward the sea. What you need to do is recognize the processes and not run away from them. Then, after you accept the truth, you can manage this part of your marital system much better.

SUMMARY

This chapter discusses the ways our emotions influence our communication in dating and marriage. It discusses the difference between emotion and thought and then defines five different attributes of emotions: source, intensity, consciousness, effects, and decreasing intensity. A general principle about emotions is then identified.

The chapter also points out that it is important for each of us to learn how to manage the emotional part of his husband-wife relationship, and it discusses nine skills. The skills are: recognizing your emotions, labeling emotions, being able to share your emotions with your partner, being able to express negative emotions in a helpful rather than harmful manner, listening with your heart as well as your head, recognizing nonverbal as well as verbal messages, accepting rather than rejecting expressions of others, keeping intense emotions from interfering with your relationship, and being able to vent emotions.

ACTIVITY 6:1
Feelings Are Different

It may come as a surprise, but many of us are not very good at recognizing the different parts of the awareness wheel shown below. We often think feelings are sensations or actions, or that intentions are feelings or sensations.

Each of the statements below represents one of the parts of the awareness wheel. Mark each one according to what it is. Just pay attention to what is said in the statement; ignore the way it is said. Use the following code:

S = A sensory statement (something happening to your five senses)
T = A thinking statement (your opinion or interpretation)
F = A feeling (or an emotion or affective experience)

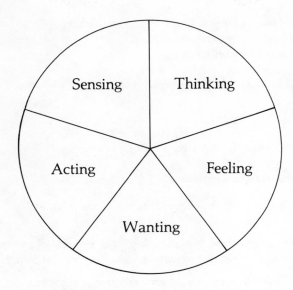

I = An intention (something you plan to do later)
A = An action (something you are doing now)

Answers*

_____ 1. I'm going to walk out of here right now.
_____ 2. I'm uncomfortable and nervous talking like this.
_____ 3. Teachers aren't very free to innovate.
_____ 4. I have such a sense of freedom and relief.
_____ 5. He's not talking as much today.
_____ 6. It's stimulating when the class gets involved.
_____ 7. It seems to me that nobody cares what happens.
_____ 8. I'd like to get some time to talk about our vacation coming up.
_____ 9. I get angry and frustrated when you don't follow through with what you say you'll do.
_____ 10. You don't even care.
_____ 11. Wow, I was excited to hear from you.
_____ 12. I'll bet you don't know what I want from you.
_____ 13. I didn't go last week.
_____ 14. He's leaning back in his chair, not smiling.
_____ 15. I think you misunderstood her.
_____ 16. I'll call Jim tomorrow morning.
_____ 17. I'm confident about it.

---

* The correct answers are on page 113.

_____ 18. I'd like to let you know what I'm thinking.
_____ 19. I smell your perfume.
_____ 20. I want to start soon.
_____ 21. I'm listening.
_____ 22. If he does, I will be furious.

ACTIVITY 6:2
Recognizing Clues to Emotions

Goal: To learn how to recognize emotions.

1. Select someone with whom you have a fairly close relationship, such as a spouse, fiancé(e), friend, or date.

2. Explain to the person that you are engaging in a project to increase your ability to recognize emotions, and ask if he or she will assist you for fifteen to thirty minutes.

3. Have the person think back to one or two emotional sensations he or she has experienced when in your presence, and then both of you try to identify several things that might have given you clues about emotions. It is important to listen hard to the person's description of the clues.

4. If the other person can identify an emotion he or she has experienced while doing step 3, have him or her identify it and then discuss things that might have been clues as to that emotion.

5. Can you now identify an emotion you have experienced while doing steps 3 and 4? If you are able to, can you also identify some ways you or someone else could recognize that emotion?

6. It is to be hoped that you have increased your ability to recognize emotions. Have you? If not, can you devise an exercise that would be more appropriate for you?

ACTIVITY 6:3
Rewarding the Recognition of Emotions

Goal: To increase the degree to which you recognize emotions by rewarding yourself when you become aware of an emotion.

1. Find something that is pleasurable to you and relatively easy to either start or stop. Some examples might be having dessert at dinner, carrying around a package of candies and eating one at a certain time, or putting money in a special bottle for something you want.

2. For the next week (or longer) reward yourself with one of the pleasures every time you consciously recognize an emotional sensation, such as happiness, anger, warmth, jealousy, or love. If you are interested in increasing your ability to recognize your own emotions, reward yourself when you become aware of an emotion you are experiencing. If you are interested in increasing your ability to recognize emotional experiences in others, reward yourself when you accurately recognize an emotion someone else exhibits.

3. At the end of the time period assess the experience, and try to determine whether or not you are recognizing your emotions more. One alternative to this exercise is to have the rewards administered by someone else, such as your spouse or fiancé(e).

ACTIVITY 6:4
Learning to Use "I" Statements

Goal: To express ownership of your own emotions and feelings by expressing to others that you are aware of these feelings, own them, have enough confidence in yourself to reveal them.

1. Identify someone who knows you well—such as a fiancé(e), spouse, or close friend—and ask him/her to join with you in an exercise that should help the two of you to understand each other more clearly.

2. Explain to the person the difference between "I" statements and "you" statements. Give him examples of each and tell why you feel that your relationship with him would be improved if the two of you were to increase your use of "I" statements and decrease the use of "You" statements.

3. Ask your partner to identify for you each time that you use an "I" or "You" statement. At the end of each day place the totals on two separate sheets of graph paper, one for the "I" statements and the other for the "You" statements.

4. Chart your progress for as long as it takes to increase the "I" statements and decrease the "You" statements to a point where you feel that you have mastered the technique.

5. One month after you have stopped recording the statements, record the data again to see if you have maintained the skill.

ACTIVITY 6:5
Understanding Personal Communication Norms

Goal: To better understand your personal beliefs about communicating about emotions.

1. Identify someone who knows you fairly well—such as a fiancé(e), spouse, or close friend—and ask him or her to help you with this exercise by having a conversation that would last at least fifteen to thirty minutes.

2. Explain the goal of the exercise to the other person, and then try to determine what you really believe about verbalizing your emotions. Talking about some of the following questions may help:

    a. Do I think I would be less of a man or woman if I were to talk about my feelings more openly?

    b. Do I turn people off by talking about my own emotions too much?

    c. If two people I know who are very open and very closed about their own emotions are opposite extremes on a continuum, where do I think I should be on that continuum?

3. Write down what you learned about your own beliefs.

ACTIVITY 6:6
Changing Personal Communication Norms

Goal: To change your personal norms so that you are more willing to talk about emotions.

1. Find a person with whom you have a meaningful relationship (a close friend, date, or spouse), who believes that people should share their emotions more than you think they should. Ask that person to help you with this exercise.

2. Make two lists on a piece of paper. One should be a list of the reasons why you think you should not talk about your feelings more than you do, and the other should be a list of the reasons the other person thinks people should share their emotions more than you do.

3. Try to identify situations in the past or relationships in the present which have influenced your belief that you shouldn't be more open about your emotions. (Often our parents' opinions have influenced us, and sometimes women and men subtly hold each other to sex-typed, traditional communicator roles, such as the "strong and silent" or "high emotional" type.)

4. Discuss the ideas you have identified in steps 2 and 3 to see whether you might want to change your opinions as to talking about emotions. If you do want to, try to identify what you want to believe and why you now think you should believe it.

ACTIVITY 6:7
Socially Desirable Methods of Decreasing Emotions

Goal: To increase the number of socially desirable ways you can vent your emotions.

1. Make a list of all the methods you now have to vent emotions. (The examples on page 107 will get you started.)

2. After you have written down all the methods you can think of—take four or five minutes to do it—engage in a conversation with several others (this can be done in a class) and try to make a new list of at least five socially acceptable methods you have never thought about.

3. Display both of your lists in some conspicuous spot. For example, tape them to the refrigerator door for two weeks and see how many times you can use the items on your new list in that time. You may want to reward yourself each time you use one.

Answers to Activity 6:1 on Pages 108-110:

1=I, 2=F, 3=T, 4=F, 5=T, 6=T (it doesn't identify that he has the feeling), 7=T (even though it would often have latent emotion), 8=I, 9=F, 10=T (but it would usually nonverbally communicate some emotion too), 11=F, 12=T, 13=A, 14=S, 15=T, 16=I, 17=F, 18=I, 19=S (and it may lead to an emotion), 20=I, 21=A, 22=T (because it is thinking what will happen rather than identifying an emotion that is occurring).

SUPPLEMENTARY READINGS

Brown, Hugh B. *You and Your Marriage.* Salt Lake City: Bookcraft, Inc., 1960, pp. 95-102.
Davitz, Joel R. *The Language of Emotion.* New York: Academic Press, 1969.
Dittman, Allen T. *Interpersonal Messages of Emotion.* New York: Springer, 1972.
Dyer, William G. *Creating Closer Families: Principles of Positive Family Interaction.* Provo, Utah: Brigham Young University Press, 1975.
Hanks, Marion D. *Now and Forever.* Salt Lake City: Bookcraft, Inc., 1974.
Johnson, David W. *Reaching Out.* Englewood Cliffs, N. J.: Prentice-Hall, 1972.
Powell, John. 1972. *Why I'm Afraid to Tell You I Love You.*
Young, P. T. *Emotion in Man and Animal.* Huntington, N. Y.: Kreiger.

7

CONSISTENCY IN COMMUNICATION

Nothing

I suppose it was something you said
That caused me to tighten
And pull away.
And when you asked, "What is it?"
I, of course, said, "Nothing."

Whenever I say, "Nothing,"
You may be very certain there is
 Something.

—Author unidentified

The following four situations illustrate an important principle in communication:

The Joneses

Sheila says, in an emphatic manner, "You hold the priesthood, so lead. You should be the leader in family home evening."

The Smiths

The home teachers leave a message about priesthood leadership, and the wife comments about how important it is to let the head of the family preside. Then, as the home teachers are about to leave, they turn the time back to the father for a closing prayer. The father stands up as he folds his arms and says, "All right, children, let's gather around so we can have a prayer." As he and the children begin to move into a circle, the mother slips off her chair onto her knees and bows her head, ready to pray.

The Barkers

Sue is excited as she tells her husband about a new development at her job. Harry doesn't seem too interested, so she says, "Are you sure you want to hear more?" He responds, "Of course, I'm listening," as his eyes continue to scan the sports page of the evening paper.

The Berretts

As Bill slips into the car seat beside Ethel, she reaches for his hand and gives it a squeeze. She then looks over at him and says, "I've really wanted to go to this play, and I appreciate your canceling that meeting. You're a jewel."

The principle involved in these situations is:

6. The Consistency Principle: The greater the consistency in communication, the better the communication.

The four situations mentioned above help us understand what is meant by consistency, and they also help us understand which kinds of inconsistencies are the most disruptive. In the Jones family there is an important inconsistency. The wife is actually assuming the leadership in the relationship as she verbally tells her husband to assume the leading role, and she does it in a demanding way. She is taking command, and when a wife does this the husband can't really be the leader, whatever he does. If he doesn't take charge of family home evenings, he won't be the leader, and if he does, he is doing it under her instructions. Either way he is still a follower. This inconsistency could be eliminated in several ways:

One way:

The wife could move out of the leadership role but still bring up the problem. She could say things like, "I have a problem, and I'd like to talk about it." Then, after they agree that it is an appropriate time to talk, she could say things like, "It seems to me that I'm the one who always gets family home evening organized and started, and I don't feel good about it." Or, more to the point, "I'm uncomfortable about our family home evenings. When I go ahead and organize them, I feel like I'm doing something that should be a part of the priesthood." This way the wife is bringing up her problem by describing her feelings and opinions. She is not giving him instructions. She is taking initiative, but she is not usurping the presider's position.

Another way:

The wife could exert more leadership in this situation but do it by consensus and under the direction of the presiding authority in the home. She could say things like, "It seems like I'm the one to get family home evening going all the time. Is that the way you (or we) want it, Fred?" In doing this, she is raising an issue for them to deal with together. She recognizes her role as a partner and also recognizes that the priesthood role in the family is one of management or directing the process rather than one in which the husband should have all of the power, initiatives, and tasks.

In the Smith family, the husband gave several verbal and nonverbal messages to the family. He verbally asked them to join in a prayer. Then, by standing up and folding his arms, he also sent the following nonverbal messages: "This time let's all stand up to pray, and we ought to get ready now. Stand up around me so that we form a circle." The wife then sent very different nonverbal messages to everyone in the room. Nonverbally, she said, "This time let's all kneel down to pray." More importantly, however, her message occurred after Mr. Smith was standing, and she therefore also communicated, "I'm the leader here. Let me, rather than my husband, indicate what ought to be done. It doesn't matter that he indicated we should stand up. Kneel down." This mixing of messages from the parents was difficult for the children to deal with and also was difficult for the parents, because the conflict all occurred on a nonverbal level. And it may have all happened unconsciously.

The Smiths could have established consistency in a number of different ways. The wife could have waited until the next visit to kneel. Another way would have been for her to use a verbal request such as, "I feel like kneeling down this time. Would that be okay?" At a deeper level, she might be unhappy with the way he leads. If she is, it would be much better for her to initiate a conversation about her feelings at another time rather than non-verbally disagreeing with him in front of the children and the home teachers. She needs to follow the skills outlined in chapter 6 of recognizing, labeling, and expressing her true feelings.

The problem in the Barkers' communication is more obvious. He is verbally telling her that he is interested in what she has to say, but then he doesn't pay any attention. This kind of inconsistency is easier to cope with because it is more in the open, and we have some conventions for dealing with it. If Sue just wanted to deal with that particular incon-sistency, she could say things like, "When you're through with the paper, I have something exciting to tell you," or "I get the feeling that I'm not being listened to," or "Hey, choose between what I have to say and the paper." This could be a unique situation, or he could have a habit of giving mixed messages. If it is a rare occurrence, it can be handled with these simple comments, or just ignored. If it is a habit, she could bring it up another time as a "problem" in their relationship, and they could try to correct it.

The Berretts are an example of the way we ought to communicate. Ethel is verbally expressing appreciation, and the nonverbal messages she is sending are all consistent with her verbal message. Reaching for his hand and giving it a squeeze reinforces the verbal messages rather than canceling them or giving a different message.

To summarize, consistency in communication means that all of the messages you send, both verbally and nonverbally, fit together. You say things that are compatible. Incon-sistency means that some of the messages you send say one thing, and others say others. When you are consistent, your communication flows smoothly and is efficient and pleasant. When you have inconsistencies, especially with nonverbal messages, you are uncomfortable. You misunderstand, and unnecessary problems appear in the relationship.

DIFFERENT TYPES OF CONSISTENCY AND INCONSISTENCY

There are three different types of consistency, and they have different effects on the quality of communication. They are verbal/verbal, verbal/nonverbal, and nonverbal/nonverbal.

Verbal/Verbal Consistency and Inconsistency

This type of consistency deals with whether all of our sentences agree. Note for example, the following situation: The school-age child does not want to go to sacrament meeting and says, "Do I have to go?" The mother responds, "No, you don't have to go. Now, put on your coat and let's get in the car."

The mother's two verbal messages were inconsistent. One sentence indicated the child didn't have to go, and the other said he did have to go. To be more consistent, the mother would have had to say something like, "Yes, you do have to go. Now put on your coat and get into the car." Or if the mother did not think the child had to go, she would need to say something like, "No, you don't *have* to go, but you should go, and I want you to go. Please decide, so those who are going can get into the car." If she were a patient mother who felt in a helpful mood, she could have said, "I realize that you want to stay home, and you may not fully understand why you need to go. Nevertheless, put your coat on and get into the car. If you want to talk about why you need to go, we can do so after the meeting."

Verbal/verbal inconsistencies are usually so obvious that most people recognize them, and when they point them out, everybody involved can see them. People learn to recognize and deal with them while they are children, and virtually everyone has these skills. They usually do one of these things: they (a) resolve the inconsistency by correcting one of the statements; (b) write the comments off as irrelevant, unimportant, or unintended; or (c) enjoy the humor in them. These inconsistencies are like detours we encounter when driving a car. They are short inconveniences that can be dealt with in a minute or two. These inconsistencies seldom seriously disrupt the overall quality of communication, probably because it is so easy to detect them and correct them.

Verbal/Nonverbal Consistency and Inconsistency

Most nonverbal messages are consistent with verbal messages. A person may wink or smile as he says hello to an old friend. You turn and face someone when you say, "What was it you said?" and your turning says nonverbally, "I'm interested," "I want to hear you," "You have my attention." When you are around someone you respect, you non-verbally act and verbally speak in a respectful manner.

If people were always this consistent it would be lovely. Unfortunately, they are not! Remember the Joneses and the Smiths and the Barkers at the beginning of this chapter? They are not rare exceptions; situations like theirs happen all too frequently in dating and in husband-wife and parent-child relationships. Some people are involved in inconsistent communication situations only occasionally. Others have a habit of being inconsistent much of the time.

What happens when this type of inconsistency occurs?

This type of inconsistency is quite different from verbal-verbal inconsistencies. This problem is (1) harder to detect; (2) harder to talk about when you do find it; (3) easier to deny and avoid when you are confronted with it; and (4) harder to solve when you want to correct it. In other words, *This type of inconsistency tends to seriously disrupt the overall quality of your communication.*

To fully understand when and how these inconsistencies occur, we need to understand several characteristics of nonverbal messages and how we send them. First, how do we send them?

Digital and analog messages. There are two ways in which nonverbal messages are sent. Communication scholars call them the *digital* and *analog* methods (Watzlawick, Beaven, and Jackson 1967). Digital messages are those in which a small bit of information is sent in one clear-cut message. If you wink at someone, this is a digital message because the wink takes only a half-second or so, and it conveys a certain message. Other gestures such as shrugging your shoulders, clenching your fists in a menacing way, and holding your hands out toward a small baby are all digital messages. All verbal messages are also digital messages since the words have a certain meaning, and when you say them you convey a clear-cut message to someone else.

Analog messages are quite different. These are messages that are continually sent for a longer period of time. For example, when you are sitting next to someone and talking with him, your presence is continually sending a message that you are there. You are also sending many other analog or continual messages. For example, you are sending a message that you are awake, male or female, of a certain age, alive, clothed, neat or sloppy, and so on.

The difference between analog and digital messages can be illustrated with the two different types of speedometers in a car. The usual kind of speedometer is an analog type, in which a needle is continuously registering the speed. If the speedometer were a blinking light that flashed electronic numbers several times a minute, it would be a digital system.

Recognizing that you send a very large number of analog messages at the same time should help you realize that you communicate a great deal more nonverbally than you do verbally. Most of your nonverbal messages are received and understood unconsciously by those around you. For example, whenever you are in a sitting or standing position, you are sending the message: "I'm awake. I'm not asleep," and people perceive this message and respond to you as though you were awake—usually. Think of all of the other hundreds of nonverbal messages you are continuously sending: "I'm doing this now rather than any of the other millions of things I could be doing"; "I'm busy" or "I'm relaxing"; "I'm in this room or chair or tub or car"; "I'm dressed, and the particular combination of clothes I have on indicates whether I am working, playing, relaxing, or ready for a formal party." These messages have prompted some scholars to suggest that "we cannot *not* communicate" (Watzlawick, Beaven, and Jackson 1967). While it is probably true that a husband and wife are *not* communicating at 3:00 A.M. when they are both asleep, it is true that whenever you are interacting with someone else, no matter how hard you may try to not communicate, you are always communicating many, many things.

Content and relationship messages. This is another set of terms that helps us understand how we send nonverbal messages. The *content* in messages is the overt part. It is *what* you say; it is the meaning of the words that are spoken. Relationship messages are communicated nonverbally by the *way* you say things. The relationship messages give information about your relationship with another person, and you usually send a large number of them with each sentence.

Think of how the relationship messages differ when the simple sentence, "Come here," is said by a policeman on a street corner, a parent holding a switch, a wife in an affectionate moment, or an elders quorum president to his bishop. Very different relationship messages are sent. Some of the relationship messages in these situations would be commands, and others would be requests. Some would imply superiority, others inferiority, and others equality. Some may imply tenderness and affection, and others may imply resentment and anger.

Another illustration of the difference between the content and relationship aspects of communication can be seen in the simple sentence, "Let's go." The content of this sentence is that a request is being made for an individual or a group to join with the sender of the message in going someplace, and this content is easily understood. This same sentence, however, could be uttered in a variety of relationships. If the statement were made even casually by a marine sergeant to his recruits, it would usually come across as a dominating statement, virtually an order. Both marine sergeant and recruits probably assume that the sergeant ought to act in a powerful, dominating manner, and the sentence would have nonverbal components that would communicate this fact. However, if the same sentence were to be used on a date, very different messages would be communicated by the nonverbal messages accompanying the verbal message. There could be a message of equality rather than of dominance, and other things, such as tenderness and affection, would probably also be communicated. If the same message were given by a small child to his parent, it is likely that the nonverbal messages would communicate deference and submission, and the sentence would be more of a request than a command.

One phenomenon that you communicate to others in your relationship messages is who has the power or control in the relationship. If a person tells others what to do, he communicates nonverbally that he thinks he has the right to tell them what they should do, and that he thinks they should be either subservient to or equal to him. When a person is subservient to another, he tends to make cautious requests rather than imperative commands.

Several other aspects of relationships are structured and maintained largely through the relationship messages in communication. One of these is the amount of privacy you feel you ought to have. You gradually learn in childhood how to tell when you are becoming too private in your interaction with someone else, and when you can become more private. You learn that in close friendship there is less individual privacy than there is in fairly formal relationships, such as teacher-student relationships. But in our society this is very seldom discussed verbally. Instead, we rely on nonverbal messages to reach agreement on the amount of privacy we should have.

Another aspect of relationships that is usually communicated nonverbally is the right to question someone's opinions, motives, or instructions. People occasionally discuss this

All forms of communication should say the same thing . . . touch, facial expressions, words, body language, etc.

verbally, but usually they merely send and receive nonverbal messages. In many families, for example, young children do not *really* have the right to question their parents.

Most of the time you do not need to be aware of these nonverbal processes because you and your spouse develop consensus about such things as who has the power and how much privacy and independence you should have. The nonverbal messages are sent and received without anyone really being aware of them—partly because there is no need to be aware of them. They are sent unconsciously, and you can focus your attention on other things.

Occasionally, however, spouses have conflicting views about what their relationship should be. If these differences deal with the parts of their relationship that they usually take care of with nonverbal messages (and hence don't usually think about), it can be difficult to identify the problems and solve them. This is illustrated by the following case history. Here two partners disagree about the nature of their relationship, and both of them are struggling to get the upper hand in their interaction:

John: Darling, you're so fond of good meat, you really should try the rib-eye steak.
Mary: Thank you, darling, but I'd much prefer the filet mignon. It's a little more expensive than rib-eye, but I do think it has a better taste.

John: (Sensing that Mary has not accepted his superior knowledge of meat.) But people order filet mignon because of its snob appeal—missing an opportunity if you don't order it. Many restaurants don't even carry it.

Mary: I really appreciate your advice, John, but I do feel like having a filet mignon tonight.

John: I'm not giving you advice. I'm just telling you the facts.

Mary: You are giving me advice, and I don't need it. If it's all right with you I'd like filet mignon—or do I have to order fish?

John: Order what you _____ well please! (Lederer and Jackson 1968, p. 165.)

This kind of interchange is significant because the nonverbal messages are inconsistent with the verbal messages; this disrupts the couple's ability to communicate. The inconsistency gets in the way. Neither partner is understood, and neither really understands the other person. And, most importantly, these verbal/nonverbal inconsistencies interfere with their emotions as they communicate. They are uncomfortable, and have a feeling that something is wrong.

Besides their disruptive influence, there is another aspect of verbal/nonverbal discrepancies that makes them important. It is that they are also elusive or hard to nail down. Unlike the verbal/verbal inconsistencies that are obvious to everyone when they are pointed out, the inconsistencies that involve nonverbal messages aren't as clear to the sender or receiver. This makes it difficult to identify them and to know what to do.

There are several skills that can help you recognize and eliminate these discrepancies, but let's first identify the third type of discrepancy before we discuss these skills.

Nonverbal/Nonverbal Discrepancies

These are the most difficult and disruptive messages of all because all of the messages involved are nonverbal. Some examples of these discrepancies may help you realize that they do occur and that they interfere with effective communication:

Courteous Only at Home

Whenever Bill and Sue are in public, Bill is a warm and attentive person. He goes out of his way to be courteous to her, and most of their friends think he is a model husband. When they are alone, however, other things seem to get in the way. He is too busy to be affectionate, and he seldom does the nice little things he does when others are around.

Wife Turns to Children

Since Mary and George got out of medical school, things seem to have changed. George's schedule is very demanding and erratic, and he is always on call. This means he is gone a lot. Mary has found an increasing fulfillment in her relationships with the children, especially the oldest boy, George, Jr. She turns to him for advice about many things, and enjoys long chats in the evenings when George is at the hospital. The resulting pattern is that Mary's nonverbal messages about a companionship type of intimacy are sent more to her older son than her husband, yet she still tries to think of George as her marital partner.

Nonverbal/nonverbal inconsistencies seem to be more rare than the other two types. This may be because they occur less frequently, or it may be because they are so difficult to identify that we just don't recognize them. When they do occur, they are extremely difficult to solve. They are harder to deal with because they are less obvious, and it is easy to deny them. They are also frequently contrary to a person's intentions, and he doesn't like to admit that he would be that inconsistent.

THE CONSISTENCY PRINCIPLE IN THE GOSPEL AND IN SCIENCE

Before we discuss the skills you can utilize with the consistency principle, you need to realize that this principle is an important part of the gospel *and* of modern science.

Its role in the gospel can be seen in the emphasis that the Savior gave it. He taught: "Not every one that saith unto me, Lord, Lord, shall enter into the kingdom of heaven; but he that doeth the will of my Father who is in heaven." (3 Nephi 14:21.)

In this verse he is dealing with verbal claims and nonverbal behavior, and he is teaching that verbal/nonverbal inconsistencies are unacceptable to him. His admonitions about prayer also teach that people should be consistent. He taught that we should not pray as the "hypocrites" do (3 Nephi 13:5), who pretend to be humble but pray without humility. His analogy of "false prophets, who come . . . in sheep's clothing, but inwardly they are ravening wolves" (3 Nephi 14:15) is an example of nonverbal/nonverbal communication.

Paul noted, "If the trumpet give an uncertain sound, who shall prepare himself to the battle?" (1 Corinthians 14:8). When part of the message gives one signal and part of it gives a different one, an uncertain sound occurs. Paul's comment about the effects of an uncertain sound suggests confusion, ambivalence, and inappropriate behavior, and that is exactly what verbal/nonverbal inconsistencies do in dating and marital relationships.

The consistency principle is also an important discovery in modern science. It was initially discovered by psychiatrists who were trying to understand several different types of mental illness. They observed that the families of schizophrenic children tended to have more inconsistencies in their communication than most families (Bateson et al. 1956). It has been difficult to empirically test this principle (Haley 1963) because it is so difficult to measure the variables with present techniques, but psychiatrists and counselors who work with troubled families have found that the principle is a very valuable insight for them.

The most recent review of the research and theory about this principle is Broderick and Pulliam-Krager's 1979 review of its role in family relationships. They suggest that a continuing pattern of inconsistencies can create several unfortunate results in families. It can lead to mental illness such as schizophrenia, and deviant behavior such as juvenile delinquency. Of course it does not always lead to these effects, because individuals can sometimes find ways to correct the problem or circumvent its effects, but it tends to create serious problems in a large number of families.

WHAT CAN YOU DO TO CREATE CONSISTENCY?

There are a number of ways you can learn to be consistent. One thing you can do is have an intellectual awareness of the consistency principle. Four other skills are: (1) learn to recognize when you are consistent and inconsistent; (2) be sensitive or alert to inconsistencies; (3) recognize that nonverbal messages are usually the most accurate; and (4) learn to metacommunicate. Perhaps it would be helpful to closely examine each of these:

Skill No. 1: Ability to Recognize Consistency and Inconsistencies

Most communication with others is consistent, and it proceeds in a normal, uninterrupted, and comfortable manner. It is therefore easy to recognize consistency, just as it is easy to tell when a car is running well or the weather is pleasant. Recognizing inconsistencies is a different matter. It is harder and takes more skill. First, you need to recognize that something is wrong, and then you need to realize that the problem is an inconsistency.

One thing you can do to learn to recognize inconsistencies is to remember, whenever you are trying to evaluate your communication, that they *do* happen. Anyone can get in situations in which communication isn't going well, and then there is a checklist of problems to think about, such as:

Are we too upset?
Are we too tired?
Is there something else bothering us?
Are we being too vague in the way we are saying things?
Is there a hidden meaning?
Is it the wrong time of the month?

We need to add at least one more question to this mental checklist:

> *Are we being inconsistent in the way*
> *we are saying things?*

There is also a unique kind of clue that can help you recognize inconsistencies: It is that they usually lead to a general, vague feeling that something is wrong. You feel uncomfortable, puzzled, or ill at ease, but it is hard to put your finger on what is causing the feeling. Other communication problems, such as not speaking loudly enough, are easily recognized because they have a specific effect in your marital system. For example:

If we speak too softly, others can't hear.
When we are highly emotional, we say things we don't mean.
When there is too much noise around us, it interferes with hearing.
If we lie, others will stop believing us.
If we don't listen, we will misunderstand.

If you are sensitive to your emotions and are alert to the possibility that inconsistencies may be causing the feelings, it will help you be skillful in recognizing them.

How many nonverbal messages can you see?

Skill No. 2: Sensitivity to Inconsistencies

Everyone pays attention to the things that he thinks are important. Physicians several hundred years ago didn't pay attention to cleanliness because they didn't think it was important. Physicians today are very sensitive about cleanliness because they know it makes a difference. Some people are like the ancient physicians; they haven't realized the importance of consistency in communication. Others are like the physicians of today; they are concerned about consistency because they know it is important.

This doesn't mean that you need to pause every few minutes and sniff the air for inconsistencies. What it means is that whenever you feel uncomfortable about what is happening in a relationship, you ought to have high on your mental checklist the possibility of inconsistencies. You ought to have an appropriate sensitivity, not too much or too little.

Skill No. 3: Ability to Recognize that Nonverbal Messages Are Usually the Most Accurate

All people sometimes say things that conceal how they really feel. Someone asks you how you are, and you respond with a "fine" even when you aren't really fine. At other times you may choose to be tactful or evasive because you don't have the time or the situation isn't right to reveal your feelings.

It is much more difficult to conceal one's true feelings in nonverbal messages than in verbal ones. This means that whenever verbal messages are inconsistent with nonverbal messages, the chances are pretty good that the nonverbal messages are closer to the truth. This, of course, isn't always true, but it occurs often enough that the following is often applicable: "How can I hear what you are saying, when what you are doing rings so loudly in my ears?"

You should also realize that sometimes the nonverbal message that is received is less accurate than the verbal message. For example, you may misunderstand the nonverbal signal, or it may be sent for a different reason than you think. This means that you need to be tentative and cautious in making conclusions, and that it is frequently useful to check out (see pages 58-62) your interpretation of nonverbal messages.

*Skill No. 4: Metacommunication**

The three skills that were just discussed will help you recognize inconsistencies, but they do little to help you correct them. There is, however, a skill that is very useful in turning inconsistent communication into consistent communication. It is called metacommunication, and is the process of talking about your communication. It occurs when you talk verbally about the verbal *and* nonverbal communication in a relationship. It is useful in resolving all kinds of inconsistencies, but it is especially useful in dealing with problems in nonverbal communication—because it turns the nonverbal messages into verbal messages.

The following example illustrates metacommunication. It builds on the Mary and John case history mentioned earlier, and it identifies both verbal and nonverbal processes.

Statement	Nonverbal Messages in the Statement
John: "I was awfully uncomfortable at dinner tonight."	John seems to be making a first attempt to bring up the earlier uncomfortable experience. This is a fairly "safe" statement in that if Mary is still too emotionally upset to talk about it, John is not exposing his feelings so much that he is likely to be emotionally hurt. A safer but more indirect way would be to say something like, "The dinner was sort of a mess tonight, wasn't it?" The fact that John has taken the initiative indicates nonverbally that this is a relationship in which he can take leadership.
Mary: "Yes, I was too. What happened?"	This indicates that Mary is probably over her anger and willing to talk about the experience. If she had made a defensive statement like, "Well, you should have been," this would

---

* The term *metacommunication* has two different meanings in the communication literature. The meaning that is used here comes from Watzlawick, Beaven, and Jackson, *Pragmatics of Human Communication,* 1967. Some scholars also use this term to refer to the nonverbal messages that accompany all of our verbal messages: for example, Keltner (1971) and Raush et al. (1979).

indicate that her emotions are still so intense that they would probably interfere with a calm conversation. Mary seems to be accepting nonverbally John's leadership in this conversation.

John:	"I'm not sure, but we really got into it."	This open, uncritical statement suggests that John thinks both were involved, and suggests also that the problem was something about the couple rather than something external to the couple, such as the food, the waiter, or in-laws. The messages up to this point in the conversation are different from the messages in the earlier conversation because they do not include connotations that one is trying to dominate the other. Rather, they imply an acceptance of the other person as an equal. It is also nonverbally assumed that the relationship is sufficiently intimate for emotions to be discussed. These statements could have an underlying nonverbal message of warmth and caring for the other person, or they could be fairly neutral in effect. They do not have the competing, aggressive tone of the dinner conversation.
Mary:	"We seem to be having kind of . . . uh . . . fight quite a bit lately."	The fact that Mary has asked a question that makes the conversation more involved, and that she has now contributed a new idea, indicates this is a relationship in which she, too, can assume leadership and not be confined to reticent, submissive roles.
John:	"Yeah . . . I wonder why. We used not to . . ."	The pauses indicated by the ellipses also communicate nonverbally. The pauses could indicate pensiveness, thoughtfulness, and an openness to ideas, and in this type of conversation they will probably create an atmosphere in which more ideas will emerge.
Mary:	"You know . . . one thing that might help us find out what's going on would be to think back about what we said to each other."	This is Mary's second initiating statement. Since John's opening comment he has been quite passive and she has had the more powerful, leading role.
John:	"You mean earlier tonight?"	John seems to be very willing to let Mary continue to play the leading role. This could be because their relationship is always that way, or it could be because of something about this

particular conversation or situation. It may be due simply to the fact that she has come up with a new idea that he doesn't fully understand, and that he's asking for clarification.

Mary: "Um hmmmmm."

This is a fairly passive response, but even this type of statement could have been made in such a way as to indicate leadership, power, and control.

John: "You mean, talk about what we said?"

The conversation does not seem to be a hectic, intense, or highly emotional experience. It is fairly low-keyed and open, and both individuals seem to have the opportunity to say what they want to without being interrupted. This, unlike the earlier conversation, permits them to talk about their feelings.

Mary: "Well, even more than that I get the feeling that . . . uh . . . some things were going on that weren't even said, and if we said them to each other we might be able to get a better picture of what happened."

Mary is now explaining what she wants to do without labeling it *metacommunication,* and she's explaining her reasons for wanting to do it. This is such an insightful comment that it is almost unbelievable that someone who has not learned about metacommunication and its value would make it.

John: "Yeah, okay . . ."

John is still willing to let Mary take the initiative, but he seems to understand what she wants to do, and seems willing to give it a try.

Mary: "It seemed to start when we were talking about what to order."

Mary is nonverbally assuming that John knows what she means by "it," and his later comments indicate that she is justified in the assumption.

John: "I remember talking about the different things on the menu . . . and you seemed to get all upset."

This is the most powerful statement John has made since the start of the conversation, and it is an initiative-taking comment. This could have been said in an aggressive manner, generating defensiveness in Mary, but, judging from her response, it wasn't.

Mary:	"Um hmmmm . . . Before that I don't think I was upset."	Mary indicates acceptance of John's comment in a passive way. She doesn't take a new initiative in the conversation.
John:	"Well, let's see what happened . . . I thought you'd enjoy that rib-eye steak."	John is taking more initiative. He seems to be trying to analyze what happened. One thing to note in this conversation is that the two are talking about thoughts (opinions or views) *and* emotions (feelings or sensations). John is not, at this point in the conversation, aware of the power-struggle aspect of the earlier conversation or of what effect his "controlling" comments had on Mary.
Mary:	"And I probably would have."	Mary seems to be content to let John take the leadership role now; nonverbally it is now apparent that in some situations in this relationship the two are flexible in letting each other be the more powerful, leading one. Pauses in conversations may contain many nonverbal clues; a deep breath, a pensive glance, or an extended index finger accompanied by an "I-just-thought-of-something-else" look can communicate complex messages.
John:	"I guess maybe I came on a little bit strong, for some reason."	John is still acting as leader, and is apparently trying to figure out what went on in the earlier conversation by reconstructing more than just the "content" in the sentences, as he is talking about how he did something, and indicating that he's not sure why he did it—or perhaps he knows but doesn't want to say why at this point.
Mary:	"Yes, and I resented it. It made me feel like you were trying to dominate me, tell me what to do."	
John:	"You know, I'll bet the reason I did was . . ."	

This conversation illustrates metacommunication about the conversation the couple had earlier. Metacommunication can also involve a discussion about the trends in a couple's communication that tend to occur in conversation after conversation. All relationships develop their own sets of norms or rules about communication, and most people never stop to identify or analyze their own norms or rules. They are aware of many social norms that are characteristic of their larger culture or society: For example, they are aware that they ought to say "please" and "thank you" at certain times in their communication, and that it is more appropriate to use "proper" language in some situations than in others. Many persons tend to be unaware, however, of many of the norms or rules that gradually develop in their marital and family relationships. Examples of such norms: "Don't talk about those subjects"; "The wife is the one who will always win in the end anyway"; "She can criticize him, but he can't criticize her"; "He has to think it's his suggestion or he won't go along with it"; "Children can't talk back to parents"; "She shouldn't get so sentimental"; and "Never make people feel guilty about something they've done." We may want to keep some of the rules in our relationships, but there are others that we would probably want to eliminate if we knew they were there.

Scoresby (1977) suggests that one or all of four basic things can be discussed when a couple metacommunicates. They are these:

1. We can clarify the literal meaning of words spoken so that correct understanding occurs. (Example: "I didn't understand what you just said.")

2. We can discuss how the nonverbal behavior and context of a message is related to what is actually being talked about. (Example: "When you told me you were happy to see me, why were you frowning?")

3. We can go back to the beginning of the misunderstanding and try to clear up the difficulty first realized, which could prevent the problem from leading to a deeper misunderstanding later. (Example: "I didn't understand what you said at first, and you didn't understand the response that I gave to you.")

4. We can discuss each person's feelings so that each can disclose what is felt and why.

Metacommunicating is not a cure-all for communication problems. But it is a technique that can get certain types of problems in the open where they can be faced and eliminated. Few people would want to spend a great deal of time metacommunicating, but most would probably benefit from some metacommunication. Activity 7:1 at the end of the chapter provides an experience to help you increase your ability to metacommunicate.

SUMMARY

This chapter discusses the effects of inconsistencies on communication. Three different types of consistency-inconsistency are identified: verbal/verbal; verbal/nonverbal; and nonverbal/nonverbal. It is pointed out that verbal/verbal inconsistencies are usually easy to recognize and correct; hence they seldom have a detrimental effect on communication. Verbal/nonverbal inconsistencies are a different matter. They are harder to detect and harder to eliminate when we do recognize them. We also tend to deny them when someone suggests that they are present. Therefore, these inconsistencies tend to disrupt the communication in the marital system. The nonverbal/nonverbal inconsistencies are the most difficult to deal with because all of the messages are in the elusive, nonverbal part of communication. Many inconsistent messages are unintended, and so people don't even know they are there.

The last part of the chapter discusses four skills that you can use to help you be a wise steward in managing this part of your marital system. The skills are: (1) being able to recognize inconsistencies; (2) being appropriately sensitive to them (not too concerned about them); (3) recognizing that when inconsistencies occur, the nonverbal messages are usually the most accurate; and (4) being able to metacommunicate. Metacommunication is the process of communicating verbally about the way you are communicating, and this means that you verbalize the nonverbal messages that you think are causing the problems.

ACTIVITY 7:1
Metacommunication

Goal: To increase your ability to metacommunicate by practicing it.

1. In a relationship such as marriage, engagement, or a close friendship, set aside fifteen to thirty minutes for this exercise.

2. Discuss how effectively you usually communicate in this relationship when you encounter a problem, a difficulty, or an issue on which you need to make a decision. Some of the things you may want to discuss are these:

   a. Does one person do certain things when communicating that the other person especially appreciates, such as being open-minded, considerate, or empathetic, or taking the time to listen rather than to think of what to say next?

   b. Does one person do certain things when communicating that the other person doesn't like, such as clamming up, not listening, dominating the conversation, or ignoring the other person?

   c. Sometimes norms or rules develop about how to communicate in a relationship, and couples are not even aware of them. You may want to think about whether you employ any of these norms and then evaluate whether you like or dislike them. Examples of these norms are these:

      1) One person can criticize, but the other can't—or at least always seems to pay a psychological or emotional price for doing so.

      2) Certain topics can never be discussed.

      3) If the two people disagree, one of the two should have more say than the other one in deciding what to do.

      4) It is acceptable for one individual, but not the other, to use covert techniques for controlling the situation (crying, getting a headache, withdrawing affection, whining, sweet-talking, etc.).

SUPPLEMENTARY READINGS

Broderick, Carlfred, and Harvey Pulliam-Krager. "Family Process and Child Outcomes," chapter 20 in W. R. Burr, R. Bill, F. I. Nye, and I. L. Reiss. *Contemporary Theories About the Family.* New York: The Free Press, 1979.

Lederer, William, and Don Jackson. *The Mirages of Marriage.* New York: W. W. Norton Co., 1968.

Raush, H., A. Greif, and J. Nugent. "Communication in Couples and Families," chapter 19 in W. R. Burr, R. Hill, F. I. Nye, and I. L. Reiss. *Contemporary Theories About the Family,* New York: The Free Press, 1979.

Watzlawick, Paul, Janet Lemick Beaven, and Don D. Jackson. *Pragmatics of Human Communication.* New York: Norton, 1967, chapters 1 and 2.

8

SOLVING
PROBLEMS

*. . . neither will ye suffer that
they transgress the laws of God,
and fight and quarrel one with another. . . .*

—Mosiah 4:14

Life has all kinds of problems—little and big, simple and complex, easy and difficult. Some of them can be handled quickly, and others are never really solved; we just learn to live with them.

Life's problems range widely in degree of complexity from the normal, routine problems that all of us face, to the severe problems or crises that are more unusual. The following lists identify some of the problems that fall on this continuum. These lists also illustrate the large number of problems that can occur in families.

Normal Problems

1. Planning activities. Where to go on vacations, whether to redecorate, what leisure activities to engage in, whether to accept Church calls, etc.

2. Role allocation. Deciding who will do which tasks or jobs, who is responsible for what, etc.

3. Disunity (conflict or disagreements). What to do when the husband wants one thing and the wife another, in areas such as money, sex, church activity, in-laws, temple work, child-rearing, etc.

4. Undesirable behavior. What to do when someone misbehaves or commits sins. How to prevent undesirable behaviors like dishonesty, cheating, infidelity, etc.

5. Getting resources. How to get enough income, get raises, not put in too much overtime, raise a garden, can food, save money, invest wisely, borrow money effectively, etc.

6. Allocation of scarce resources. How to budget, keep track of money spent, buy wisely, use charge accounts. When to buy new cars, insurance, house, clothes—and which kind to buy.

7. Interaction with other systems. Dealing with school problems, the medical community, in-laws, neighbors, church, unions, volunteer organizations, little league, etc.

8. Development changes or tasks. How to cope with changes in children as they grow up, menopause, retirement, losing physical attractiveness, losing athletic ability, children leaving home, children getting older and more independent and having opinions that differ from parents' views.

9. Resolving questions or issues. Whether to move, whether to have additional children, etc.

10. Normal membership changes in the home. Grandparents coming to live in the home, Indian child living in home, children leaving home, birth of a new child, adopting a child, hospitalization, etc.

11. Dilemmas. Situations in which you must choose between two desirable situations and can't get all of the advantages of both. For example: you want to buy things and also save your money. You want to have the advantages of living in a city but still live in a rural area.

Severe Problems or Crises

1. Sudden disasters. A flood, tornado, hurricane, automobile accident, airplane crash, etc.

2. Unusual membership change in the home. Unwanted pregnancy, death, desertion, divorce, illegitimacy, runaway, imprisonment, suicide, institutionalization for mental illness, child born retarded or handicapped, war separation or reunion, return of deserter, hospitalization.

3. Extremely undesirable behavior. Nonsupport, infidelity, alcoholism, drug addiction, delinquency, chronic illness, child abuse, wife beating, rape.

4. Sudden change in status. Major depression, prolonged unemployment, sudden wealth or fame, political revolutions, wars, persecutions, refugee migrations.

THE DESIRABILITY OF PROBLEMS

In weak or tired moments in your marriage, it would be only natural for you to think that life would be better if you could do away with problems and crises. While it is true that life would be more simple and less painful if you encountered no problems, this is actually a very short-sighted view, as it takes into consideration only the enjoyment of the present moment. When you back off and take a long-term view of life, you arrive at a very different conclusion. If you look at the eternal scheme of premortal, mortal, and post-mortal life, you will realize that problems are actually *desirable.* This is another paradoxical aspect of life, that the problems you experience—even those that are extremely painful and difficult—are also desirable.

One reason we need to encounter difficulties is that it is only as we experience pain, frustration, disappointment, tragedies, and other adversities that we are able to experience the deepest and most satisfying joy, happiness, and peace. Consider, for example, the situation of Adam and Eve in the Garden of Eden. They did not have problems, frustrations, difficulties, sin, opposition, or adversity. They were in the condition that some of us occasionally think would be ideal—free from problems. Unfortunately, their sterile and uneventful life was also without happiness or growth. As the scriptures teach, they were "in a state of innocence, having no joy, for they knew no misery; doing no good, for they knew no sin" (2 Nephi 2:23). The paradox is that opposition is necessary. Problems and happiness, difficulties and satisfaction, misery and joy, go together. You cannot have one of these opposites without the other.

A second reason why problems are desirable is that without them you would be incompetent. You wouldn't grow and progress. When you face problems, you can learn to deal with them in creative, imaginative ways, and they can help you develop resourcefulness and a capacity to get things done. If you did not face obstacles you would remain forever in a state of ignorance and inability as well as innocence. This would frustrate you even in this life if you truly want to grow and progress. Also, when you think about your eternal goal—to become as God is—you realize that it will be important to learn how to cope with problems and difficulties. You will need to learn these things if you are to be an effective leader. And you can only learn the skills you will need by having problems and then learning how to stand on your own two feet to deal with them.

It is also important to realize that problems are not unique to our mortal life. They existed before we came to this earth, and we will have them eternally with us. Some of us mistakenly think that heaven will have only positive qualities such as joy, peace, beauty, and rest, but this is not so. We can only conjecture, for example, what our heavenly parents went through as one-third of their spirit children defied their wise plan and chose to follow Lucifer in a course of rebelliousness. Our Father and mother are *in* heaven, and what they are experiencing is what their exalted children will also experience. They have the challenge of dealing with the problems we give them in our earthly life, and they also have many other difficulties and adversities. It is true that certain problems that occur on the earth will not be present in heaven. For example, sicknesses and physical afflictions of the body will be removed when our "corruptions shall put on incorruption" (Mosiah 16:10). This should not, however, lead us to the conclusion that all other problems will also disappear. Probably they will be eternally with us, and we need to learn how to overcome, oppose, and deal with them in effective and desirable ways.

Why Should You Improve Your Problem-Solving Skills?

The preceding paragraphs have identified two main reasons why you should improve your problem-solving skills: (1) Your happiness is at least partially dependent on your problem-solving ability. This is because it is only as you are able to face and deal with adversity and opposition that you will experience the greatest joy. (2) You need to become highly proficient at problem solving if you are to attain your ultimate destiny—godhood. You will do this in a line-upon-line manner, wherein you improve a little here and a little there. Much of this learning can be done in this life, and each of us ought to do what he can to become a good problem solver.

There are several additional reasons why it is wise to improve your problem-solving skills in this life. They are:

(3) *Problem solving is different for couples than for individuals.* Most people learn early in life to make decisions and deal with their problems as individuals. They learn to make many decisions about their lives, such as what type of clothing to wear, which classes to take at school, whom to have as friends, and so on. This type of problem solving is very different from the kind they will be doing as adults and in the postmortal life. It is different because they have been making these decisions as individuals. After two people marry, they make decisions as a pair, and the process of making pair decisions is often different from that of making individual decisions. Most of you who read this book are in your twenties; you are in the middle of the process of moving from individual to couple decisions, and haven't had much practice at the latter. As a result, most have considerable room for improvement, and would be wise to improve their *couple* problem-solving ability.

(4) *Many of you have been too sheltered from problems.* As you grew up in your family, your parents made most of the important decisions about your life. You may not have had the opportunity to make your own decisions, and as a result you may not have developed much skill in problem solving. It is only when you need to make decisions and you have the responsibility for your own life and the freedom to do your problem solving in your way that you really learn how to do it. In this process you stub your toes a few times. You make some bad choices, and you then have to live with their consequences. This process helps you learn how to make good decisions. Your newfound independence as an adult makes this an ideal time to improve your problem-solving ability.

(5) A final reason it is important to improve your problem-solving skills is that there is a principle to be learned that will pay off in your marriage. This principle is this:

7. The Problem-Solving Principle: The better you can solve problems, the better your marriage and family life.

This principle is not a simple linear relationship in which any increase or decrease in your ability to solve problems increases or decreases your marital satisfaction. It is probably a curvilinear relationship like the one shown in Figure 8:1 below. Any change (an increase or decrease) in your ability makes the biggest difference when you have relatively little ability to begin with. When you have a moderate or higher-than-average ability to cope with problems, increases or decreases have less effect on the quality of your marriage.

The shape of this relationship has several implications. One is that those people who are already quite proficient in solving problems as a couple will get little benefit from trying to find ways to improve their problem-solving ability. If they were to take classes on it, read books on it, or enroll in problem-solving workshops, it wouldn't help their marriage a great deal. Even the best problem-solvers can learn some things that will help, but the return on their investment of time and energy may be less in this area than it would be in some other parts of their lives. For example, they might get much more from reading a book on

Figure 8:1   The Relationship Between Problem-Solving Ability and the Quality of Marriage

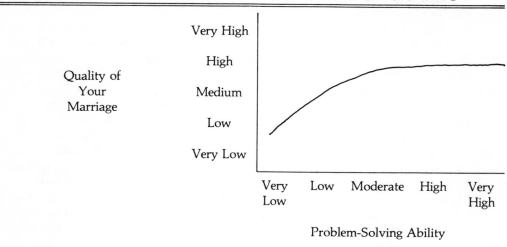

cooking or gardening than from reading one on problem solving. On the other hand, those who aren't very good at solving problems as a couple may benefit a great deal from some work in this part of their lives—until they get to the moderately good level.

One other aspect of this principle is that problem-solving ability isn't like height or weight, where one single factor goes up or down. As in all complex systems, 99 percent of it can be in tip-top shape, but if one crucial part operates poorly, the whole system suffers. It is a little bit like a chain; a chain is only as strong as its weakest link. Your problem-solving ability isn't as weak as its weakest part because, unlike chains, you can get by with a weak link or two. A few weaknesses, however, add up quickly, and they disrupt the whole process. For example, crucial things like listening carefully to each other's opinions, being decisive when it is necessary, and following through on decisions are crucial skills in problem solving. You can be highly proficient in many of the other parts of the process, but if you do several of these crucial things poorly, your overall problem-solving ability suffers. Thus one's problem-solving ability is not the sum of all of its parts. It is a complex process in a system, and gradations between poor and good problem solving can be determined by a few parts of the process.

All marriages have problems, and the successful marriages are the ones in which couples learn how to deal with those problems successfully, turning them into assets rather than liabilities. President Spencer W. Kimball has discussed this principle many times in pointing out that effective problem solving can eliminate the need for divorce. He has counseled as follows:

> There is a never-failing formula that will guarantee to every couple a happy and eternal marriage; but like all formulas, the principle ingredients must not be left out, reduced, nor

CLOUD NINE

Why is it
whenever I reach for the sky
to climb aboard cloud nine,
it evaporates and rains
upon my dreams?
Is it a matter of science,
or simply a matter of fact,
that not even a cloud
with a silver lining
can hold the weight of our dreams
without some precipitation?
I think I've found the answer
to this dilemma—
keep on reaching for the sky,
but don't forget your umbrella!

—Susan Stephenson

limited. The selection before courting and then the continued courting after the marriage process are equally important, but not more important than the marriage itself, the success of which depends upon the two individuals—not upon one, but upon two.

When a couple have commenced a marriage based upon reasonable standards, no combination of power can destroy that marriage except the power within either or both of the spouses themselves; and they must assume the responsibility generally. Other people and agencies may influence for good or bad; financial, social, political, and other situations may seem to have a bearing. But the marriage depends first and always on the two spouses, who can always make their marriage successful and happy if they are determined, unselfish, and righteous.

Later in this address, President Kimball said:

It has come to be a common thing to talk about divorce. The minute there is a little crisis or a little argument in the family, we talk about divorce, and we rush to see an attorney. This is not the way of the Lord. We should go back and adjust our problems and make our marriage compatible and sweet and blessed. (1976, pp. 16-17, 30.)

USING SPIRITUAL RESOURCES TO IMPROVE YOUR PROBLEM SOLVING

Knowledge is very limited in this mortal life. You came to the earth as an infant and then gradually learned as you grew up. But even as an adult, there are many truths that are hidden from you by the veil that separates you from the spiritual realm. Your limited knowledge can be increased dramatically, however, if you can get in touch with the spiritual part of life and then use it. Using your spiritual resources will be an invaluable aid in dealing with your problems in marriage and family living.

How Do You Receive Spiritual Assistance?

The scriptures teach that spiritual truths are learned in a very different way than natural truths. We learn natural truths by focusing the mind, thinking about natural things, and reasoning to make sure they are consistent with our previous experiences. We use our natural senses of hearing, seeing, touching, smelling, and tasting, and we couple these with our mental process of reasoning. The result is knowledge of the natural world around us.

The things of God are learned in a very different manner. They are sensed with senses that are different from the five senses we use in learning natural things. Spiritual truths are learned through becoming in tune with the Spirit of God, and the senses we then use are the senses that can recognize spiritual truths. Each of us knows the delicate feeling inside that whispers to us as we go out of our way to do something right. A different spiritual sense operates when we do something that we know is wrong. We get an uncomfortable feeling, a dullness, a twinge, a hurt. These two feelings, a feeling of rightness and one of wrongness, are two spiritual senses. They do not occur first in the head or mind. They do not occur first in the eyes or ears or mouth or nose or fingers as they would if one of our five senses were the source of the information. They occur in what is referred to as the "heart"—not the organ that circulates the blood, but that part of the body or soul that receives spiritual messages.

We can learn a little more about how to receive spiritual messages by reading several scriptural passages closely. By comparing an idea or message to a seed, Alma explained how to "listen" for spiritual information.

> Now, we will compare the word unto a seed. Now, if ye give place, that a seed may be planted in your heart, behold, if it be a true seed, or a good seed, if ye do not cast it out by your unbelief, that ye will resist the Spirit of the Lord, behold, it will begin to swell within your breasts; and when you feel these swelling motions, ye will begin to say within yourselves—It must needs be that this is a good seed, or that the word is good, for it beginneth to enlarge my soul; yea, it beginneth to enlighten my understanding, yea, it beginneth to be delicious to me.
>
> Now behold, would not this increase your faith? I say unto you, Yea; nevertheless it hath not grown up to a perfect knowledge.
>
> But behold, as the seed swelleth, and sprouteth, and beginneth to grow, then you must needs say that the seed is good; for behold it swelleth, and sprouteth, and beginneth to grow. . . .
>
> And now, behold, are ye sure that this is a good seed? I say unto you, Yea; for every seed bringeth forth into its own likeness.
>
> Therefore, if a seed groweth it is good, but if it groweth not, behold it is not good, therefore it is cast away. (Alma 32:28-32.)

The key phrases of Alma's message are these: "behold, it will begin to swell within your breasts," "feel these swelling motions," "enlarge my soul," "enlighten my understanding," "delicious to me," and "sprouteth." These are the sensory experiences that occur when we are receiving spiritual messages that something is good and true.

The Lord describes this process by saying, "By my Spirit I will enlighten them, and by my power will I make known unto them the secrets of my will" (D&C 76:10). Joseph Smith has also described the process of receiving spiritual insights:

A person may profit by noticing the first intimation of the spirit of revelation; for instance, when you feel pure intelligence flowing into you, it may give you sudden strokes of ideas; so that by noticing it, you may find it fulfilled the same day or soon; i.e., those things that were presented unto your minds by the Spirit of God, will come to pass; and thus by learning the Spirit of God and understanding it, you may grow into the principle of revelation, until you become perfect in Christ Jesus. (*History of the Church* 3:381.)

Joseph F. Smith later explained that all of us can receive revelation to help us in our lives:

I believe that every individual in the Church has just as much right to enjoy the spirit of revelation and the understanding from God which that spirit of revelation gives him, for his own good, as the bishop has to enable him to preside over his ward. Every man has the privilege to exercise these gifts and these privileges in the conduct of his own affairs, in bringing up his children in the way they should go, and in the management of his farm, his flocks, his herds, and in the management of his business, if he has business of other kinds to do it is his right to enjoy the spirit of revelation and of inspiration to do the right thing, to be wise and prudent, just, and good in everything that he does. I know that this is the thing that I would like the Latter-day Saints to know. (Smith 1917, p. 34.)

It is possible to change so that you are highly receptive to spiritual messages. But it is also possible to change yourself so that you cannot hear or sense these messages. There are two things you can do to make these changes: *First,* you can change the overall level of your righteousness. If you try to live correctly, you will become increasingly sensitive to these messages, but if you live incorrectly (if you sin), you become increasingly deaf to these messages. The keys are to desire (Alma 32:24) to improve yourself, and to repent of your mistakes (D&C 58:41-43) so that you can become increasingly worthy to receive spiritual help. President Marion G. Romney gives a fourfold formula for increasing spiritual sensitivity:

If you want to obtain and keep the guidance of the Spirit, you can do so by following this simple fourpoint program.
One, pray. Pray diligently. Pray with each other. Pray in public in the proper places, but never forget the counsel of the Savior:
"When thou prayest, enter into thy closet, and when thou hast shut thy door, pray to thy Father which is in secret; and thy Father which seeth in secret shall reward thee openly" (Matthew 6:6).
Learn to talk to the Lord; call upon his name in great faith and confidence.
Second, study and learn the gospel.
Third, live righteously; repent of your sins by confessing them and forsaking them. Then conform to the teachings of the gospel.
Fourth, give service to the Church.
If you will do these things, you will get the guidance of the Holy Spirit and you will go through this world successfully, regardless of what the people of the world say or do. (1980, p. 5.)

A *second* thing you can do to increase or decrease your ability to hear spiritual messages is to listen and respond, or to ignore and not respond when the messages come. The more you listen for the messages and respond appropriately to them, the more you are able to hear them. This, in turn, allows your spiritual senses to become more keen. And the opposite is also true. The more you ignore the messages, the less able you are to hear them.

Alma explained this process very well by showing how it will ultimately lead to the extremes of knowing vast amounts or losing all of our ability to hear spiritual messages:

> And now Alma began to expound these things unto him, saying: It is given unto many to know the mysteries of God; nevertheless they are laid under a strict command that they shall not impart only according to the portion of his word which he doth grant unto the children of men, according to the heed and diligence which they give unto him.
>
> And therefore, he that will harden his heart, the same receiveth the lesser portion of the word; and he that will not harden his heart, to him is given the greater portion of the word, until it is given unto him to know the mysteries of God until he know them in full.
>
> And they that will harden their hearts, to them is given the lesser portion of the word until they know nothing concerning his mysteries; and then they are taken captive by the devil, and led by his will down to destruction. Now this is what is meant by the chains of hell. (Alma 12:9-11.)

The Savior had a slightly different way of explaining this same process. He was aware that we have natural ears to hear natural sounds, *and* also spiritual ears to hear spiritual messages. This is why he commented, "He that hath ears to hear, let him hear" (Matthew 11:15; 13:9). Moses was another who talked about spiritual communication, as he observed that he could not see God with his natural eyes:

> But now mine own eyes have beheld God; but not my natural, but my spiritual eyes, for my natural eyes could not have beheld; for I should have withered and died in his presence; but his glory was upon me; and I beheld his face, for I was transfigured before him. (Moses 1:11.)

In summary, the things of God are known by the Spirit of God. Therefore, if you want spiritual help in solving your problems, you must be spiritually in tune. You become in tune by living the commandments as well as you can, repenting when you make mistakes, and increasing your ability to receive spiritual messages.

What Should You Do When You Want Spiritual Help?

The Lord gave some very specific instructions to Oliver Cowdery as to how he was to ask and not ask for divine assistance in translating from the plates of the Book of Mormon. The instructions are also useful in assisting you as you solve marital problems. Oliver Cowdery was told:

> Behold, you have not understood; you have supposed that I would give it unto you, when you took no thought save it was to ask me.
>
> But, behold, I say unto you, that you must study it out in your mind; then you must ask me if it be right, and if it is right I will cause that your bosom shall burn within you; therefore, you shall feel that it is right.
>
> But if it be not right you shall have no such feelings, but you shall have a stupor of thought that shall cause you to forget the thing which is wrong; therefore, you cannot write that which is sacred save it be given you from me. (D&C 9:7-9.)

The Spirit of the Lord can help in other ways. For example, James taught:

> If any of you lack wisdom, let him ask of God, that giveth to all men liberally, and upbraideth not; and it shall be given him.

But let him ask in faith, nothing wavering. For he that wavereth is like a wave of the sea driven with the wind and tossed. (James 1:5-6.)

Sometimes you may have problems for which you feel you need wisdom before you can study them out in your mind and get confirmation about your decision. When this occurs, it is appropriate to pray for wisdom concerning what you should do. This was what Joseph Smith did in the Sacred Grove in Palmyra, New York. No doubt he had previously studied the matter out in his mind to the extent that was possible, but there was just not enough information available for him to come up with a tentative conclusion that he could take to the Lord. So he went in supplication, asking the Lord what he should do. Anytime you are likewise perplexed about a problem you can do the same, and if you are in tune the Lord will help you in the way he deems best.

When Should You Seek Spiritual Help?

Amulek gave one of the great sermons in the Book of Mormon; in it he touched on the issue of appropriate times to seek spiritual help. He gave this counsel:

> Yea, humble yourselves, and continue in prayer unto him.
> Cry unto him when ye are in your fields, yea, over all your flocks.
> Cry unto him in your houses, yea, over all your household, both morning, mid-day, and evening.
> Yea, cry unto him against the power of your enemies.
> Yea, cry unto him against the devil, who is an enemy to all righteousness.
> Cry unto him over the crops of your fields, that ye may prosper in them.
> Cry over the flocks of your fields, that they may increase.
> But this is not all; ye must pour out your souls in your closets, and your secret places, and in your wilderness.
> Yea, and when you do not cry unto the Lord, let your hearts be full, drawn out in prayer unto him continually for your welfare, and also for the welfare of those who are around you. (Alma 34:19-27.)

Amulek's examples were drawn from the daily conditions of the primitive people he was addressing. Applying his message to modern conditions, it seems to imply that you should ask for divine assistance about daily things such as classes in school, examinations, and dates. You ought to pray about such mundane decisions as which class to take, whether to buy a car, where to shop, whether to accept a date, whether to get a part-time job, and how you can help the family next door.

There is, however, another side to this issue. Some people have the impression that the Lord will always give them the answer about what they ought to do if they just trust in him, ask, and live righteously. They forget that the Lord's ways are higher than and different from our ways (Isaiah 55:8-9). He will assist his children in his own time and in his way. You are on the earth to learn by your experiences, to learn how to stand on your own feet, to learn how to make decisions with your spouse, and to learn by making mistakes. If you were always provided with answers about what you should do, you would never mature, never learn, and never really grow. Therefore, much of the time, at his discretion, the Lord answers prayers in ways you don't understand. He always hears your prayers, but sometimes his answer is silence; he leaves you alone to grow and develop. At other times, for reasons you don't understand, he may assist you without your even asking. At other times he even helps people against their own will (see Acts 9:1-10).

Therefore, you need to remember that you should seek divine assistance and be sensitive to divine messages, but should not be inappropriately dependent on the Lord. The Lord will provide the assistance he deems fit. He will enlighten your understanding, give you wisdom, and assist you, but he will not give you an answer to every question you ask, solve all of your problems, or "baby" you. He will not remove adversity, opposition, ambiguity, dilemmas, and problems. They are there, and you need to learn how to live with them. He will help you in his way, his time, his manner, and in his wisdom. President Spencer W. Kimball makes this point clear:

> If all the sick for whom we pray were healed, if all the righteous were protected and wicked destroyed, the whole program of the Father would be annulled and the basic principle of the gospel, free agency, would be ended. No man would have to live by faith.
>
> If joy and peace and rewards were instantaneously given the doer of good, there would be no evil—all would do good but not because of the rightness of doing good. There would be no test of strength, no development of character, no growth of powers, no free agency, only satanic controls.
>
> Should all prayers be immediately answered according to our selfish desires and our limited understanding, then there would be little or no suffering, sorrow, disappointment, or even death, and if these were not, there would also be no joy, success, resurrection, eternal life, or godhood. "For it must needs be, that there is an opposition in all things . . . righteousness . . . wickedness . . . holiness . . . misery . . . good . . . bad . . ." (2 Nephi 2:11).
>
> Being human, we would expel from our lives physical pain and mental anguish and assure ourselves of continual ease and comfort, but if we were to close the doors upon sorrow and distress, we might be excluding our greatest friends and benefactors. Suffering can make saints of people as they learn patience, longsuffering, and self-mastery. The sufferings of our Savior were part of his education. "Though he were a Son, yet learned he obedience by the things which he suffered; And being made perfect, he became the author of eternal salvation unto all them that obey him" (Hebrews 5:8-9). (Kimball 1979, p. 172.)

Using the Patriarchal Order

The way to get spiritual assistance with problems is to use the proper priesthood system. This system, known as the patriarchal order, provides an efficient, harmonious method of solving problems as well as directing other processes in your complex marriage system. The patriarchal order is explained in more detail in chapter 10 of this volume, and that discussion is very relevant to the issues discussed here. You should realize that the information covered there will be very helpful in getting valuable spiritual assistance in dealing with your problems.

USING THE SOCIAL SCIENCES TO IMPROVE YOUR PROBLEM SOLVING

The social sciences have discovered a number of techniques that can also help us solve problems. One of these is the division of the problem-solving process into several stages. Five stages* in problem solving are these:

1. Identify the problem.
2. Agree to work (or not work) on the problem.
3. Identify and evaluate alternative solutions.
4. Make a decision by selecting one of the alternatives.
5. Implement the decision.

One of the important skills in problem solving is being able to tell which of these stages you are in. This is important because when the wife is in stage 4 and she's ready to make a decision, and the husband is way back in stage 1 (he doesn't even know what the problem is), the method of problem solving is itself one of the problems. There are also a number of other skills that can help you in each of the five stages. They are discussed in the following paragraphs.

Skills for Identifying Problems

Skill no. 1: To be able to tell when you are in this stage. How can you tell when you have a problem? Usually one spouse becomes aware of a problem or need and communicates his or her concern to the other. In a family, one member senses the problem and then others are told about it. The following statements are typical of this problem-defining stage:
"We need to talk about . . ."
"What is really bothering you, dear?"
"I feel we ought to make some changes around here."
"As I see it, the problem is that . . ."
"I have a problem, and I'd like us to do something about it."
Since communication always occurs in this stage of decision making, the principles and skills discussed in chapters 5-7 can help make the communication effective. Since defensiveness is one of the common reactions when a spouse tries to bring up a problem, the ideas that deal with ways to decrease defensiveness are also very useful in this situation.

Many times, previous events in your relationship permit you to move very quickly over this stage. Sometimes such indicators as the way a person acts, a gesture, or just a certain type of silence can communicate that a problem needs attention. But other times you can

---

* Many scholars use this five-stage paradigm, but there are many other sets of stages. Some have condensed problem solving to two or three stages, but others have expanded it to more than five. For example, Bales and Strodtbeck (1951) divided decision making into orientation, evaluation, and control stages. Blood (1962, p. 245) changes this slightly to orientation, evaluation, and execution. Thomas (1977) has seven steps. Aldous (1971, p. 266) refers to the five stages of identifying and defining of the problem, collecting information relevant to the problem, producing action alternatives, choosing a course of action, and evaluating the consequences of the action. Among the longer lists is the one used by Duvall (1971, p. 177), who identifies nine stages: face the problem, look at the causes, set some goals, get more knowledge and understanding, be the other person, consider what to do, make a plan of action, check the plan with the goals, plan the follow-up.

assume too much when you rely on gestures or other nonverbal methods of identifying problems, and you later find out you did not really have consensus about whether a problem or issue existed or what it was. The best way to identify a problem is to use words, to describe it in sentences, trying not to threaten the other person's self-esteem.

Skill no. 2: Using "I" statements. Whenever you try to identify problems, it is useful to make "I" statements rather than "you" statements. This skill was discussed in detail on pages 96-97.

Skill no. 3: Using "summary" statements. One effective way of making sure that there is consensus about the definition of a problem is for one person to make a summary state-ment. This can be a very brief statement about what the problem or issue is, with which the other person can then either agree or disagree. When the feelings, reactions, or behavior of one member of the couple is the problem, one way to summarize is to reverse roles and see if that member can describe the problem. One advantage of summary statements is that they tend to move couples into the next stage of decision making after they agree on what the problem is. Sometimes, of course, they can mutually recognize a problem nonverbally, and when this happens, summary statements are unnatural and useless. But at other times these summaries are very helpful.

Skill no. 4: Turning an "individual" problem into a "couple" problem. When you are solving problems alone, you can go on to the second stage as soon as you are aware of a problem. But when you are part of a couple, it is very different. If one member of the couple recognizes a problem, it is at that moment the individual's problem, not the couple's problem. Only when one person communicates to another that there is a problem, and the other person recognizes the problem, does it become a couple problem. And, as many married couples know, the process of convincing a spouse that there really is a problem is sometimes a very difficult task. In fact, it is occasionally impossible, and the individual who has recognized the problem has to treat it as his or her own problem rather than as a couple problem. One of the useful observations made by Waller and Hill (1951, pp. 312-16) is regarding what they term *insightful adjustment,* namely, that the member of a couple who is sufficiently insightful to become aware of a problem may be at a disadvantage. If that member cannot convince the other member that there really is a problem, he or she may have to do all of the changing or adjusting.

There are several techniques that can help you turn individual problems into couple problems. For example, if you have strong feelings about something, you can share these feelings, and this may help the other person realize that there really is a problem. You can also compare problems by saying things like, "Look, this is as big a problem to me as when we . . ." or, "I'm more upset about this than . . ." You can also avoid making a mountain out of every molehill that comes along. If you thought that everything was a serious problem, it would be like the "wolf, wolf" story. Your spouse would justifiably learn to ignore your attempts to convince her or him that you indeed had a problem.

Skill no. 5: Being sensitive to the emotions that accompany this stage. Little problems like, "Who's going to pick Jane up at the bus station?" or, "Should we go to the movie or concert?" create few emotions. But many problems are more complex, and when you bring them up there are intense feelings involved. In marriage, many problems are closely tied to

Turning an individual's problem into a "couple" problem is sometimes a challenge.

feelings of masculinity or femininity, feelings of adequacy or inadequacy as a person, and delicate feelings of love, acceptance, tenderness, and caring; any attempt to bring up problems in these areas can create strong feelings. Many times, in marriage, the emotions that accompany a problem are much more important than the problem itself. It is therefore useful to go slowly when you are trying to identify a problem, and also to pay close attention to the overall situation. Ask yourself: "Is it a good time? Are there other feelings that will get in the way? Do we have enough privacy? Will the other person be threatened? How do I feel about the situation? And, would we have enough time to deal with the problem?" If you haven't been able to find a time, you may want to only mention that you have a problem that you need to talk about as soon as it can be arranged. Above all, you ought to be as supportive as possible of each other when problems are identified that create negative emotion; and beautiful processes like tact, patience, caring, consideration, and gentleness are tremendously important. *As valuable as these loving behaviors are when things are going well, they are much more valuable when problems are being discovered.*

Skills in Identifying and Evaluating Alternatives

In some ways the process of identifying solutions is similar to that of identifying a problem. Both situations evoke emotions, and you need to be sensitive to the feelings that are created. Also, both demand attention, listening skills, and the ability to express yourself in nonthreatening ways. In other ways, the process of thinking of solutions is different, and it demands unique skills. Following are several of the skills that are unique to this stage:

Skill no. 1: Being able to recognize when you are in this stage. You can move into this stage when there is consensus between partners about what the problem is. Sometimes this is simple and automatic, and both spouses recognize it at the same time. At other times, you may need to check out whether you are ready to move to this stage or whether you are already in it. You may say things like, "Are we ready to try to figure out what to do?" or, "Okay, we agree on what the problem is. What can we do about it?"

While you are identifying alternatives, statements like the following are called for:

"One thing I've thought of is . . ."

"You know what _____ did about that?"

"Have you got any ideas about what we can do?"

"As I see it, we've got two choices . . ."

"I'm wondering what you'd like to see done about it."

After several alternatives have been proposed, you can evaluate them by discussing their consequences. These can be catalogued as disadvantages or advantages, according to your personal value system, and each alternative can be weighed against the others. You can also try to change some of the alternatives so that they are more desirable. The following statements are characteristic of this process:

"Well, if we stay home we'll at least have the benefit of air conditioning."

"Hey, look, maybe we could do a little of each."

"Grandma is apt to be too busy to visit with us if we go at the end of the month."

"We can invite him to dinner, but it will make me miserably uncomfortable."

"Yes, but it would be really hard to . . ."

"It seems to me that if we do that it will make it easier to . . ."

Skill no. 2: Being creative. Research (Aldous 1971) shows that creativity is very valuable when you are identifying alternatives. This means that you ought to work blindly as you are trying to find ways to solve problems. Let your mind go. Think up alternatives that are unusual, different, and even bizarre. Since you will be evaluating the alternatives later and can then reject the inappropriate ones, there is no harm in getting some "creative" solutions on your list. This is an open-ended part of the problem-solving process, and there is no harm in having a few useless or impractical options that will need to be discarded later. One of the advantages of letting your mind go in this stage of decision making is that creativity is contagious, and the far-out, unusual things you think of that *won't* work may help you think of some new things that *will* work. Being careful or cautious tends to restrict thinking, and it may keep you from finding new and novel solutions.

Skill no. 3: Avoiding the evaluation of alternatives when you are trying to be creative. One characteristic of humans is that certain mental activities encourage similar activities and discourage different activities. For example, when you are in a reverent or sacred mood there are a number of behaviors that are encouraged and a number that are discouraged. Reverence tends to create quiet and respectful behaviors such as speaking softly and moving slowly, and loud or boisterous activities are then inappropriate. If you are cheering at an athletic contest the opposite behaviors are called forth.

Some scholars have suggested that this is important in problem solving because being creative in thinking up new alternatives and evaluating those alternatives call for opposite mental processes. When you are doing one it will tend to discourage the other. This means that when you want to be creative in thinking of new alternatives, you may want to refrain from evaluating the alternatives. You can write the new ideas down on a piece of paper and add to the list. Then, after you are through brainstorming, you can shift into the evaluative processes, where you are more cautious and more hesitant to think up new ideas in a carefree manner.

You might recognize this process in your experiences. When you are in a group that is being creative, one idea seems to stimulate another; one funny or far-out idea seems to lead to others, and some of them that seem at first to be too wild or unworkable later turn out to be the best ideas. In other situations, you may notice that evaluations tend to turn off the process of coming up with new ideas. When someone comes up with a fairly unusual or seemingly unworkable idea, and someone else who is in the evaluative mood comments, "I don't think that will ever work," it can be a wet blanket. It makes everyone more hesitant to come up with ideas.

One thing you can do to foster a creative frame of mind is to agree beforehand that the next few minutes will be used only to think up as many ideas as possible. You can call it a "brainstorming time." You can then be as creative as possible and not make any negative or evaluative comments during that time. Then, after the brainstorming is over, the ideas can be sorted, evaluated, and modified.

Skill no. 4: Getting several alternatives. Some couples usually make up their minds about what to do as soon as they think of the first good solution. This is illustrated in the following situation:

> *Phil and Jennifer, an engaged couple on a tight budget, were deciding where to look for housing. "Basement apartments are usually most inexpensive," said Jennifer. Phil agreed, and they looked in the newspaper listing, jotting down the addresses of basement apartments. They found one they liked pretty well, and decided to take it although they didn't like the neighborhood.*

It may be this couple have found an apartment that fills their needs well, but the small number of options they considered may have excluded other possibilities that would have been wiser choices. For example, they might have found a mobile home, an upstairs apartment, or a duplex that would have given them a better combination of their desires in housing, but these possibilities were excluded by their narrow range of alternatives. Research in this area* shows that the quality of decisions is usually lower when very few alternatives are identified, and it tends to improve when more alternatives are identified.

Apparently, however, after an optimum number of alternatives has been identified, attempts to find additional alternatives tend to interfere with decision making. This may be because couples get bogged down in considering too many alternatives. Since generating alternatives takes time, thought, energy, creativity, and stick-to-itiveness, it may sometimes

---

* See Turner (1970, pp. 112-13) for a discussion of this idea and an evaluation of the research on it.

Evaluating the alternatives on paper can help with important decisions.

be desirable for couples to seek alternatives from someone else. They could use several different sources, such as friends, teachers, counselors, or the mass media.

Research on problem solving in organizations has shown that people usually have a very narrow range of alternatives in decision making, as they tend to think of frequently encountered similar situations in the past and only suggest the things that were done before, or very slight variations (Feldman and Kantor, 1965, pp. 620-23). It has been the authors' experiences in marriage courses that when students complete the Number of Alternatives Activity (8:1 at the end of this chapter), many are surprised to learn how few alternatives they usually consider when making decisions. Most discover that their usual pattern is to identify one possible solution and then decide whether or not to do it. Only when that alternative is undesirable do they usually try to find a second. Those who want to change their habits by increasing their alternatives will also find Activity 8:2 at the end of the chapter to be useful.

Skill no. 5: Changing and reorganizing the alternatives. Sometimes there is little you can do with the alternatives. For example, if you are deciding whether to go to a ball game or a movie, you may wind up with a simple choice of one or the other. Many times, however, you can be creative in shaping up one or two alternatives so that they are more attractive.

As an example, suppose a couple has a problem of the wife wanting her husband to pick up his clothes and put them in the hamper rather than leave them lying around, for he has a rather deeply ingrained habit of leaving them all over the place. They have talked about it many times, but the wife hasn't changed her expectation and he hasn't changed his behavior. The only alternatives they have identified are that she quit being so fussy or that he pick up his clothes. Had they been a bit more creative, they could have also thought of the additional alternatives of his at least throwing them all in the same corner so it would be easier for her to pick them up, of getting three more hampers so it would be easier for him to pick them up, and of getting a valet (chair with a rack on the back) so he would have a place he could hang things easily.

After getting these five alternatives they could combine or modify them in creative ways. For example, they could agree that the clothes he may use again soon could be put in a certain place such as over a chair or valet, and all of the dirty clothes could be placed in a new hamper that could be placed in the bedroom.

Skills in Selecting an Alternative (Deciding)

Skill no. 1: Recognizing when you are in this stage. Some couples are very skillful at the decision-making practice. They have a knack for knowing when they are ready to make a decision. They can also tell when they have made the decision and are ready to move on to implementing it. Others aren't so blessed. They can't make up their minds or aren't sure what the decision is when they're finished. They find themselves saying things like, "Oh, I thought we decided to . . ." or, "But we were going to . . ."

Here are some of the comments typical of this stage:

"Okay, Rod, which do you think is best?"

"It looks to me like the best way to handle this is for us to have separate closets. What do you say about that?"

"Then let's do a little of both, but . . ."

"It sounds as though we agree best on that last idea. What do you say we go ahead on it?"

Skill no. 2: Being decisive. One essential ingredient in decision making is to come to a conclusion about what to do or not do. Some couples raise issues and problems and talk about the relative advantages and costs of various alternatives, but they find it difficult to come to a conclusion about which course to take. This is illustrated by the following situation:

> *Fran and Roger were upset about some of the behavior of their three-year-old son. They had discussed the matter and had recognized that a large part of the problem was that each of them responded to him differently—they sensed that they were defeating each other's goals. They made a few suggestions but agreed upon no plan. Time went on, and their son's troublesome behavior continued.*
>
> *It is easy to see that Fran and Roger did not really come to a decision; it is this decisiveness that is important.*

As with so many other skills, the first step for you is an introspective analysis to determine what you usually do as a couple or a family. Are you too indecisive? Or does one member of the couple move to the deciding stage too quickly? Or is this an area that is not a problem in your relationship? Whatever your needs, the action plan on pages 42-43 can help you change what you are doing.

Skill no. 3: Taking appropriate risks. Turner (1970, pp. 113-14) has suggested that willingness to take risks is also related to the quality of decision making. As he points out, too little or too much risking hinders the quality of decisions.

Each couple, of course, needs to decide just how risk-taking they should be. Some couples may be more daring than is wise, while others may be so afraid of breaking traditional patterns that they make much less wise decisions than they could. Activity 8:3 at the end of the chapter can help you determine how optimal your usual patterns are.

Skill no 4: Being able to work out quid pro quo's. A *quid pro quo* is "something for something" (Lederer and Jackson 1968, pp. 177-80). It is an arrangement in which one person's behavior stimulates the other person to behave in a certain way. Many *quid pro quo's* are unconscious and automatic. For example, we all know that a smile is contagious; if you smile at someone, he will tend to smile in return. In a marital relationship you soon become conditioned to the quid pro quo pattern even though you don't realize it. Each of us informs the other of his response pattern with little clues, and we each learn how to recognize the responding clues of the partner.

The value of quid pro quo's in this stage of decision making is that you can consciously work out some reciprocal arrangements as strategies for solving problems. If the husband wants the wife to behave in a certain way and she doesn't, it may be possible to solve his problem and, at the same time, solve one of hers if a quid pro quo can be worked out. He can agree to do something that he hasn't previously done if she will also make the desired change. An example is a situation in which the wife wants the husband to express his affection with words by saying things like "I love you" more often, and the husband wants the wife to respond to his sexual advances more frequently. They may find that a quid pro quo in which he agrees to be more verbally affectionate and she agrees to be more physically affectionate will solve both problems and add considerable pleasure for both of them.

Skills in Implementing Decisions

Making a decision does not solve a problem unless the decision is actually carried out. Sometimes this involves some detailed planning about what the couple or family is going to acquire or how things will have to be changed. Several scholars who have analyzed decision making (Duvall 1971, for example) suggest that this stage should also include some way of evaluating the plan of action later to make sure that the solution is really solving the problem. Here are some comments that are typical of this stage of decision making:

"Now that we've decided what to do, how are we going to do it?"

"Where are we going to get the money for . . . ?"

"For the next two weeks I'll . . ."

"Could you help me . . . ?"

"There isn't any way we can . . ."

This stage of problem solving calls for many of the same skills that are needed in other stages, but it also demands some unique skills. Some of these are discussed below:

Skill no. 1: Sticking with it until a method of implementing the decision is found. Some couples think a problem is solved when they agree on decisions and solutions. And sometimes it is. When problems are mere choices between several desirable things, they are solved when a decision is made, providing the person concerned follows through. However, most of the problems that occur in dating and marriage are more complex, and couples need to stay in a problem-solving mode after they have selected a solution. Usually the most difficult process is over. They're over the crisis, or over the hump, but there is one final thing that must be done if they are to be effective in problem solving:

> *They need to take the time to figure out how to implement*
> *the decision, and then implement it.*

This demands a "stick-to-itiveness" that is difficult for many couples.

Skill no. 2: Showing an increase of love (D&C 121:43-44). Another thing that can help after problems are solved is to take the time to provide reassurance, support, or love to make sure that everyone feels good about the situation. You ought to go out of your way to be supportive if any feelings were hurt or if some things that were said were hard to swallow or unkind. Research has shown that supportiveness is an important ingredient in problem solving, and you ought to be sure to include it at the end. It will help put the problem behind you and help you to be less reluctant to deal with other problems in the future.

Some Skills That Are Not Unique to Stages

The skills discussed on the last few pages apply fairly specifically to certain stages. For example, one needs to be decisive and risk-taking only when he is in the deciding stage of problem solving. But there are many other skills that are useful in all of the stages of problem solving. Scholars such as Aldous (1971) and Klein and Hill (1979) have summarized the research in this area; they have identified many factors that are related to effectiveness in problem solving. Five of these seem particularly relevant to marital problems, and therefore useful for those who study this book. They are:

Skill no. 1: Showing charity. First of all, the patience, consideration, and love that come with charity are priceless in all of the stages of problem solving. Those who are slow to anger when they have problems will find that they can solve those problems better than those who have quick tempers. If you think of the needs and welfare of others and worry about what will be fair for them, you will find hidden blessings. Charity has been stressed in earlier chapters, but it is so important that it deserves this repetition. To relate a famous scriptural passage to marriage, the authors respectfully suggest the following adaptation of Paul's message in the 13th chapter of 1 Corinthians,

> Though we are very skillful in our communication, if we have not charity our efforts at problem solving will be empty and futile, and our problems won't go away. They will stay.
> And though we have the gift of finding alternatives and evaluating them carefully, and we

understand all that is said by everyone, and we have great insight and are decisive and even pay attention to feelings, if we have not charity, our problem solving is nothing.

And though we bestow all our wisdom on those around us, and use "I" statements—as valuable as they are, and though we get consensus and even seek spiritual helps, if we have not charity, it profiteth us nothing in solving our problems. For in our problem solving we must suffer long and be kind, and not think too much of ourselves, or seek our own things.

We must not be easily provoked, and must think of no evil, but we must bear many things willingly, without malice or grudge, and without thinking that we must get even. For we know what happens in marriage only in part, and since we know only in part, we must give in much more than our share.

And now abideth faith, hope, and charity in problem solving, but the greatest of these is charity.

Skill no. 2: Participating. Considerable research indicates that when people are left out of the decision-making process, they tend to be unhappy about the decisions that are made. Conversely, when they are included, they tend to be more satisfied. Participation involves more than just how much a person says in the discussion. As Tallman points out, "It is the sense that one has played an important role in contributing to the problem's solution" (1970, p. 96). The low end of this continuum can be seen in the following situation:

Frank's wife-to-be came over to his apartment two weeks before the wedding with a notebook under her arm. "It's budget-discussing time," she announced, and she explained to him the categories she had laid out and noted the monthly amounts of money she had allotted to each category. "Well, that's it," she concluded. "Now are you ready for our date?" He was not happy about the amount of money in the recreation and food categories and had reservations about living within the budget.

A family member may be left out of decisions in ways other than physical absence. For example, he may be reticent or afraid or may not care to participate, or he may think that his ideas will probably not be understood or considered. Also, an idea may not be developed well enough for a person to be willing to venture into a discussion, or his self-esteem may be so precarious that he does not dare risk rejection. He may feel so inferior to others that he preevaluates his ideas and censors them as not being worthwhile. Then, too, a person may not care enough about the decision being made to contribute, or he may not have done enough thinking to have many relevant ideas to express. Here are some other times when participation is like to be lower than optimum:

—When partners don't allow enough time to discuss decisions;

—When one partner is overly certain that his own views are best;

—When one person thinks that the other doesn't care what his opinion is;

—When a person articulates his ideas poorly (in which case others tend to "tune him out" and behave in ways that reflect to him a lack of interest in hearing more);

—When listening skills are not well developed;

—When one person's self-esteem is low, and he reacts by trying to be controlling.

Activity 8:4 at the end of this chapter can help you determine how much each individual in one of your ongoing relationships is involved in decision making.

Skill no. 3: Paying attention. Turner (1970) has identified another factor that influences the quality of decision making in marital and family situations. He calls it the *quality of the attention* that is given to suggestions made by others. As he points out: "Suggestions made by a child are often received with a friendly pat on the head and given no serious thought . . . thus if the father is viewed or views himself as omnipotent relative to other family members, he is less likely to take their suggestions seriously, and the quality of family solutions will be poorer" (p. 113). The same type of depreciation may be applied to the opinions of a date or a spouse, and it will apparently have the same effect.

Most of us have been in situations where attention is given to opinions, and we have been in others where it is not given. Here are some of the comments that occur at these times:

"Hmmm, let's consider that. What do the rest of you think about it?"

"Tell us what you mean. Let's hear a little more about that."

"Fine, dear" (and the conversation goes on essentially uninterrupted without dealing with the son's ideas).

"But I think that we ought to . . ." (which changes the topic right after someone suggests a new idea).

Quality attention involves more than just turning your head and passively listening to what someone is saying. It includes an alertness to subtleties of tone, posture, gestures, and facial expressions, and an interest in the other person's contributions. Also, it frequently has ramifications beyond the quality of a particular decision, because whether people's ideas are ignored or viewed as important can influence how they will feel about themselves. If people are ignored, they tend to experience feelings of inadequacy or unimportance and often withdraw from a situation. But if others treat their ideas with respect and attention, they are more likely to feel respected and hence respectable, and to feel that they have important contributions to make. Good listening basically entails focusing one's attention on understanding what the other person means. Some skills that can be used to give high-quality attention are (1) keeping the focus of the speaker; (2) using invitations to speak; (3) checking for understanding; (4) attending to feelings; (5) sticking to the issue being discussed; and (6) attending to nonverbal cues.

Several qualifications probably should be made in regard to using this skill in your personal life. It is wise to take into account the maturity of the individual who is giving opinions. A suggestion of the three-year-old that the family go to Africa for their vacation may not be a very reasonable alternative. Serious attention to such opinions would interfere with the quality of decision making—especially when time is precious. On the other hand, the spontaneity and the creativity of children frequently provide alternatives that older individuals wouldn't think of. Also, it seems reasonable that paying attention to children's views may pave the way for more serious participation later.

Skill no. 4: Dealing with emotions first. The following five situations all have one thing in common. What is it?

Holly and Ted had just become engaged the night before. It had been an exciting day, telling friends at work of their marriage plans and then phoning some relatives in the evening. To add to the excitement, Ted's parents had just given the couple their first wedding gift, which was extra money for their honeymoon. Holly and Ted sat down and decided to drive to Yosemite National Park for their honeymoon. Weeks later they had to change their decision when with some thoughtful planning they realized that the drive would be too far and too exhausting.

It is dinner time. The parents want to have the family make a decision about scheduling the use of the car. The teenage daughter is chewing her food as quickly as possible in order to leave for a play rehearsal.

A girl and her boyfriend are deciding how much time they can spend together this week. The girl says, "But it takes you so long to do your homework. Why do you take so long on it for such mediocre grades?"

It is 5:30 P.M. A wife is dividing her attention between frying pork chops, tending the baby banging his spoon on the high chair, setting the table, and watching the boiling pudding. Her watching husband comes into the kitchen and says, "What should we do about this offer to sell the house?"

The newlywed husband has just come in the door with his arms full of groceries. He has gone seven dollars over the weekly budget and is feeling very disappointed in himself and pretty low about his ability to manage money. His wife says, "Okay, let's sit right down and decide how to handle this budget business."

What do these situations have in common? The emotions were so intense that they interfered with effective problem solving. *The solution? Whenever feelings are strong, deal with the feelings first.* Put off the problem solving whenever possible until you can cool off or calm down enough to be effective. This is especially important if the feelings are negative emotions such as anger, resentment, jealousy, fear, hurt, depression, or anxiety. These feelings get their way. They influence us against our will so much that they seriously interfere with problem solving. The solution, to put off the problem solving, isn't a natural way in our society, but it is wise.

One of the important aspects of this skill is being able to recognize when your lack of control is interfering with the decision-making process. A second part is being able to do something about it when you realize your relative irrationality. Both of these skills were discussed in chapter 6, and the exercises identified there (pages 108-113) are helpful in the present context. In addition, you can do many other things to increase your rationality in decision-making situations. One thing is to change the conditions that impair your rational control: eliminating distractions like loud music or fatigue, postponing an appointment you might have been hurrying to get to, taking the time to establish rapport, counting to ten, or just trying harder to remain rational when it is difficult to do so. Activity 8:5 can help you recognize your level of control.

Skill no. 5: Agreeing who the leader is. Whenever you are working on a problem, it is a good idea to get consensus on who the instrumental leader is. The instrumental leader is the one who keeps the couple or group moving. He is the person who takes charge by doing such things as getting the group or couple together, moderating when it is necessary, directing the attention to the key issues, noticing who is left out and including them, and moving the group to the next stage when it is time.

This type of leadership is different from the social or emotional leader, who helps people feel good about each other. Research has shown that when no one takes the instrumental leadership role, the discussion wanders inefficiently and problem solving is fairly ineffective.* Also, when more than one person tries to be the leader at the same time the power struggle tends to get in the way rather than help solve the problem. The solution? Make sure everyone understands who the leader is at that time, and let that person lead.

Some people think it is part of the patriarchal order for the man to always be the instrumental leader, but this isn't true. The head of the house presides, but that doesn't mean he is always the instrumental leader. He may be, but he may also not be. There is a difference between presiding and conducting. The presiding official in a priesthood setting always presides, but he may arrange situations so that others do the conducting. *The instrumental leader is the one who conducts.*

There are two key ideas in this issue. One is that it is wise to know who is in control when you are trying to solve a problem. The other is that anybody who is competent can be the leader in any situation, since leadership in these situations is a separate process from presiding. The patriarch always presides, but others may direct certain processes and have the most say about specific aspects of the marriage or family life.

SUMMARY

This chapter has identified a number of things you can do to solve the problems that occur in marriage and family living. First, you need to realize that problems are not just bearable or unavoidable. They are, paradoxically, desirable. You wouldn't want to be without them. As you try to solve problems, you ought to seek spiritual assistance, and the chapter discusses several ideas about how to do this. It discusses some methods of getting in tune so you can "hear" spiritual messages, some ways to seek help, and times when you ought to seek help.

The chapter also suggests that you need to recognize the different stages of problem solving so that you know what you are trying to do—what the issue is. Five stages are identified, and the next part of the chapter discusses several skills that can help you in these stages.

The last part of the chapter discusses five skills you can use in any of the stages of problem solving. These last skills are (1) being charitable; (2) letting those who are involved in the outcome participate in the process of solving the problem; (3) paying attention by listening carefully rather than ignoring or doing other things; (4) dealing with emotions first

---

* See Bavelas (1950), Leavitt (1951), Blau and Scott (1962, pp. 116-28), Guetzkow and Simon (1955), Guetzkow and Dill (1957), Tallman (1970).

(This means you may need to forget about a problem temporarily while you cool off or find some other method of venting a feeling. This is especially important for negative feelings); and (5) getting consensus as to who the instrumental leader is in the situation. The leadership can be passed around in a family, since leading in specific situations is different from presiding. The husband-father always presides, but others can conduct, and the conductor is the one who makes things happen.

ACTIVITY 8:1
Number of Alternatives

Goal: To determine how many alternatives you usually think about in decision-making situations.

1. Think about the way you usually make decisions in a relationship with someone such as your spouse, date, or roommate, and identify what you think is the *average* number of alternatives you usually consider in making fairly unroutine decisions. (Exclude such routine decisions as whether it is time for lunch or how to get to work or school.) Write the number down.

2. At the end of each day for the next week, take a few minutes and identify two or three decision-making situations that have occurred during the day. Identify decisions that you made with someone else rather than decisions you made alone, and try to identify fairly unroutine decisions. Count the number of alternative solutions that were identified in each decision-making situation and record the average number of alternatives per decision.

3. At the end of the week compare your predicted average number and the actual number. If the actual number is lower or higher than the predicted one, you are among the majority. If the numbers are the same, you are among the insightful minority.

ACTIVITY 8:2
Increasing Alternatives

Goal: To increase the number of alternatives that you usually consider in decision making.

1. Usually when you are making decisions you get to a point where you are ready to decide what to do. At this point you make comments like, "So let's . . ." or, "I think we ought to . . ." or, "Then we'll . . ." For the next week, at least once during each day, stop the decision-making process—quit working at the process of deciding what to do. Hold up your hand. Stand up and turn around if you need to to get things stopped, but stop the decision making.

2. Once the decision-making process is stopped:

   a. Itemize and count the alternatives that have been identified. Count them on your fingers or write them on paper, but explicitly identify each alternative and count how many have already been brought into the open.

   b. Have the group or couple focus their attention briefly on the following question: "Are there any other possible solutions we ought to consider?" Try to think of at least one or two more and add them to the list. Then resume the normal process of coming to a decision.

   c. At the end of the week think about several times you have been in other group decision-making situations, and note whether you have found yourself interrupting or stopping yourself at that certain place in the decision-making process to see whether or not there are other alternatives you might want to consider. If you have changed your usual behavior so that you interrupt yourself in decision making, you have accomplished the goal of this exercise. You are sensitized to the process of identifying alternatives, and you probably will be identifying more alternatives than you were before. You may want to try the "Number of Alternatives" exercise again to see just how much you have changed.

ACTIVITY 8:3
Riskiness

Goal: To gain a better understanding of how bold you tend to be in decision making.

1. One way to gain more insight into how risky your behavior usually is, is to get feed-back from others about what they think you do. To do this, ask three people who know you fairly well how they would evaluate you on the following question (try not to bias their opinions before they commit themselves): "When I'm in a problem-solving or decision-making situation, which of these statements best describes my usual behavior?

   a. Eager to take chances or gamble with new and novel solutions—even if they involve some risk.
   b. More willing than most to take chances.
   c. Somewhat willing to take chances.
   d. Usually quite reluctant to agree to risky solutions.
   e. Very unwilling to take chances.

2. Use this feedback and your own perceptions to assess how risky you tend to be, and what implications this has for your decision-making ability.

ACTIVITY 8:4
Amount of Participation

Goal: To determine how much each individual usually tends to be involved or uninvolved in decision making in one of your ongoing relationships.

1. Identify one of your ongoing relationships, such as with your parent's family, with your spouse, or with a roommate.

2. Observe the decision making in this relationship for one week without letting the others know you are observing the interaction.

3. Try to determine which individuals are highly involved in the decision-making process, and whether anyone is excluded or left out of the decision making. Do not try to change what seems to be naturally happening until the week is over. Even if you are unhappy about the situation, it has undoubtedly existed for some time, and a few more days will make little difference. You ought to take the entire week to be sure that the patterns that disturb you are repetitious enough to be a problem.

4. Evaluate what effect participation or lack of participation has on the satisfaction of the individuals in regard to their decision making. You may or may not then want to intervene in the situation to try to change people's participation.

ACTIVITY 8:5
Recognizing Self-Control

Goal: To increase your ability to recognize when your self-control tends to be high or low.

1. Get someone who knows you well to help you recognize when you are high or low in self-control. This will take ten to fifteen minutes daily for one week.

2. At the end of each day, do two things with the other person:

   a. Identify (and list on a piece of paper) three situations in which you had discernibly less control.

   b. Identify the clues that helped either of you to tell whether the control was high or low, and list these clues on the piece of paper. Discuss these clues enough so that both individuals understand what they were.

3. At the end of the week, evaluate the effects the week's activities have had on your ability to understand self-control.

SUPPLEMENTARY READINGS

Aldous, Joan, ed. *Family Problem Solving.* Chicago: Dryden Press, 1970.

Blood, Robert O., Jr. *Marriage.* Glencoe, Ill.: The Free Press, 1969, chapter 17.

Kieren, Dianne, June Henton, and Romona Marotz. *Hers and His: A Problem Solving Approach to Marriage.* Hinsdale, Ill.: Dryden Press. 1975.

Tallman, Irving. "The Family as a Small Problem Solving Group," *Journal of Marriage and the Family.* 32:94-104 (February), 1970.

Lee, Harold B. *Decisions for Successful Living.* Salt Lake City: Deseret Book Co., 1974.

Ellis, Albert, and Robert Harper. *A Guide to Successful Marriage.* Hollywood: Milshire Book Co., 1975, p. 286.

9

CREATING
UNITY

*There is no disparity in marriage
like unsuitability of mind and purpose.*

—*Charles Dickens*

Finally, be ye all of one mind.

—*1 Peter 3:8*

Scriptural teachings and scientific research suggest that unity is important in marriage. In one of the first scriptural comments about the relationship of man and woman, we are told, "Therefore shall a man leave his father and his mother, and shall cleave unto his wife: and they shall be one flesh" (Genesis 2:24). There are few themes that are then repeated in the scriptures as often as the messages of oneness and unity (See, for example, 3 Nephi 11:28; D&C 38:27). The Savior said many times that he and his Father are one (John 10:30; D&C 35:2), and he prayed for and admonished the saints to be one—even as he and his Father were one (John 17:11). Since marriage is the most enduring personal relationship of all, it is understandable that this relationship is singled out as one in which unity is especially important. As Paul taught, the husband and wife should be one (Ephesians 5:31), and Amos poetically asked, "Can two walk together, except they be agreed?" (Amos 3:3).

Scientific researchers have studied the issue of unity to determine how important it is in the marital relationship, and there are few areas where the evidence is as massive, consistent, and conclusive.* Scientists have used slightly different words to study this phenomenon. For example, they have used terms such as consensus, similarity of beliefs, conflict, homogamy, and heterogamy, to study different aspects of unity. The research has

---

* The first research studies of factors related to marital success found support for this idea (Bernard 1934; Burgess and Cottrell 1939; and Terman 1938). Later studies using longitudinal methods (Burgess and Wallin 1953) further reinforced the idea, and many studies since then have added additional confirmation (Luckey 1960; Blood and Wolfe 1960; Rollins 1961; Mangus 1957; and Locke 1951). Those who are interested in further reading about research in this area will find Kirkpatrick (1963, chapters 15-18), Burgess, Locke, and Thomas (1963, chapter 15), Bernard (1964), and Burr (1973, pp. 105ff) useful beginning places. Wirth (1948), in his presidential address to the American Sociological Society, has even proposed that studying consensus is the central task of sociology.

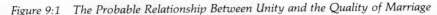

Figure 9:1   The Probable Relationship Between Unity and the Quality of Marriage

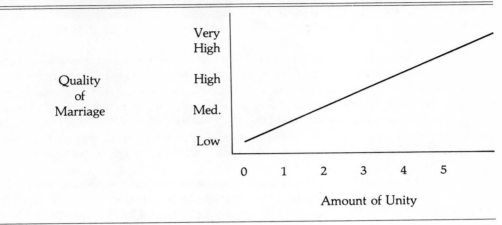

indicated that the similarity or unity of two people before they marry is a good predictor of how successful they will be if they marry. It has also been found that similarity after marriage correlates very highly with marital success. The higher the unity, the less the chance of divorce, desertion, violence, child abuse, adultery, criticism, and neglect. Unity is also related to the more positive aspects of marriage. The higher the unity, the more happiness, love, peace, companionship, friendship, and satisfaction in the marriage, and the better the relationship with the children.

There is thus a massive amount of evidence for the following generalization:

8. The Unity Principle: The greater the unity between marriage partners, the greater the happiness in the marriage.

Before going further, we need to define *unity*. It is the degree to which two people agree on such matters as their attitudes, norms, role expectations, values, goals, or philosophy of life. If two people have little similarity in their beliefs and values, they have low unity. The more they agree, the higher their unity. You should also realize that unity deals with your mind rather than your behavior. It refers to whether you agree in your thoughts, beliefs, or ideas. It is indirectly related to behavior because your beliefs influence how you act, but it is unity in the mind that is the key.

It is also useful to realize that the relationship in the unity principle is probably linear. This means that any increase or decrease in unity seems to have an effect on the marriage. Even small increases or decreases seem to have an effect, and there is not a plateau or point where you can have too much unity, or where changes in unity cease to have an effect. This is shown in Figure 9:1.

DO SOME AREAS MAKE MORE DIFFERENCE THAN OTHERS?

When you first realize that unity is an important factor in marriage, you may wonder whether unity, or the lack of it, is more important in some areas than in others. The answer is definitely yes!

The areas where unity makes the most difference are in the deeper, more basic beliefs. Beliefs about the nature of man, God, eternity, and the purpose of life probably matter most because they are the foundation on which most other beliefs rest. These basic issues in one's philosophy of life then give rise to values and goals, and these are probably the areas that are the next in importance in marriage. Your values and goals deal with such matters as the style of life you want and the importance of such basic concerns as religion, education, leisure, freedom, independence, autonomy, truth, honesty, virtue, social status, responsibility, power, and pride.

Your basic philosophy, values, and goals give rise to a number of specific beliefs about how you and your partner ought to act as spouses. These beliefs deal with issues such as these: Should you be affectionate or not? Should the husband be the head of the house? Should the wife have a career? Should the wife be able to criticize the husband as much as he criticizes her? Should either spouse have the freedom to spend large amounts of money without consulting the other, and should you discuss marital problems with others such as parents and friends? These beliefs are called *role expectations,* since they are the expectations you have about how a person should behave in the "role" of spouse. The research shows that it is very important that couples have high unity in their role expectations in those areas that the individuals believe are important. The following list identifies some of the expectations that most people think are important, and some that most think are relatively unimportant:

Role Expectations *Most Think Are Important*	*Role Expectations* *Most Think Are Unimportant*
Spouses should not hit each other.	Toothpaste tubes should be squeezed in the middle.
Spouses should tell the truth to each other.	Parents should attend PTA meetings.
Sexual involvement should be confined to the marriage.	Spouses shouldn't snore.
Spouses should have considerable patience.	Husbands should bring flowers home.
Spouses should not flirt with others.	Spouses should always say, "Thank you."
The husband should be able to provide a living.	The windows in the house should be washed regularly.

What about other aspects of life? Is it important that a husband and wife be unified about everything? For example, if the wife prefers to do the washing with a certain kind of detergent, is it important that the husband also think this brand is the best? If the husband is a White Sox fan, is it important that the wife also be a White Sox fan? And is it important for the husband and wife to like to do the same type of things in their leisure time?

Clarifying our role expectations (desires, wishes) can help create unity.

The best answer to these questions is that it is important to be unified in the things that are *relevant* for the marital part of your life and *important* to you. Is there anything that is irrelevant to a marriage? Yes, for example:

The route that a person takes while driving to and from work.
Whether you prefer a lot of catsup on your hamburgers or just a drop or two.
Whether a husband likes to work on the car.
Whether the wife likes her pillowcase ironed.
Political preferences.

Some leisure-time interests take little time and energy, and it is not very important that you be unified in these. For example, the wife may like to read novels and the husband may prefer to listen to music. Or the wife may enjoy a quiet walk in the evening and the husband may prefer to read the newspaper. You ought to allow for these types of individual differences. However, if something is a dominating interest in one person's life, unity then becomes more important. For example, the husband may like to live in a sports-oriented world. He may want to participate whenever possible as an athlete or spectator. When this occurs, it is good for him to have a wife who agrees. If the wife is so involved in an activity that it dominates her life, it is probably important for her husband to agree that it is desirable for her to spend her time the way she wishes.

In summary, it is extremely important that spouses be unified in their basic philosophies of life, values, goals, and important role expectations. Unity is less crucial in areas of life that are less important and not connected to a marriage.

HOW CAN YOU CREATE UNITY BEFORE MARRIAGE?

One way to create unity before marriage is to associate with people who are similar to you in background and personality. Every person is very strongly influenced by his childhood experiences, and whenever he develops a relationship with someone from a substantially different background, he is decreasing the likelihood of achieving unity after he is married. Sometimes you are romantically attracted to someone because he or she is different from you, but this difference loses its glamour and becomes the source of problems and difficulties when you settle down to the serious tasks of raising children, budgeting, and living together for a long period of time. The kinds of background characteristics that frequently make a difference are: race, religion, ethnic background, social standing in the community, rural vs. urban background, style of interacting in the home, and education level.

The object: Marry someone who is as similar to yourself as possible. This will make it easier to create and maintain unity in your marriage. This specific advice was also given by President Spencer W. Kimball when he said:

> We are grateful that this one survey reveals that about 90 percent of the temple marriages hold fast. Because of this, we recommend that people marry those who are of the same racial background generally, and of somewhat the same economic and social and educational background (some of those are not an absolute necessity, but preferred), and above all, the same religious background, without question. (Kimball 1976, p. 11.)

WHAT CAN YOU DO WHEN DIFFERENCES APPEAR AFTER YOU ARE MARRIED?

First of all, will this happen to *you*? Will you have differences of opinion that will be difficult to eliminate, that will get in your way? Unfortunately, yes—everyone does. These differences appear in all marriages; none of us are exempt. Some people think that they are different; they tell themselves that they are unique, and that they have so much going for them that it won't happen to them. They eventually learn that having differences is a natural and inevitable part of life. Each spouse has grown up in a different family and had different experiences, and this leads to differences of opinion.

Some people think that if they are able to work out all of their differences before the wedding or shortly after the marriage, this will eliminate them, and they won't have to face important differences later. Unfortunately, this, too, is idealistic. As you move through the cycles of early marriage, rearing children, and then the empty nest, you encounter new experiences and your opinions change. Many of your opinions as a couple will change together, but differences will also appear. Also, you will likely discover differences you have had all along that never came up. For example, it is impossible to identify all of your important opinions about raising children or managing a house before you are in the middle of it.

Another reason new differences will appear in marriage is because you are living in a rapidly changing world, and changing social conditions will bring about some changes in your opinions. The women's movement is an example of how changing social conditions influence unity in marriages. The women's movement created an awareness in many women that the discrimination and inequities in America were much worse than they had realized, and they changed some of their opinions about women's roles. These changes were sometimes resisted by husbands who had benefited from the inequities, and the resulting disunity had to be dealt with.

President Spencer W. Kimball has repeatedly recognized that differences in marriage are not only normal, they are inevitable:

> Two people coming from different backgrounds soon learn after the ceremony is performed that stark reality must be faced. There is no longer a life of fantasy or of make-believe; we must come out of the clouds and put our feet firmly on the earth. Responsibility must be assumed and new duties must be accepted. Some personal freedoms must be relinquished and many adjustments, unselfish adjustments, must be made.
>
> One comes to realize very soon after marriage that the spouse has weaknesses not previously revealed or discovered. The virtues that were constantly magnified during courtship now grow relatively smaller, and the weaknesses that seemed so small and insignificant during courtship now grow to sizeable proportions. The hour has come for understanding hearts, for self-appraisal, and for good common sense, reasoning, and planning. The habits of years now show themselves; the spouse may be stingy or prodigal, lazy or industrious, devout or irreligious, kind and co-operative, or petulant and cross, demanding or giving, egotistical or self-effacing. The in-law problem comes closer into focus and the relationship of the spouses to them is again magnified. (Kimball 1976, pp. 12-13.)

What Are Your Options?

When differences appear after you are married, you have four alternatives. Three of these alternatives are healthy, good choices; the other one is undesirable. The healthy alternatives are these: (1) one spouse can change his or her opinion so that it is the same as that of the other spouse; (2) the two can work out a compromise in which both change their opinions; (3) they can agree to disagree but find a way to live happily with the difference. The less desirable solution is to continue to disagree and have one or both spouses uncomfortable about it. The following pages discuss some ways to arrive at one of the three suitable alternatives.

One person can change. Sometimes, as in the following situation, it is easy for one person to change:

> *Sue grew up in a family where care was taken to prepare thoughtful presents on birthdays, and the presents were always carefully wrapped and given with considerable fanfare—such as in a treasure hunt or at a restaurant while going out to dinner. Bill grew up in a family where they gave each other money or gift certificates, so the person*

receiving the gift could get things he needed or would really want. The first few birthdays led to some disappointments, even though Sue smiled about the gift certificates and thanked Bill. When their differences were finally brought into the open, they talked about how they felt and why they both assumed the other one would think the way they did. After some discussion, Bill decided he liked the romance attached to the gifts and that he could easily change his opinion. They then used Sue's way of exchanging gifts.

It is easy to have one person do all of the changing in situations where some new information changes one person's mind. It is also easy to do all of the changing in areas that are unimportant to you but important to your spouse. Occasionally, it is also very gratifying to give in to someone you love, just to be kind, thoughtful, and loving.

Sometimes, however, you will find yourself in situations in which it is neither easy nor pleasant to give in. What can you do then? One strategy is to try to create a "win-win" situation. This means to structure the situation so that neither spouse feels that he or she is losing by doing all of the giving in. When you are in a situation where one spouse "wins" and the other "loses," especially if this happens very often, it creates resentments that interfere with love. Win-lose situations usually turn into lose-lose situations. Therefore, you should try to create a win-win situation. Sometimes this can be done by one spouse agreeing to give in in one area and the other agreeing to give in in a different area, so that the net effect is to solve two differences and keep a win-win situation. In other situations, the spouse who gives in will not have a feeling of losing if the other person shows an appropriate appreciation or thankfulness for the sacrifice that has been made.

Compromise. Compromise occurs when consensus is created by both individuals changing their opinions. It is sometimes easy to arrive at a compromise, and at other times it is very difficult. Compromising is easy in minor and unimportant areas where you don't have intense feelings. It is much harder when you feel strongly and your opinions are important to you.

There are two main ways to compromise. One is to accept a middle course that is between two extremes. For example, if the wife wants the husband to express his affection verbally more than he cares to, they could agree on a compromise in which he will be slightly more affectionate. The net result is that he will be more affectionate than he has previously been, and less affectionate than she would prefer. The second way to compromise is for each spouse to take turns in getting what he or she wants. An example of this occurs when both want to spend every Thanksgiving with their own parents, and they agree to take turns.

There are two key parts of a compromise that some people ignore. These two parts are: (1) the two individuals must agree on the solution; and (2) the solution must feel emotionally satisfying. If you don't agree on the solution or you don't feel good about it, you don't have a good compromise.

Agree to disagree. This happens when two people agree to live with a difference of opinion and find ways to feel good about it. If we lived in an ideal world, we would never need this alternative, but in our very real world we mortals are limited and frail in many ways. The result is that all marriage partners sometimes find it necessary to use this alternative.

Strategies for Creating Unity

1. *Use information in earlier chapters.* The most important thing that can be said in discussing how to resolve disagreements is to use the information in chapters 5, 6, 7, and 8. Also, chapter 3 discusses charity, and discovering a charitable way of approaching differences is immensely helpful.

In addition to being charitable, it is also wise to use the idea in chapter 6 that helps us get to the feeling level. It is probably true that

> *When you have differences (disunity in marriage),*
> *your feelings about the differences are more*
> *important than the differences themselves.*

This means that it is always useful to deal with your feelings whenever you have differences. You need to recognize what you feel, and you need to find verbal and nonverbal ways to communicate these feelings to your spouse without hurting him or her. You need to understand the feelings your spouse has, accept them for what they are, and then deal with them as you find solutions for the disunity. If the solutions are not comfortable you haven't really created unity. Sometimes it takes much longer to deal with the emotions than it does to deal with the differences in the ideas or opinions.

Chapter 5 discusses many different skills that you can bring to bear whenever you have differences. For example, you can be sensitive to nonverbal messages, listen carefully, check out your understanding with questions or paraphrasing, give feedback and support, and pay attention to the many environmental factors such as the time of day and outside pressures. Chapter 7 discusses the importance of having your communication be consistent; there is no setting where this is more important than when you are trying to create unity in your relationship.

2. *Strive for consensus.* The Lord has indicated that the decisions in the quorums of the priesthood should be unanimous decisions. For example, in giving instructions to the First Presidency and Quorum of the Twelve he said:

> And every decision made by either of these quorums must be by the unanimous voice of the same; that is, every member in each quorum must be agreed to its decisions, in order to make their decisions of the same power or validity one with the other—
> A majority may form a quorum when circumstances render it impossible to be otherwise—
> Unless this is the case, their decisions are not entitled to the same blessings which the decisions of a quorum of three presidents were anciently, who were ordained after the order of Melchizedek, and were righteous and holy men. (D&C 107:27-29.)

All of the decisions made by a husband and wife ought to be unanimous or by consensus. If they are not, the partners "are not entitled to the same blessings" they would have if their decisions were unanimous.

Doing things together creates unity.

Lest this idea be misunderstood, having a unanimous decision does not mean that every individual must have originally preferred the final decision. Occasionally, there needs to be an extensive discussion of what to do, and decisions need to be made without unanimity. It is important, however, to try to get unanimous consent whenever possible, which everyone agrees to intellectually and emotionally, with his head and heart.

3. *Make mutual rather than unilateral attempts to change.* One scholar has pointed out (Spiegel 1957, pp. 545-64) that attempts to resolve differences in marriage should be made by the couple rather than by only one member of the couple. When one person alone tries to create unity, it is usually disruptive and unproductive, as the other person is almost always resisting.

Dr. Spiegel, a psychiatrist, observes that when one person is trying to create unity, the methods of changing that usually occur are coaxing, coercing, withholding something, refusing to do something, defying, pressuring, manipulating, masking or covering something up, postponing, and forcing. It is interesting to observe how close these techniques are to the Lord's list of undesirable ways to use the powers of the priesthood. The Lord has said, "When we undertake to cover our sins, or to gratify our pride, our vain ambition, or to exercise control or dominion or compulsion upon the souls of the children of men, in any degree of unrighteousness, behold, the heavens withdraw themselves; the Spirit of the

Lord is grieved" (D&C 121:37). These methods of trying to change someone else attempt to take away his free agency, to change him against his will. This is seriously inappropriate.

Whenever you want something changed in a relationship, you should first identify your desire to get a change and discuss whether you and your partner agree to try to make the change. The process of changing things is then a mutual activity, rather than a unilateral pressure by one person. This greatly increases the likelihood that a change will occur, and it decreases the negative consequences that unilateral pressure causes. These negative reactions are resentment, anger, opposition, and frequently a more intense determination not to change. It is also very likely that the positive feelings of love, appreciation, tenderness, and affection that are so precious in a marriage will be undermined very quickly by the unilateral pressures.

What this means is that the wife who wants her husband to change some of his beliefs (such as opinions about going fishing on Sunday, being more talkative, spending more time at home, going to church, exerting more leadership in the home, picking up after himself around the house, or driving more carefully) should be very careful. She should not try to change his opinions or way of behaving *until he, too, agrees that he should change.* She shouldn't encourage, persuade, nag, coax, plead, entice, seduce, withhold, cajole, or do anything else to try to change his opinion until they mutually decide that his changing is a desirable goal.

If wives were to learn this one skill in creating unity, it would help marriages greatly!

This also means that husbands who want their wives to change some of their beliefs should act the same way. When a husband wants his wife to be on time more, clean the house better, keep the kids neater, be more responsive sexually, keep herself up better, talk on the telephone less, be more thrifty, stay at home more, or get more active in Relief Society, his attempts to tell her what she ought to do, get after her, poke fun at her in front of others, beg, encourage, persuade, force, call her to righteousness, physically abuse, or do anything else to try to change her opinions are disruptive rather than helpful. He has no business trying to change her until they mutually decide that her changing is a desirable goal.

If husbands were to learn this one skill in creating unity (and presiding in a home) it would help marriages greatly!

This idea is not merely consistent with the gospel; it is a fundamental part of the gospel. The Lord has indicated that he teaches line upon line and precept upon precept (D&C 98:12). This means that he is willing to let us live with many of our imperfections without trying to change us until we are ready. He taught in parables so that only those who were ready for his message would understand it (Matthew 13:10-13), and he repeatedly commented that his message was only for those who had ears to hear and eyes to see, who wanted and were able to hear his suggestions. Also, notice how his suggestions are presented and how attempts to change should come: "Only by persuasion, by long-suffering, by gentleness and meekness, and by love unfeigned; By kindness, and pure knowledge" (D&C 121:41-42).

Joseph Smith taught that love is the most powerful force there is for changing people:

> You need not be teasing your husbands because of their deeds, but let the weight of your innocence, kindness and affection be felt, which is more mighty than a millstone hung about the neck; not war, not jangle, no contradiction, or dispute, but meekness, love, purity—these are the things that should magnify you in the eyes of all good men. . . .
>
> Nothing is so much calculated to lead people to forsake sin as to take them by the hand, and watch over them with tenderness. When persons manifest the least kindness and love to me, O what power it has over my mind, while the opposite course has a tendency to harrow up all the harsh feelings and depress the human mind. (Smith 1938, pp. 227, 240.)

The Lord wants people to serve, if they "have desires to serve" (D&C 4:3), and Alma taught that when a person is trying to change others he should do it in the spirit of a beloved brother, when *they* desire it: "And now, my beloved brethren, as ye have desired to know of me what ye shall do . . ." (Alma 32:24).

Should it not be the same in marriage? Should you refrain from trying to change your spouse, until he or she desires it?

Yes! Yes! Yes!

4. *Give in more than your share, instead of keeping score.* People have a natural tendency to want justice in all relationships, and this is especially so in marriage. Whenever one spouse has to give in on something that is important to him or her, it creates a subtle obligation for the other spouse to give in on something. Or if one person grants a favor, it creates a feeling that the other person should also grant one. One scholar has called this process a universal "norm of reciprocity" (Gouldner 1960). This process is healthy in marriage because it keeps things fair and spreads blessings and burdens around. In resolving disagreements, it is useful because it keeps couples from developing a pattern of one person doing all of the giving in. There is, however, a danger if you become too meticulous in keeping track of who gives in, and then insist on not giving in more than your share. The marital relationship seems to work best when you adopt two rules:

1. Avoid keeping track. Don't keep track of who gives in unless there seem to be serious inequities.
2. Give in according to the needs and goals of the couple rather than according to percentages.

Some research (Murstein et al., 1977) has shown that it is important to keep track of favors and obligations in friendships. It helps the friendships grow and be pleasant. However, in more intimate relationships (parent-child and marriage), keeping track seems to get in the way. It makes the relationship too much a matter of bargaining and bartering. It is much better to have a giving relationship in which each partner is willing to give in much more than his share of times.

There are several reasons why this is true. One is that you see life only from your own point of view, and so you don't see the whole picture. You see only your side. Since each of you is highly concerned about himself, your record keeping will tend to emphasize your side and shortchange others. Therefore, most people need to be willing to give in most of the time to actually come out even.

Second, marriage is such a complex relationship that you can't really count all of the favors, rewards, or obligations. Many of them are subtle, intangible things that you can't even express, let alone count. Therefore, it is much better to be willing to give in as needed rather than to only give in a certain percent of the time. You ought to try to assess the needs of the individuals and the circumstances, and give in according to the goals and needs you have as a couple. When you do this you create a unity, a oneness that rises above the more superficial bargaining or exchange-oriented relationships that occur in the marketplace or with more casual acquaintances.

Most marriages go through periods when one spouse has to give much more than the other. When illnesses or accidents strike, you need to rally around and give out of a sense of love and concern even if it is not "your turn." And you need to give without the expectation that the other person then owes you something. Also, you may have occupational demands or deep-rooted habits or tendencies that you find difficult to change, and when this occurs, the best solution will be for the other person to give more than his or her share.

A final reason why it is wise to give in according to your needs rather than because it is your turn is because this is a higher law, which when lived will lift you up and ennoble you. The process of keeping track and living by a law of justice in this life is a lesser law—a terrestrial law. It is certainly better than such less desirable processes as exploitation and coercion, but it is only at an intermediate level. The higher law is *mercy*. Those who have mercy give in to others around them, to help them in a charitable spirit. Alma's discourse on the difference between justice and mercy (Alma 42) shows that justice insists on equality and a fair return, while mercy shows compassion and is willing to do more than its exact share. They are both necessary, two sides of the same coin. In marriage, however, you can at times forego justice, or being even, and be merciful to your spouse. Therefore, those who can live the laws of mercy as they resolve differences in their marriages will have the most rewarding and joyful relationships. Those who can live only a law of justice may have good relationships, and perhaps will eventually be able to be merciful. Those who demand more than their share will find their marriages much less than ideal, and they ought to strive for justice—and then later strive for mercy.

SUMMARY

This chapter has discussed one type of problem solving: resolving differences of opinion. It has shown that your ability to manage your differences has a great influence on the quality of your marriage. Most of the time the best way to manage differences is to eliminate them—create unity—but this is not always possible. When you can't eliminate the differences you can try to find ways to keep them from being disruptive. You can do this by ignoring them or by agreeing on a course of action that is acceptable even though it is less than ideal.

Four other strategies for creating unity are also discussed. They are: (1) using the ideas about charity and communication discussed in earlier chapters; (2) striving for consensus rather than one person getting his way; (3) trying to change the other person only when that person agrees that it would be desirable to change; and (4) being the kind of person who will give in much more than his share, rather than keep score about whose turn it is to give in.

SUPPLEMENTARY READINGS

Deutsch, Morton. *The Resolution of Conflict.* New Haven: Yale University Press, 1978.
Romney, Marion G. "In the Image of God," *Ensign,* March 1978, pp. 2-4.
Scoresby, A. L. *The Marriage Dialogue.* Reading, Mass: Addison Wesley, 1976.

10

THE PATRIARCHAL
ORDER IN
MARRIAGE

No power or influence can or
ought to be maintained by virtue
of the priesthood, only by
persuasion, by long-suffering,
by gentleness and meekness,
and by love unfeigned.

—D&C 121:41

Latter-day Saint men and women live in a world that is changing dramatically. Many of the norms for behavior that used to be accepted are now being questioned or rejected. Minority groups are no longer tolerating unequal treatment. Premarital and marital sexual attitudes and behavior are changing. Many women are reexamining the traditional roles they have been given and are finding them no longer acceptable.

Statements by well-known feminists challenge the traditional roles of wife and mother, suggesting that women do not have the same opportunities as men for education or jobs and that marriage and family are instruments of women's oppression. They speak of the beauty and sacredness of motherhood as an archaic and inappropriate concept.

After being bombarded daily with statements like these, Latter-day Saint women then listen to the conference addresses and hear statements such as the following by President Spencer W. Kimball:

> When men come home to their families and women devote themselves to their children, the concept will return; then to be a mother will be the greatest vocation in life. She is a partner with God. No being has a position of such power and influence. She holds in her hand the destiny of nations, for to her comes the responsibility and opportunity of molding the nation's citizens. (Kimball 1975, p. 7.)

Latter-day Saint couples are living in an age when many groups are advocating one set of norms for marriage while family behavior experts and Church leaders are stressing another. The result is a mental tug-of-war to determine how they should act. We hope this chapter can assist in resolving some of these pressures.

AN ETERNAL PERSPECTIVE

One thing that can help you resolve these conflicts is to back off and make sure that your basic perspective is correct. If it is not, you may be like the four blind men who were

> Woman was made from the rib of man.
> She was not made from his head, to top him.
> Nor from his feet, to be stepped upon.
> She was made—
> From his side, to be equal with him;
> From beneath his arm, to be protected by him;
> Near his heart, to be loved by him!
>
> —Author unidentified

feeling the elephant to determine what elephants were like. As one felt the leg, another felt the ear, another the tail, and another felt the side, they each came up with a very different —and incorrect—conclusion. As with the blind men, you need to gain an overall view if you are to make sure of a correct perspective so that you can make wise decisions about both male and female roles.

Two opposing perspectives about male-female roles dominate the current controversy. One is well-intentioned and partly true. Unfortunately, it is also shortsighted and partly false. It can be called the "earthly" perspective. It assumes that social roles are created only by earthly conditions such as economic systems, traditions, migration patterns, and a gradual evolution over time. It also assumes that there is no limit to the ways roles can be modified and rearranged whenever circumstances change—for example, whether one is living in a rural or an urban environment.

The second perspective is quite different. An eternal perspective asserts that earthly life is only a part of the eternal experience, and that pre-earthly as well as post-earthly lives have an influence on the roles men and women should have. This perspective affirms that social conditions should justify some changes in roles, *but there are limits to the amount of change that should be made.* Some roles should not change at all, and some can change only within certain previously established limits.

These two incompatible perspectives lead to very different views of male-female roles. The earthly perspective allows people to rearrange such roles according to temporary conditions. Those who adopt this perspective see nothing wrong with radical changes in roles, such as eliminating distinctions between the roles of men and women in a highly industrialized society. This view is called unisexism or androgeny. The eternal perspective allows people to rearrange male-female roles only within certain limits that are imposed by pre-earthly and post-earthly conditions.

People in either group can learn something from the other. Those with an earthly perspective would be better off if they were to recognize pre-earthly and post-earthly conditions, and in the long run they will make some foolish mistakes if these conditions don't influence what they do in their roles. Even so, two wrongs don't make a right, and some of

"Husbands and wives are equal partners, particularly Latter-day Saint husbands and wives."
Marion G. Romney.

those who have the eternal perspective have been more rigid than the eternal truths justify. They have sometimes forced men and women into culturally dictated roles and have mistakenly thought them to be eternal. Latter-day Saint couples need to recognize that there are many ways in which male-female roles can change according to customs and cultures, and then feel free to make the appropriate changes.

THE PATRIARCHAL ORDER

The next step in recognizing the roles men and women ought to have in marriage is to have an accurate understanding of the patriarchal order. The underlying purpose of the patriarchal order is to *create order,* not to elevate one spouse above the other or to encourage servant/master roles in marriage. To create order, the patriarchal system specifies a division of responsibility between the marriage partners. Each spouse has a specific stewardship, assigned by law and appointment, and it cannot rightfully be abdicated to the other. In this manner, both the husband and the wife can feel they have a place and a purpose in an eternal plan.

When properly administered, the patriarchal family order is one of equality between the marriage partners as they approach life together. President Marion G. Romney (1978) emphasizes this point:

> They (husband and wife) should be one in harmony, respect, and mutual consideration. Neither should plan or follow an independent course of action. They should consult, pray, and decide together. . . . Remember that neither the wife nor the husband is the slave of the other. Husbands and wives are equal partners, particularly Latter-day Saint husbands and wives. They should so consider themselves and so treat each other in this life, and they then will do so throughout eternity.

This statement emphasizes the equality of the marriage partners; it is not a doctrine of "sameness." It is very different from the worldly view that there are few, if any, inherent psychological and emotional differences between the sexes—that all differences are learned from our culture. This worldly view claims that most roles now being performed by men could as easily be done by women, and vice versa, with no harm to society or children. Though many roles can be given as well to men as to women, there are some basic differences that should not be ignored. Elder Boyd K. Packer (1977) has provided some unique insights into these differences:

> We recognize men and women as equally important before the Lord, but with differences biologically, emotionally, and in other ways.
> We cannot eliminate, through any pattern of legislation or regulation, the differences between men and women.
> There are basic things that a man needs that a woman does not need. There are things that a man feels that a woman never does feel.
> There are basic things that a woman needs that a man never needs, and there are things that a woman feels that a man never feels, nor should he.
> These differences make women, in basic needs, literally opposite from men.
> A man, for instance, needs to feel protective, and yes dominant, if you will, in leading his family. A woman needs to feel protected, in the bearing of children and in the nurturing of them.
> Have you ever thought what life would be like if the needs of men and women were naturally precisely the same?
> What would it be like if they both naturally needed to feel dominant all the time, or both naturally needed to feel protected all the time? How disturbed and intolerable things would be. When God created male and female, He gave each important differences in physical attributes, in emotional composition, in family responsibility. We must protect and honor the vital differences in the roles of men and women, especially in respect to the family.

Some disagree with Elder Packer, but many in the scientific community agree. One such is John H. Crook:

> The biological roots of human sexual behavior are different in the two sexes and likely to be fundamental determinants in the differentiation of mature personality. . . . The naive idea of a psychological "equality" of the two sexes and of their total interchangeability in the performance of social roles has gained support from certain studies purporting to demonstrate that gender role is determined simply through developmental conditioning. This view ignores totally the significance of genetic and physiological differences between the sexes that in current research are shown to exert profound effects during the behavioral maturation of the growing organism. . . .

Those concerned with Women's Liberation would be wise to ponder the biological and psychological complementarity of the two sexes and their deep emotional needs for partnership as a counter to the notion of a poorly defined equality. (Crook 1972.)

While we may not yet understand in every instance which of the many differences between men and women are inherent and which are created by our cultures, it would be unwise and premature to conclude that they do not exist.

The Husband's Role in the Patriarchal Order

In a pamphlet dated 1973, the Church has provided some specific guidance as to the duties included in the role of husband/father:

> Fatherhood is leadership, the most important kind of leadership. It *has* always been so, it always will be so. Father, with the assistance and counsel and encouragement of your eternal companion, you preside in the home. It is not a matter of whether you are most worthy or best qualified, but it is a matter of law and appointment. You preside at the meal table, at family prayer. You preside at family home evening, and as guided by the Spirit of the Lord, you see that your children are taught correct principles. It is your place to give direction relating to all of family life.
> You give father's blessings. You take an active part in establishing family rules and discipline. As a leader in your home you plan and sacrifice to achieve the blessings of a unified and happy family. To do all of this requires that you live a family-centered life. (*Father, Consider Your Ways,* pp. 4-5.)

This statement does not mean that the husband is to make all of the decisions for the family. It means that the husband is to *direct the process.* We need to keep in mind President Romney's statement that neither the husband nor the wife is to plan or follow an independent course of action. They are to consult, pray, and decide together, and neither is the slave of the other. To preside does not mean to dominate and dictate, but to coordinate and to guide.

While keeping these truths in mind, you should also remember that the Lord occasionally intervenes by revealing his will. This happens in many ways, but usually through revelation to one or both spouses. When the revelation comes to only one spouse, it is important that the other spouse be willing to comply. Sometimes the revelation comes to the husband. An example of this was when the Lord spoke to father Lehi in a dream, directing him to leave Jerusalem. Even though Sariah was not enthusiastic about leaving her home, still she followed the direction given to her husband. At other times the revelation may come to the wife, as when Rebekah was told why she was expecting two sons when she had previously been barren (Genesis 25:22-23). In this instance, the husband was supportive of the revelation given to the wife.

The Wife

One of the questions often asked by women in the Church is, "If the husband is to preside over and lead the family, can the wife really be considered an equal? If so, how?"

The answer has at least partially already been presented in this discussion. From Elder Packer: "We recognize men and women as equally important before the Lord, but with differences biologically, emotionally, and in other ways." From President Romney: "Husbands and wives are equal partners." A further quotation from an apostle will help determine just how partners can be equal even though one presides:

> Woman does not hold the Priesthood, but she is a partaker of the blessings of the priesthood. That is, the man holds the Priesthood, performs the priesthood duties of the Church, but his wife enjoys with him every other privilege derived from the possession of the Priesthood. This is made clear, as an example, in the Temple service of the Church. The ordinances of the Temple are distinctly of Priesthood character, yet woman has access to all of them, and the highest blessings of the Temple are conferred only upon the man and his wife jointly.
>
> The Prophet Joseph Smith made this relationship clear. He spoke of delivering the keys of the Priesthood to the Church and said that the faithful members of the Relief Society should receive them with their husbands. . . .
>
> This division of responsibility is for a wise and noble purpose. Our Father in Heaven has bestowed upon His daughters a gift of equal importance and power, which gift, if exercised in its fulness, will occupy their entire life on earth so that they can have no possible longing for that which they don't possess. The "gift" referred to is that of motherhood—the noblest most soul satisfying of all earthly experiences. If this power is exercised righteously, woman has no time nor desire for anything greater, for there is nothing greater on earth! This does not mean that women may not use to the full their special gifts, for the more woman exercises her innate qualifications the greater is her power for motherhood. Woman may claim other activity but motherhood should take precedence in her entire scheme of life. (Widtsoe 1954.)

It almost appears that the priesthood and its presiding role may have been given to men as compensations, so they could be equal to women. Without man's leadership role, he would be stripped of much of his purpose and identity. Thus there is complementarity in roles rather than similarity, coordination rather than duplication, and order rather than confusion.

It may help you to understand that a division of labor does not imply inequality if you compare the husband-wife division to offices in the Church. A bishop is called to preside over a ward, usually for several years. Does this mean that during those years he is superior to the other ward members? Is he better or more powerful as a person? Is he smarter or wiser than other members of the ward? No—his calling doesn't mean any of these things. He is asked to perform a service, do a job. He has a unique responsibility. He is to direct the processes in the ward by doing what he can to see that things are done properly. It is an assignment, not a condition of superiority or inferiority. The Relief Society president has a different task, as does the president of the elders quorum, and these are differences in assignment, not in degree of superiority. After a few years, the bishop will be released, and he may become the group leader of the high priests while someone who was a Sunday School teacher becomes the bishop. All remain equally important, contributing, and involved. None are better than others merely because of particular positions assigned to them. It is the same in the home. The husband is assigned the responsibility to preside, and the wife is to give birth and have the main responsibility in rearing the children.

Accountability

Within the family all members have an accountability for their stewardships or assigned roles. This accountability is explained in 1 Corinthians 11:3: "But I would have you know, that the head of every man is Christ; and the head of the woman is the man; and the head of Christ is God." This can be diagrammed as follows:

God ◄ Christ ◄ Man ◄ Woman

From this it can be seen that the husband is not excluded from having to submit to someone who has a stewardship over him. The husband is commanded to submit himself in righteousness to the will of the Savior, and the wife is counseled to submit herself to her husband as he obeys the Son, who in turn obeys the will of the Father.

There is, however, an important qualification for submission within the patriarchal order—that of *righteousness*. The husband should have no qualms about submitting his will to the Savior's will, as Jesus Christ is always consistent and is perfect in his love and administrations, as is the Father. The wife, however, is required to submit to a mortal man who is but a god in embryo, a novice who is trying to become perfect—who has not yet arrived. It is interesting to note that the Hebrew word for husband is *baal*, which has two meanings: (a) lord and master, and (b) *false god*. The latter meaning is probably closer to the truth much of the time.

In the meantime, what does the woman do who marries an egotistical, lord-and-master type who is in fact a spiritual midget? Of course it would have been best not to marry him in the first place. It has been said that individuals should go into marriage with both eyes wide open. If, however, it's too late for that, a woman can choose to keep both eyes half-closed. If a husband is striving for perfection, the wife has an obligation to help him grow spiritually. On the other hand, Brigham Young (1854) offered the following counsel:

> But I never counselled a woman to follow her husband to the devil. If a man is determined to expose the lives of his friends, let that man go to the devil and to destruction alone. (P. 77.)

Slavery, oppression, inequality, and unrighteous dominion have no part in the patriarchal order. A woman is not obligated to suffer this type of oppression. As to when enough is enough, that will have to be prayerfully considered as the problem arises.

Presiding in Righteousness

For the husband who desires to preside in righteousness, but is not sure exactly what this means, the best place to look for the answer is D&C 121:39-46:

> We have learned by sad experience that it is the nature and disposition of almost all men, as soon as they get a little authority, as they suppose, they will immediately begin to exercise unrighteous dominion.
>
> Hence many are called, but few are chosen.
>
> No power or influence can or ought to be maintained by virtue of the priesthood, only by persuasion, by long-suffering, by gentleness and meekness, and by love unfeigned;

By kindness, and pure knowledge, which shall greatly enlarge the soul without hypocrisy, and without guile—

Reproving betimes with sharpness, when moved upon by the Holy Ghost; and then showing forth afterwards an increase of love toward him whom thou hast reproved, lest he esteem thee to be his enemy;

That he may know that thy faithfulness is stronger than the cords of death.

Let thy bowels also be full of charity towards all men, and to the household of faith, and let virtue garnish thy thoughts unceasingly; then shall thy confidence wax strong in the presence of God; and the doctrine of the priesthood shall distil upon thy soul as the dews from heaven.

The Holy Ghost shall be thy constant companion, and thy scepter an unchanging scepter of righteousness and truth; and thy dominion shall be an everlasting dominion, and without compulsory means it shall flow unto thee forever and ever.

From this passage it becomes evident that most men do *not* automatically and innately know how to preside correctly. Presiding is a skill that must be learned. This scripture does not end by stating that most priesthood bearers cannot lead in righteousness—it goes on to list ten ways men can lead properly in the patriarchal order and in other priesthood roles. Consider, if you will, the authors' interpretation of these concepts below, and consider also the manner in which these traits are made manifest in *your* home:

1. *Persuasion.* This is likely the chief tool of priesthood leadership. It means an attempt to convince one's spouse and family through the presentation of ideas and concepts. It is the opposite of force or tyranny. It is talking and reasoning—without raising one's voice or threatening. It is sharing ideas to show others the wisdom in what one desires. Whenever one *persuades,* the other person is free to agree or to disagree according to his free agency.

2. *Long-suffering.* Patience and a willingness to overlook imperfections in one's mate are important parts of priesthood leadership. This is the opposite of impatience, fault-finding, and expecting perfection.

3. *Gentleness.* A gentle husband is one who respects his wife and considers her his equal. A gentle husband is sensitive to his wife's needs, both emotional and physical, and is never guilty of forcing his own desires upon her.

4. *Meekness.* To be meek is to be teachable and willing to conform to the gospel standards and thus submit one's will to the will of the Lord. The meek husband is not a law unto himself. He cares about others' feelings and is willing to be taught by them.

5. *Love unfeigned.* An unfeigned love is one that is sincere, not counterfeit or hypocritical. It is genuine. Under this principle we do not love our mates simply for what they can do for us; we love them as persons of unique worth in and of themselves. Their lives are as important to us as are our own lives.

6. *Kindness.* Kindness is an attitude that should moderate the actions of priesthood leadership at all times. It is the opposite of cruelty, revenge, and being nonforgiving. Perhaps the highest form of kindness we can show others is to forgive them completely.

7. *Pure knowledge.* To preside with pure knowledge is to lead one's family by revelation and inspiration. Pure knowledge comes from God and is undefiled and unpolluted by the theories of men. How fortunate is the family that has a patriarch at its head who is able to use this gift to bless his family!

8. *No hypocrisy.* The father-husband within the patriarchal order should not be guilty of requiring his wife and family to sacrifice, work, go the extra mile, do without wants or necessities, forego recreation or hobbies, etc., if he himself is not willing to live by the same rules. There cannot be two codes of conduct based on the assumption that the one spouse has an inherent right to more privileges than the other.

9. *No guile.* To lead guilefully is to lead with deceitful cunning, by duplicity (or doubleness) of thought, speech, or action. There is no place for this type of presiding within a true patriarchal order. Instead, all eventual members of the celestial kingdom will have overcome this mortal weakness, as is explained in D&C 76:94: "They who dwell in his presence are the church of the Firstborn; and they see as they are seen, and know as they are known, having received of his fulness and of his grace." To see as we are seen and know as we are known is to be without guile and to be completely genuine.

10. *Charity.* Charity is the pure love of Christ; it is discussed in depth in chapter 3. It is an essential character trait of the patriarchal leader. Couples who manifest charity are promised confidence, understanding, the constant companionship of the Holy Ghost, and an everlasting dominion of righteousness and truth. (D&C 121:45-46.)

METHODS OF PRESIDING AND FOLLOWING

Within the patriarchal order there is some flexibility as to how a husband presides and how a wife submits to his leadership. The Lord has provided some guidelines, some do's and don't's—but to live within the bounds of the order is not to be "commanded in all things." In fact, individual differences are desirable and even essential, as long as you stay within the bounds the Lord has set. The rest of this chapter discusses several techniques that couples have found useful in working out their own styles of presiding and following. It is likely that readers can identify additional ideas they will find useful.

Presiding and Conducting Are Different

Presiding is quite different from conducting. While the difference between presiding and conducting is readily understood in Church meetings, many of us blur and confuse the distinction in our homes.

The presiding responsibilities are not passed around or rotated in a priesthood organization. One person is always identified as the one to preside, and whenever that person is present, he or she is presiding. If that person is absent, another person is identified as the one to preside during the absence. Since the patriarchal order in a family makes it a priesthood organization, this same procedure should be followed there. The father should preside, and this function should be delegated to someone else only when he is absent.

Conducting, on the other hand, is quite different. The person who is conducting a particular function takes the initiative to organize things, get things going, direct activities to make sure they run smoothly, and stop things when they should be stopped. The conducting person is the one who speaks up and actually manages the operations. The conducting is done under the direction of the one who is presiding, but the presiding role can be passive much of the time. The usual custom in priesthood organizations is to rotate the conducting role among those who are leaders in the organization.

In families the function of conducting can be rotated in several ways. Even when children are very small, they can begin to have a turn conducting certain family activities. Children who are in elementary school can learn to conduct such activities as family home evenings, picnics, trips to the movie, and birthday parties. Later, as the children become teenagers, they can learn how to conduct more complex family activities such as family councils, reunions, camping trips, shopping trips, and spring housecleaning. This process of passing around the conducting has several advantages. It teaches the children some very valuable skills, such as learning how to lead and how important it is for people to be willing to follow a leader rather than oppose and ignore him. It gives the children a feeling of importance because they are making a contribution to the family that is visible, respected, and important. It also keeps the father from always being the conductor, and this can actually increase respect for him in his position as the presider.

The wife can also be involved in conducting various family activities. This can be done according to the interests, personality, and abilities of the wife. Some wives would rather not conduct family activities; they would prefer to make their contribution to the family in other ways. Other wives would prefer to have equal turns in conducting activities, and some like to conduct most of the time. Certainly the freedoms within the patriarchal order allow for these differences to be arranged in whatever manner a couple prefers. In some situations, the husband may not desire to conduct certain activities such as family council, but the wife may have an energetic personality and be skillful in organizing and directing the decision-making process in those councils. There would be nothing wrong with a couple such as this deciding that the wife would always conduct family councils.

Delegate and Report

Those who are familiar with the priesthood quorums recognize that the dual process of delegating and then reporting is an important part of priesthood activities. In delegation, the person who is conducting asks someone to take an assignment. The assignment is an agreement to do something, to have a specific task. The person receiving the assignment can volunteer or be asked to accept the assignment. Then there is the provision for the person with the assignment to report back to the quorum or presidency that gave the assignment. If it can be completed in a short period of time, the person usually reports back after the job is completed. He indicates what he did and the contribution he made. If the assignment is a long-term responsibility, the person periodically reports on how things are going with his stewardship. This can be done monthly, annually, or as often as the group wishes.

It is important to realize that the process of delegating and reporting is more than just a convenient way to get things done. It is the method the Lord used in heaven before the earth was created, the method he uses now, and the method he will use in the future. It is the method that we too will use when we return to live with him. It is, therefore, an eternal way of organizing things, and we would do well to learn how to use it in this life.

A number of terms are used to label the assignments that are given in priesthood quorums. They are sometimes called *stewardships*. They are also called *responsibilities* or *assignments*. The scriptures also use the term *callings*. Families can use the terminology that they find comfortable.

If couples were to use the process of delegating and reporting in their families, many of the discontentments and frustrations that have given rise to the women's movement would be taken care of to everyone's satisfaction. The way to proceed is for each married couple to begin early in marriage to follow the example of the scriptures by having family councils to decide how to organize themselves. "And the Gods took counsel among themselves and said: Let us . . ." (Abraham 4:26).

Couples ought to counsel together and decide who should have which assignments in their marital systems. This should never be a process in which the husband tells the wife what she ought to do, or in which the husband gets his way more than she does, or in which the husband gets the last word. *These are not priesthood privileges.* The husband and wife should talk about how to organize themselves until they can acquire a consensus (D&C 107:27-29) that they both feel good about. In making these agreements, they should not be fettered by the cultural traditions inherent in society. They should feel free to arrange their family in the way they feel will be the best for their personalities, interests, and preferred lifestyle. If this means that the wife conducts family councils because she likes to and is good at it, so be it. If it means that the wife mows the lawn and the husband does the laundry, so be it. If it means that the husband has the most say in buying cars and recreational equipment, while the wife has the most say about buying furniture and houses, so be it. And if you decide to organize your family in a way that is very different from your parents' family, so be it.

The key in this process is to remember that the husband presides over the family as a whole. This means he *directs the process* of family life. He does not get his way more than the others. In fact, he may get his way less because he needs to sacrifice for the whole. He is not a dictator, and is not the boss. He has a God-given assignment to make sure that the family system operates with order, and he is to do it by patience, requests, love, suggestions, asking others to accept assignments, receiving reports about the assignments so he knows how things are going, occasionally conducting meetings himself, encouraging, and respecting the rights and wishes of those around him. Recognizing that the greatest among us is a servant, he serves.

Different Levels of Perfection

In this area, as in all others, all people are at different levels of perfection. Some are at a high level and can live the instructions in section 121 of the Doctrine and Covenants. They can be kind, long-suffering, meek, and patient, and employ gentle persuasion. Others are not up to that level; in fact, some are far from perfect in this area. For example, one person known to the authors has a difficult time controlling his temper. He frequently hits and pushes and in other ways physically abuses the others in his family. He is trying to repent and rise above his undesirable ways of interacting. He tries now to remember to hit other things, like a punching bag he has recently installed, instead of his wife and children.

To help each of us select our goals, the following paragraphs describe the authors' views of three different levels of perfection in this area. We should all ultimately seek the highest level, but some of us need to set intermediate goals as steppingstones. Then, as we master those goals, we can set our sights on the next set and thereby gradually perfect ourselves.

Highest level of perfection. At this level, the patriarch tries to always lead the family in such a way that they achieve consensus in making decisions. The Lord has instructed that when you are able to get consensus, you receive more blessings (D&C 107:26-28). If you have to resort to less desirable practices, such as majority votes, you receive fewer blessings. When you can't get consensus, the husband does not get his way any more than anyone else. All are equal in power and say.

At this level, you also follow the Savior's admonitions in the Sermon on the Mount and in D&C 121 to be kind, merciful, patient, loving, forgiving, nonjudgmental, and long-suffering. You ought also to try very hard to be empathetic and use effective communication techniques such as establishing rapport, getting feedback, listening with your heart as well as your ears, respecting the subjective rightness of everyone's opinions, and making sure that people get to participate whenever they would like.

Intermediate level of perfection. Some fathers believe they should think about how the family should be organized and what decisions should be made, and then call a family council to get a sustaining vote. Though this is certainly a better system than some of the strategies that will be discussed below, it has several disadvantages. It often creates resentment because it gives the father too much control, and it does not encourage the same development in the children as when they are actively involved in the whole decision-making process.

Another system at this intermediate level is to have the father get information from all of the members of the family and then to be the one to make the decision. This method also puts the father in a slightly higher position. It assumes that he is the one who has the most or best information about everything, and it makes him just a little "holier than thou" as compared with the others. Some people in the Church think this is the optimal method in the patriarchal order, but the authors disagree. We think that this is a pattern that has crept into our culture from the traditions of society, and that it fosters inequality between husbands and wives in an inappropriate way. There are many areas in which the wife may be better informed than the husband. There are also situations in which the wife may be more insightful or sensitive than the husband. When this occurs, it may be best for the husband to preside but to let the wife make the decision.

Some other ways of behaving at an intermediate level are to only appear to listen to others; to let other members of the family express their opinions before forcing one's will on them; to use subtle methods of getting one's way such as bribing, whining, and being stubborn; and to bargain in a way that produces only justice, rather than being willing to be merciful and charitable.

Lower level of perfection. Some fathers think being the patriarch means that the father should make all of the important decisions. Some think he has no obligation to even ask the opinions of other members of the family. He is the leader, the head of the house, and the others ought to do what he says, just because he says it. These men would do well to listen to the others' opinions.

Some people use undesirable methods—such as coercion, force, losing their temper, and physical abuse—to get their way. Some also refuse to admit they are wrong, even after they know that they are. Some also use profanity and threats to enforce their opinions. They would do well to identify these undesirable ways of behaving and gradually try to eliminate them.

Lead with Gentleness

A beautiful example of how a husband is to preside was given by President Spencer W. Kimball. In at least one situation in which he was presiding over a meeting in the temple, rather than telling the others that he would give the prayer, he asked, "Is it all right if I give the prayer?"* He phrased it as a question to those over whom he presided, rather than just telling them. It was more like a gentle request than an instruction or order. The difference between gentleness and force, between softness and coercion, may be small in words, yet it is great in effect. How often did the Lord speak of being merciful, kind, peacemaking, forgiving, gentle, and loving? How much should a partner in marriage act in these ways, either in presiding or supporting?

President Kimball has suggested that we should have "a style of our own." This applies in the way we preside and follow in our homes. We ought to adopt the style advocated by the Savior—of patience, mercy, kindness, love unfeigned, and softness. Were this to occur, we would find much more joy and peace than most of us ever thought possible.

Allow for Agency

One of the most difficult challenges for a husband as he presides is to find the proper balance between the interests of each family member and those of the family as a whole. Each family member should be able to exercise his own free agency, yet he cannot have complete freedom because excessive freedom may interfere with the rights of others. This is an important issue in the occupational world, educational institutions, hospitals, and wherever there are organized groups. It is especially important in marriage and family life because members spend so much of their time together, and family life is the hub of the wheel of life.

---

* Personal correspondence.

When children are small, they are given little freedom, simply because they lack wisdom and experience. They are told what time to go to bed, what time to get up, what to eat, how to act at the table, and so on. When small children resist their parents' control, they are reminded that they "have to" do what they are told, and this is enforced with a firm tone of voice, punishments, and control over rewards. Children experience little free agency and a lot of benevolent coercion.

As these children grow up, two things change. They are allowed more and more freedom, and the parents gradually learn to change the methods they use to obtain compliance. The parents learn to ask more and tell less. They learn to make suggestions and give advice, and the children are gradually allowed enough freedom and independence that they can choose to accept or reject suggestions and advice.

Allowing for agency is more complex in a marriage relationship, because both partners are adults. They both deserve and desire certain freedoms and independence, and occasionally they even want freedoms that interfere with their marriage or family life.

There are no simple solutions to this dilemma, but there are several things that are good to remember. First, both extremes are unhealthy. You can have too little or too much freedom. Second, most individuals in our modern culture err in allowing too little freedom to those around them. They want people to do things their way. They want too much control over what their spouses and older children want to do. Every adult needs to recognize that *each person* in the family needs to make choices and learn by the good and bad decisions he makes. Satan's plan in the pre-earth life was to coerce people into narrow limits by denying their agency, by not giving them the freedom to make mistakes and learn by suffering the consequences. The Savior's plan is to give advice and suggestions and then to allow people freedom in making their own choices, while being ready to forgive their mistakes when they repent. Many tend to use Satan's plan too often and to ignore the wisdom of the Savior's plan.

SUMMARY

This chapter discusses the fundamental parts of the patriarchal order and describes several things that each of us could do to use this system of government wisely. The patriarchal order provides a division of labor wherein the man is to preside in the family and the woman is to give birth to the children and have the primary responsibility for rearing them. In both areas the other spouse is to assist. This creates a harmonious complementarity that does not elevate one sex above the other. Both have important responsibilities. This provides order and equality, but not sameness.

There is considerable freedom in the way you can administer the patriarchal order in your home. The wife can accept assignments that give her a great deal of leadership and influence in the home, if the partners prefer to structure their lives in that manner. If, on the other hand, she prefers to not be very involved in leadership activities, this too can be arranged. The role of presiding in the home means that the husband is responsible to organize the family in a way that accomplishes what needs to be done in a harmonious manner. He is not a dictator, because being a priesthood leader means that he should *direct the process* in the home rather than always have his way. He is to make sure that things get done, and the best way he can accomplish this is to be a gentle leader who gets consensus about decisions, makes assignments, delegates responsibilities, and monitors what is happening to determine when new decisions need to be made. He is therefore a steward, a servant, and a manager, rather than a drill sergeant or dictator. The methods that he should employ are gentleness, persuasion, kindness, love, encouragement, affection, and softness.

SUPPLEMENTARY READINGS

Tanner, N. Eldon. "No Greater Honor: The Woman's Role" *Ensign,* January 1974, pp. 7-10.

Turner, Rodney. *Woman and the Priesthood.* Salt Lake City: Deseret Book Company, 1976.

Widtsoe, John A. *Priesthood and Church Government.* Salt Lake City: Deseret Book Company, 1954, ch. 7.

11

COPING WITH UNDESIRABLE BEHAVIOR

He that is without sin among you,
let him first cast a stone.

—John 8:7

Most of the time we act as we should. We're polite, cooperative, affectionate, and considerate. We're charitable and kind and patient. Sometimes, though, we all act in undesirable ways.

Some undesirable behaviors occur because man is in a mortal condition in which no one is perfect. As the scripture indicates, "all have sinned, and come short of the glory of God" (Romans 3:23). People become impatient when they are tired or when they have the pressures of final examinations or when they are paying the monthly bills. They feel resentful and want to get even when someone takes advantage of them. And some stretch the truth when they are in a tight spot.

Not all undesirable behavior is so wrong that it can be called sin. Sometimes it is a result of differences in background, as with the neighbors of one of the authors.

Peter grew up in a family where the mother handled the family money and paid all of the bills. Sue was raised in a family where the father took care of the finances. When they were married, each assumed that the other one would be the one to handle the money. For the first few months of their marriage, the bills stacked up. In fact, the light bill and telephone bill were so much overdue that the power and telephone were turned off twice. Both partners felt more than a little frustrated because the other one wouldn't assume his or her "rightful" obligation in this part of their marriage.

Is this a case of "undesirable behavior"? Definitely! When Peter did not pay the bills, it was undesirable to Sue, and vice versa. Situations like this are common, yet they are quite different from sinful behavior such as physical abuse, dishonesty, adultery, exploitation, excessive drinking, or cruelty.

Since everyone is imperfect, and since all husbands and wives grow up in different kinds of homes, individuals must learn to recognize and then cope with both types of behavior problems in marriage. They need to learn to manage their marital systems so that they turn these situations into productive rather than destructive experiences. This chapter discusses several strategies that can help you deal with these situations.

A GENERAL PRINCIPLE

Social scientists have discovered a general principle that can help you deal with undesirable behavior in marriage. The principle uses four terms that you will need to understand: (1) role expectations; (2) role behavior; (3) congruence of expectations and behavior; and (4) the importance of expectations.

Role Expectations

This concept was defined on page 162. It refers to your beliefs or opinions about how people should act. Whenever you use words like *should, should not, ought,* or *ought not* to describe what you consider to be good or bad behavior, you are identifying your role expectations.

Role Behavior

Role behavior is the way you act when you are playing a role. This is different from *role expectation,* since an expectation is the belief as to how you should or should not act. The behavior is what you actually do. For example, a husband may be like the following man who does not verbally express affection to his wife: "Look at all I do that shows her I love her. I provide a good living. I don't run around. I'm home in the evenings, and I help take care of the kids. If she needs anything, I do my best to help her get it. That ought to be enough to show her I love her. Anybody can say words. It's actions that count." A husband who understood the role expectations of most women would behave quite differently. His role behavior would include at least occasional physical *and* verbal expressions of affection.

Congruence of Expectations and Behavior

Congruence occurs when your expectations and your perceptions of behavior are the same. If the wife believes her husband should be considerate and cooperative, and thinks he *is*, there is high congruence. If, however, she expects him to be considerate and cooperative, and thinks he is inconsiderate or uncooperative, there is low congruence. In other words, congruence is whether you act the way you should—whether you get what you want. If you want a person to act in certain ways and he does—high congruence; if he doesn't—low congruence.

There are two main ways in which incongruence occurs: intrapersonally and interpersonally. Intrapersonal incongruence occurs when you have expectations for yourself, but your own behavior is not in harmony with your expectations. For example, you may think you should be patient, but keep losing your temper. Or you may think that you should

> There is a set of terms that is simpler than *role expectations, role behaviors* and *role discrepancies*. It is not quite as precise, but it still does the job. It is our "BB's". Our role expectations are our *beliefs* about how we ought to act—one of the "B's". Our role *behavior* is the other "B". The key is to keep our BB's the same. When our BB's are out of whack, it fouls up a marriage. If our BB's are out of harmony, we can change either one—the beliefs or the behavior—to get things back on an even keel. Or, if we can't change either of the B's, we can try to say, "Oh, well. It doesn't matter that much."

pick up your dirty clothes and put them in the clothes hamper, but forget half the time. Interpersonal incongruence exists when either spouse has expectations for the other person and the other person doesn't act that way.

The Importance of Expectations

Some role expectations are very important, and others are not. For example, expectations regarding adultery, desertion, deception, and cruelty are very important to most people. Some expectations that are usually less important are not biting fingernails, closing the cupboard doors after you open them, not squeezing the toothpaste in the middle of the tube, putting books back on a shelf neatly, and folding napkins when there are guests.

The Principle

The principle that uses these terms is very important in marriage, because it helps you understand what is really happening when undesirable behaviors occur. It also gives you vocabulary that can help you talk with your spouse, and when you fully understand the principle, it helps you know how to cope with misbehavior. The principle is:

9. The Congruence Principle: The greater the perceived congruence between role expectations and role behavior, the higher the marital and family satisfaction (especially with important expectations).

Considerable research* concerning this principle has been done, and the research shows that it has a linear relationship as shown in Figure 11:1. What this means is that each incongruence has a detrimental effect in a marriage, and each congruence helps the marriage to be successful.

---

* Ort 1950; Luckey 1960; Kotlar 1961; Hawkins and Johnson 1969; Burr 1971; Brinley 1975.

Figure 11:1   The Relationship Between Marital Satisfaction and the Congruence of Expectations and Behaviors

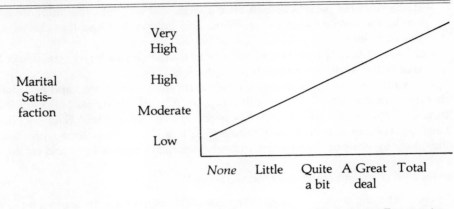

APPLYING THE CONGRUENCE PRINCIPLE

Think Incongruence Rather Than Right and Wrong

The first thing one should do in learning how to use the congruence principle is to think about the undesirable behaviors that occur in a marriage in terms of the *congruence of expectations and behavior.* In other words, when the wife thinks the husband is spending too much time with his friends and too little time with her, she should not take the simple way out by telling him that he's wrong and he ought to stay home. It is not that simple! She needs to realize that there are no absolute laws about how much time a husband spends at home. Instead, this is a situation where expectations and behavior seem incongruent. She has expectations, he has expectations, and he has certain behaviors. His expectations and behaviors may be just as correct and wise as hers, if she were to completely understand his view of things. By thinking in terms of the congruence principle, one realizes that this situation is not one in which one spouse is right and the other wrong. Both have beliefs and both have behaviors, and their relationship would be better if they could make some changes.

This sounds simple, but most people are not very good at it. They assume that their opinions about what should be done are the Truth (with a capital "T"). For example:

—If the wife doesn't want to do the housework, and he thinks she should, he thinks he is right, right, right, and she should shape up.

—If he thinks that kids should not be spanked, and she disagrees, she assumes he ought to change—pronto.

—If she visits her parents at least once a week and he thinks that monthly is enough, he thinks she should be more reasonable and independent and that she ought to be the one to change.

—If he can't keep on the budget because he's an impulsive buyer, she thinks he ought to change his behavior and be more responsible.

A person tends to think in terms of absolute right and wrong, and he usually assumes that he is the one who is Right (with a capital "R"). *People would be so much better off if they would approach all situations in terms of expectations and behavior.* Both partners have expectations and both have behavior. It is a lot easier to cope with situations when they think in terms of expectations and behavior rather than of right and wrong.

Is the Basic Problem Disunity or Incongruence?

The next thing to do in coping with undesirable behavior is to approach the situation as a problem, and use the problem-solving techniques discussed in chapters 8 and 9. The first stage in problem solving is to determine what the problem is.

You may say to yourself, "That's easy! The problem is that someone is misbehaving. Someone is not doing what he ought to do. The problem is the behavior, so let's change the behavior." If you say this, you may be falling into a trap and will probably create more problems than you will solve. You need to realize that most of the time when there appears to be a behavior problem, its root or basis is not behavioral. The problem is usually not that someone is misbehaving; most of the time the root of the problem is *disunity.*

What is the difference?

Examine the situations of the following three couples. Some of their problems are only behavior problems (in which behavior is incongruent with expectations), but some of them involve disunity.

The Smiths

Incongruence only: She thinks he should pick up his soiled clothes rather than leave them where he takes them off. He agrees, but he gets so busy that he forgets every other night.

Expectations: Both agree. There is unity.
Behavior: His behavior is incongruent with both of their expectations.

Incongruence and disunity: She thinks he should pick up his clothes rather than leave them where he takes them off. He disagrees. He thinks that part of her tidying a bedroom in the morning ought to include gathering the soiled clothes from the chairs. It is easier to do it in the morning than to go to the bother at the end of the day when people are tired. So he leaves them on the chair.

The Possibly Perfect Partner

or

What Is the Eggbeater Doing in the Silver Chest?

You've fallen in love, you two who were friends. You look at each other and the world around you with an eye single to your own world, this one face is your kind of face: this one smile, the warming one.

You build your dreams, set the date, and go through the motions of becoming betrothed. And while the enchanting spell spreads over you, you marry. Then, holding hands, you walk off into the sunset to live happily ever after.

New in your discovery of each other's ways in the daily tasks of life, you are full of wonder—you wonder how you could not have known that this marvelous skiier decorates the bedroom with socks, ties, and used lift passes. And when he dries the dishes, he absent-mindedly puts the eggbeater in the silver chest.

He wonders how you, his beautiful and sensible wife, could possibly emerge as a toothpaste tube mutilator, a cap leaver-offer, and a financial hazard with the check book. What's more, you starched his no-iron shirts.

You each wonder if two people so different, cloaked with love and some frustration, can ever become one.

It is at such moments that you are glad that you are friends as well as husband and wife. You are thankful for an understanding of the plan of life and the potentiality of the human spirits. In all your differences there is one important quality you share—imperfection and the right to grow.

So you pick up the socks; he replaces the toothpaste cap; you retrieve the eggbeater; he copes with the overdraft one more time. Then you kiss each other.

Maybe not the perfect partner yet, but you keep trying because you promised you would.

Two imperfect children of God who look at each other and the world around them with an eye single to another's needs—friends still and forever. . . .

—Author unidentified

Expectations: They disagree. There is disunity.
Behavior: Congruent with his expectations but incongruent with hers.

The Johnsons

Incongruence only: He thinks they should visit their folks at least monthly, and so does she. He's "so busy" that he doesn't go very often. She takes the kids and visits the folks monthly.

Expectations: Both agree. There is unity.
Behavior: His behavior is incongruent with both expectations.

Incongruence and disunity: He thinks they should visit the folks weekly. She thinks that is too often. She thinks once a month is plenty, and once every other month would be best. They visit them weekly.

Expectations: Disunity. They disagree.
Behavior: Congruent with his wishes but incongruent with hers.

The Tuckers

Incongruence only: He thinks the house should be much straighter than it usually is, in case someone drops in. He also thinks it is the wife's job to keep it clean. She agrees that it is her job and that it should be straighter, but with five small children it is not straight very often.

Expectations: Unity. They think the same.
Behavior: She is not behaving the way they both think she should.

Incongruence and disunity: Same situation as above, except that she thinks that while the children are small it is all right for the house to be less clean. She thinks that it is straight enough.

Expectations: Disuinity. He wants it neater than she does.
Behavior: Her behavior is consistent with her expectations, but not with his.

There are two reasons it is important to know whether a problem is merely an incongruence or whether there is also disunity. First, whenever you have disunity it is a more basic or fundamental problem than the behavioral problem. Beliefs precede behavior. This means that you have to deal with the disunity problem before you can solve the behavioral problem. If you try to solve the behavioral problem when you have disunity, it is like trying to fix a flat tire by putting air into it before you fix the hole. And as long as the disunity is there, it will somewhere cause incongruence between beliefs and behavior. You are just kidding yourself if you think you can solve the behavioral problem while you have disunity. For example, if the husband wants more affection shown than the wife, and they have had little affection (as the wife wants), they can solve his problem by becoming more affectionate. Unfortunately, this merely makes the behavior incongruent with the wife's views rather than the husband's. It transfers the problem from him to her; they still have the same problem as a couple.

The second reason why it is important to know whether there is disunity whenever there is undesirable behavior is that you solve the two problems very differently. When you have disunity problems, you solve them with the techniques discussed in chapter 9. You talk about your beliefs; you try to change your opinions, your wishes, your desires, and your expectations. While there may sometimes be emotional or psychological overtones, this is dealt with as a mental issue, since it concerns differences of opinion.

When the problem is incongruence of expectations and behavior, you have more options. You can change your expectations *or* your behavior, *and you use very different techniques to change your behavior.* Trying to solve disunity problems by changing behaviors is like putting a cast on your arm to cure a sore throat, or getting the car tuned up because the TV won't work, or vacuuming the rug because the dishes are dirty. These analogies may seem ridiculous, but many people actually make similar mistakes in their marriages. You try to get your spouse to change something he is doing *because you think it should be changed,* when the problem you need to solve is not the behavior at all. *It is the difference of opinion.*

In summary, whenever you have a behavior problem in your marriage, you need to find out whether you are unified in the problem. If you don't have unity, you back up to the ideas in chapter 9 and try to create unity. Then, *after* you have created unity in your expectations, or have found a way to live happily with your disunity (such as finding a way to agree to disagree), you try to cope with the behavioral part of the problem.

Remember—Deal with Feelings First

After you have learned that you have a problem, what do you do next? Do you jump right into the process of solving it? Only if you like to fight and destroy precious things like love and peace. The answer? *Wise couples deal with their feelings first.* Some of these skills are discussed in chapter 6, where it is suggested that we ought to deal with our emotions in ways that will be beneficial instead of destructive. In resolving behavior problems, it is extremely important to use these skills, since such discrepancies are often accompanied by intense feelings. Therefore, before entering into a discussion you should ask yourself, "Is the total environment right? Is the time of day right? Will there be distractions, noise, outside pressures interfering? Am I in control of myself? Is my partner receptive? Is he or she defensive, preoccupied, tired, overworked?" You should check out these questions with your partner by asking him or her if the time is right before you sit down for the discussion. If everything seems to be in order, you are ready to move ahead.

The next step is to gain an understanding of how each of you *actually feels* about the incongruence. As you do this you are building the foundation for other processes to occur *after* each of you has an understanding of the other's feelings about the discrepancies.

What Are Your Alternatives?

After you understand each other's feelings, you can then turn your attention to resolving the discrepancies. What is the next step? As with any other problem (as discussed on pages 145-149 in chapter 8), step two is to *identify and discuss your alternatives.* When undesirable behavior occurs, there are four main alternatives: (1) change the expectations, (2) change the behavior, (3) change the importance of the expectations, or (4) learn how to

A sense of humor is a valuable asset.

live with what is seen as less than ideal behavior. The following situation can help you understand these alternatives:

Glenda's side:
Harry and Glenda have been married for six months, and their marriage isn't what she thought it would be. She thinks Harry spends too much time with his buddies. Since he is working and still finishing school, he doesn't have much free time, and what he has seems to go to his friends. There aren't very many spare minutes left for her. This leaves her with a lot of time on her hands. At first she didn't mind, but she resents it more all the time.

Harry's side:
Harry has some close friends, and he doesn't want his marriage to mean that he has to give them up. It takes time to keep friendships. He does spend a lot of time with his friends, but he also spends a lot of time with Glenda. His marriage is first, but it is not the only thing.

Assume that this is a behavioral problem, not a disunity problem. They have agreed that they should spend a lot of time together. Assuming this, consider their alternatives:

1. *Change expectations:* It may be that their expectations are unrealistic. Both want to spend time together, but they have so many other things they also want that there aren't enough hours in the day, especially for Harry. Therefore, they may help solve the problem by adjusting their expectations. They could change them in several different ways. For example, they could decide to spend less time with friends, even though that might be painful. Or they could agree to get by with less interaction with each other than they would like—temporarily, until they get out of school. Or Harry could take an extra year to finish school.

2. *Change behavior:* It may be that Harry has not yet fully realized some of the changes that occur with marriage. He has assumed that his spouse would be his best friend, but he hasn't realized this means that some of his other friends must become less important. In trying to keep everybody happy, he has unwittingly neglected Glenda. If this is so, the problem could be solved by his adjusting his behavior so that he spends more time with her and less with his friends. They could also make sure that the time they do spend together is "quality" time.

3. *Change the importance.* It may be that they can't find a way to change their expectations or behavior enough. He just can't give up his buddies even though he realizes he should. The best solution they may be able to come up with is to live with their problem, letting Harry spend a lot of time with his buddies. Glenda may be able to change her opinion about how important it is by saying to herself, "This certainly isn't the most important thing in our marriage. It would be nice to have it better, but it is not necessary. He recognizes that he has a fault in this area and will try to improve, but it is not as important as some other things, and we are going to work on them first."

4. *Learn to live with it without any changes:* (This is what people do when they can't find a better solution.) Harry continues to see his friends a lot and Glenda can't tell herself

it isn't important because it *is* important to her, and it is important to him. What can they do about it? They realize they have a lot of other great things going for them in their marriage, and aren't going to let this one problem ruin their life. They try to avoid the issue and just accept it as a "less than ideal situation." They tell themselves, "After all, all couples have a few areas where things aren't perfect. Besides, Harry is a good husband in many other ways."

There are a number of strategies that can help us with each of these alternatives. The following pages discuss some of them.

STRATEGIES FOR COPING WITH UNDESIRABLE BEHAVIORS

Methods of Changing Expectations

Talk about why. Set aside some time to talk about the reasons for your expectations. In the case of Harry and Glenda, they could talk about why she wants him to be with her more and why he wants to be with his friends a lot. When a couple spend a few evenings talking about their feelings and all of the subtle variations and possibilities, they frequently find a way to rearrange their views so that these are compatible or change them so that they are more workable or realistic.

Another advantage of this strategy is that it helps you better understand each other. Also, just spending the time together creates a feeling that the other one cares enough to do what he can in working things out. It can help you feel that your partner is trying to understand your point of view. That type of emotional support is very helpful.

Talk with other couples. It can be very helpful to talk with others about their expectations in marriage. You can make statements such as these:

—We have some differences of opinion about _____ and we're interested in getting some other opinions.

—How do you work out a budget?

—What do you do when one person does . . . ?

You need to be careful in using this strategy to make sure that you do not discuss parts of your marriage that would be better kept to yourself. For example, it would be unwise for couples to discuss the intimacies of each other's sexual interaction or to use these conversations to embarrass or coerce either person. There are, however, hundreds of areas in marriage about which it is useful to get opinions from others. For example, it can be very useful to discuss ways of relating to in-laws, budgeting, disciplining children, what to do about insurance, finding time to get everything done that you'd like to, how to buy a house, etc.

Recognize that most expectations should be flexible. There are a few role expectations that are tied to important moral and ethical ideals. For instance, you should not physically abuse a spouse, you should never be cruel to each other, you should not commit adultery, and you should not bear false witness about each other. But these rigid and inflexible expectations are surprisingly few in marriage. Most of your expectations are cultural beliefs that you glean from your parents or some other part of your culture, and they can be altered and changed according to your personal needs and wishes. Notice how flexible all of the following issues are:

—Who should handle the money?
—Who should do the cooking, cleaning, and ironing?
—Should the main meal be in the middle of the day or in the evening?
—How often should we visit in-laws?
—How should we discipline the children?
—How much influence should in-laws have?
—How often should we express affection?
—How frequently should we go out?

Most individuals grow up assuming that their way of doing things is the right way. They need to learn that their way is only *one* way. There are other ways that can be equally good and wise. Thus you can have a tremendous amount of flexibility in how you arrange or rearrange your interactions in marriage.

Avoid unrealistic expectations. Sometimes couples set their goals so high that they assure failure. You need to realize that you both need a little time to attain perfection, and you may need more than a *little* time. You climb mountains one step at a time, and you need to progress and grow the same way. This means that you can have long-term, ultimate goals of being at the top of some high mountains, but your immediate goals and desires should be some short-range goals that are within your immediate reach.

The Lord has given us the ultimate goal, "Therefore I would that ye should be perfect even as I, or your Father who is in heaven is perfect" (3 Nephi 12:48 and Matthew 5:48), but it may take some of us millennia to achieve this. His plan, therefore, provides for repentance and allows us to work at a pace that is realistic and manageable. Those who set unrealistically high standards for themselves create excessive guilt and anxiety about themselves and others, and this actually impedes their progress. They would be so much more wise to set realistic goals that they can attain, and temporarily accept some of their limitations and their spouses' limitations more gracefully.

The common pattern in the Latter-day Saint culture of setting unrealistic goals and then feeling guilty and defeated when they are not reached is delightfully illustrated with the tongue-in-cheek description of Sister Patti Perfect.

This is not to say that you should go to the other extreme and abandon all of your high standards and goals. You need to find a middle ground. You ought to keep your lofty long-term goals and realize they are just that—long-term. You ought to also have many intermediate goals and short-term goals so that you are "anxiously engaged" in improving yourself. And this can include some "godly sorrow" about the imperfections that are yours; but it ought to also include confidence and pride in what you are able to do. You should have enough goals and areas you are working on to make you stretch and lengthen your stride, but you ought not to try to run faster than you can lest you stumble on your own intentions.

Patti Perfect
by
Margaret B. Black
Midge W. Nielson

Many LDS women unconsciously compete with an idealized image of the already-perfect wife and mother who successfully incorporates all the demands of family, church, and society into her life. Although we have never met such a woman, we persist in believing she's out there somewhere. We can just imagine what she must accomplish in a day . . .

Patti gets up very early and says her personal prayers. She zips her slim, vigorous body into her warm-up suit and tiptoes outside to run her usual five miles (on Saturday she does ten). Returning home all aglow, she showers and then dresses for the day, in a tailored skirt and freshly starched and ironed blouse. She settles down for quiet meditation and scripture reading before preparing the family breakfast. The morning's menu calls for whole wheat pancakes, homemade syrup, freshly squeezed orange juice, and powdered milk (the whole family loves it).

With classical music wafting through the air, Patti awakens her husband and ten children. She spends a quiet moment with each and helps them plan a happy day. The children quickly dress in clothes that were laid out the night before. They cheerfully make their beds, clean their rooms, and do the individual chores assigned to them on the Family Work Wheel Chart. They assemble for breakfast the minute mother calls.

After family prayer and scripture study, the children all practice their different musical instruments. Father leaves for work on a happy note. All too soon it is time for the children to leave for school. Having brushed (and flossed) their teeth, the children pick up coats, book bags, and lunches they have prepared the night before and arrive at school five minutes early.

With things more quiet, Patti has storytime with her preschoolers and teaches them a cognitive reading skill. She feeds, bathes, and rocks the baby before putting him down for his morning nap. With baby sleeping peacefully and the three-year-old twins absorbed in creative play, Patti tackles the laundry and housework. In less than an hour, everything is in order. Thanks to wise scheduling and children who are trained to work, her house never really gets dirty.

Proceeding to the kitchen, Patti sets out tonight's dinner: frozen veal parmigiana that she made in quantity from her home-grown tomatoes and peppers. She then mixes and kneads twelve loaves of bread. While the bread rises, Patti dips a batch of candles to supplement her food storage. As the bread bakes, she writes in her personal journal and dashes off a few quick letters—one to her congressman and a couple of genealogy inquiries to distant cousins. Patti then prepares her miniclass lesson on organic gardening. She also inserts two pictures and a certificate in little

Paul's scrapbook, noting with satisfaction that all family albums are attractive and up-to-date. Checking the mail, Patti sees that their income tax refund has arrived—a result of having filed in January. It is earmarked for mission and college savings accounts. Although Patti's hardworking husband earns only a modest salary, her careful budgeting has kept the family debt free.

After lunch, Patti drops the children off at Grandma's for their weekly visit. Grandma enjoys babysitting and appreciates the warm loaf of bread. Making an extra call, Patti takes a second loaf to one of the sisters she is assigned to visit teach. A third loaf goes to the nonmember neighbor on the corner.

Patti arrives at the elementary school where she directs a special education program. A clinical psychologist, Patti finds this an excellent way to stay abreast of her field while raising her family. Before picking up her little ones, Patti finishes collecting for the charity fund drive.

Home again, Patti settles the children down for their afternoon naps. She spends some quiet time catching up on her reading and filing. As she mists her luxuriant house plants, the school children come through the door. Patti listens attentively to each one as they tell her about their day. The children start right in on their homework, with mother supervising and encouraging them. When all schoolwork is done, Patti and the children enjoy working on one of their projects. Today they work on the quilt stretched on frames in a corner of the family room.

Dinnertime and father arrive, and it is a special hour for the whole family. They enjoy Patti's well-balanced, tasty meal, along with stimulating conversation. After dinner, father and the children pitch in to clean up so that mom can relax. She enjoys listening to the sounds of laughter and affection that come from the kitchen.

With the teenage children in charge at home, mother and father attend an evening session at the temple. During the return trip, they sit close together as in courting days. "Well, dear," says Paul Perfect, "did you have a good day?" Pat reflectively answers, "Yes, I really did. But I feel I need more challenge in my life. I think I'll contact our family organization and volunteer to head up a reunion for August."

Methods of Changing Behavior

Sometimes it is easy to change behavior. Here are some examples:

Sam never calls Sue when he's going to work late, and she would like him to. Sue tells him how important it is to her, and from then on he does it.

Jack hasn't been praying as regularly as he should. He has good intentions; he just forgets. He and Jill decide that they will have their prayers at the same time, as that will help him remember. After that, he prays each morning and evening.

Bernard thinks Barbara toasts the bread too dark. He recognizes that she grew up that way because her whole family likes it dark, but it prefers it just barely a light brown. She thanks him for letting her know how he wants it and toasts his lighter.

At other times it is hard to change behavior. Some habits are formed over many years and are difficult to change. It takes a lot of discipline and work to change them even a little.

What can you do to change these behaviors?

There are many things you can do to change behavior. Four of these are: (1) change habits a little at a time, (2) use conditioning, (3) use Deutsch's principle, and (4) discuss the consequences.

Changing habits a little at a time. You haven't built your habits overnight; you have built them slowly and gradually. You break them the same way. Those who think they can break a deeply ingrained habit quickly are apt to discover later that they haven't really changed it.

Habits are like threads in a rope. If you try to break one thread or small piece of string, you can do so easily. If you put two pieces of thread together, it is a little harder, but you can still break them. When you put three or four together, it is difficult; but if you wrap the threads around your finger and pull hard, they pop. Breaking this many at once hurts your hand a little. When you add a few more and try to break them, it hurts you to try, and you can't break them. If you were to continue to add threads one by one, you would gradually create a piece of twine and then a small rope. Then you'd have a large rope, and then a massive rope that could tow the largest of ships and hold up thousands of tons. Gradually it would become so strong that there is no way it could be broken by pulling on it.

But even the strongest rope can be broken by reversing the process. You can take one thread away from the large rope and break it; then another, and then another. As you do this, gradually even the largest and strongest rope will slowly get smaller and weaker. Eventually you will only have one or two strands left, and you can easily break them. In this manner, the strongest ropes on earth can be broken by the weakest of people.

What does this teach you?

Habits are like ropes. They are made up of small, thin little acts that are easy to change when you change them one at a time. When you act the same way hundreds and thousands of times, you have a habit—and, like the rope, it is so strong that it is impossible to break immediately. You can try as hard as you can, and all it will do is hurt you to try. You cannot break the habit. You cannot change your behavior all at once. You can, however, change the way you act in any small moment. That time won't break the habit, and it takes concentration to go against it; but, just as with the threads on the rope, even the weakest person can take one thread and break it. Then, after you have changed one act many times, you will observe that your habit is becoming weaker. It then gets easier and easier to take a thread away and break it (change the way you act). Gradually you can break the most troublesome and difficult habit.

This has many implications for how you ought to act in marriage. For example, it means that you need to be patient and long-suffering with yourself and with your partner when you are trying to break bad habits. It means that some of them take months and years, even a lifetime, to break. And since you may have several different bad habits (large ropes), you cannot work on all of them at the same time and with the same energy and dedication. This means that you may have to live with some of them for a while, while you work on others. It means that you ought to be accepting and tolerant of your limitations and imperfections and be willing to forgive and forgive and forgive while you are in the slow process of perfecting yourself.

Use conditioning. You have undoubtedly heard about the Russian scientist Pavlov and his dogs. As all dogs will in such circumstances, his dogs would salivate when they saw him bringing their food. Pavlov started to ring a bell when he brought them the food, and he kept doing this till eventually the dogs would salivate when he rang the bell and didn't bring food. They had been *conditioned.* They had learned to associate the bell and the food so closely that they responded to the bell the same way they did to the food. This discovery about a century ago led scientists to more and more discoveries about how humans learn to do some things and avoid others. You can use these discoveries to help you change your behavior in your marriage.

One of the best ways to use conditioning employs a principle that Homans calls the success principle (Homans 1967, p. 33). It is a simple idea:

10. The Success Principle. The more often a person's activity is rewarded, the more likely he is to perform the activity.

The opposite is also true: The more a person is punished, the less likely he is to repeat an activity. How can you use this principle to help change your behavior? You can use it by going through several simple steps. These are:

1. First, use this principle in connection with specific actions that you can easily observe and count. You can use it to help do specific things like doing three kind acts a day or giving one compliment a day to someone else or "giving in" every other time when you have a disagreement.

2. Before you try to change, spend a period of time monitoring how you really do act. It is usually best to do this on paper. You ought to chart, count, tally, or check your behaviors for several days. This gives you a clear indication as to what you are doing, and sometimes you are surprised.

3. Next, think of some way to reward yourself for doing something right or punish yourself for doing something wrong. Even little ways can do it, like putting pennies in a jar every time you act the way you should. You can also tell yourself that you will get a certain reward, such as a movie, new dress, ball game, or dinner out, when you have performed at a certain level.

4. While you are trying to change, you need to again keep track of how you are actually behaving. This means you need to go through the tedious process of counting, monitoring, tallying, etc.

In today's society, people value economic and materialistic things, and so these things can be very effective reinforcers. You can use them to reward yourself and deny them to

yourself or take them away to punish. You need also to learn that there are social reinforcers. These are more subtle, less obvious, but they can be extremely powerful. Things
such as recognition, attention, praise, encouragement, thanks, affection, and closeness can
have extremely powerful effects. In fact, modern scientists believe that many undesirable
behaviors are learned through reinforcement patterns having social rewards. For example,
when you were a child you may have unconsciously learned that the only way you could
get your parents' undivided attention was to misbehave. When you did things right you
were ignored; you just blended into the woodwork. But when you got into trouble, your
parents were right there, and they were concerned about you, really concerned. Gradually
you learned to misbehave, and thus you created some undesirable habits.

There are two other aspects of this process that you ought to remember if you are going
to use it in your marriage. These are so important that if you ignore them, you may be like
your parents and experience unintended, undesired consequences. *You may actually do
more damage than good in your marriage.* What are these cautions?

First, rewards make much more difference than punishments. As the old saying has it, "It
is easier to catch flies with honey than vinegar." If you use punishments to change your
own behavior or the behavior of others, it creates resentments, animosity, and anger.
Therefore you would be well advised to use rewards liberally and punishments very rarely
and cautiously.

Second, most adults resent it when they are manipulated by others. They like to be in
control of their own lives. They like to do things the way they want to do them. They
appreciate their free agency, and they don't like to have it threatened or taken away.

What does this have to do with conditioning?

If you use conditioning on someone against his will or in a way he wouldn't like, you are
taking away part of his agency. You are *manipulating* him, and this is unkind, unethical,
and usually unwanted. It can cause very undesirable side effects in a marriage. So what do
you do? Whenever you want to use conditioning to change someone else's behavior, you
need to be sure that he would agree with the goals you are trying to reach. If you are trying
to change some undesirable behavior, it ought to be a *mutual* decision. You need to make
sure that you are unified in what you are trying to do. The person who is being conditioned has the right to decide that this is what he or she wants.

This means that the well-intentioned wife who wants her husband to be more active in
the Church should not punish him for his behavior. She should also not try rewarding him
with such things as affection or attention when he does things her way. Such behaviors will
build resentment and animosity toward the wife and the Church—and most of the time the
husband and wife will not know what is happening.

Another thing this means is that the husband who wants his wife to stay more within the
budget will just make matters worse by getting after her, scolding her, or berating her
(punishing her to get her to change her ways). They need to first find out if they are unified
about what ought to be done, and then, after they are unified, work out a plan together to

> There is so much good in the worst of us,
> And so much bad in the best of us,
> That it's hard to tell which one of us
> Ought to reform the rest of us.
>
> —Author unidentified

change the behavior. When this is done the wife (or husband) agrees to the reward or punishment arrangement, and not only will it be more effective, it will create solidarity in the relationship rather than divisiveness.

Use Deutsch's Law. Deutsch's law was discussed on pages 31-34, but it is so useful in changing behavior that it needs to be applied in this situation. The principle is this:

> *The more you act in a certain way,*
> *the more others around you*
> *also tend to act in the same way.*

This idea can help you change behavior when you want to help your spouse change his (or her) behavior. If you want him to become more considerate or kind (and he agrees that he wants to change), you can become more considerate or kind yourself, and this will help him change. If you want him to become more generous or helpful, you can become more generous or helpful. If you want another person to give in more, you can give in more than you have been doing. If you want your spouse to be more attentive, you can pay more attention to what the other person is saying. If you want the other person to be more sensitive to your feelings and goals, you can be more sensitive to his feelings and goals.

This principle is beautiful to use because it is so subtle and soothing in relationships. It is giving some of yourself to and for the other person. It is going the second mile. It is like oil on troubled waters, soft music, or a gentle rain. It usually creates more of what you want than you would think possible, and somehow it also makes other things better as you feel good about the changes you are making, and you feel closer and more deeply in love with each other. Perhaps this is why the Savior relied so much on this principle in his teachings about going the second mile, judging not, returning good for evil, turning the other cheek, the classic rule of doing unto others as you would have them do unto you, and the ultimate commandment of all—to love even as the Savior has loved us.

Evaluating consequences. Social scientists, in evaluating different ways of trying to change behavior, find that one of the effective ways is to evaluate the effects of what you are doing (Hoffman 1970; Rollins and Thomas 1979). You accomplish this by asking yourself and each other questions such as:

"What will happen if I keep doing what I am doing?"

"Is that what I want to happen?"

"If I act in this way, what will be the consequences or results?"

"How will it affect me and those I love and care about?"

"Will it make things better or worse?"

Social scientists have discovered that this is a very effective strategy for guiding children. It helps them discover some of the reasons for acting in correct ways, and then they feel much better about doing the right thing. It is much more effective than telling a child to do something "because we said so." It is the same with yourself and your spouse. As you think and ponder about the effects of what you do, it helps you find the strength and determination to correct undesirable things, and it gives you reassurance and confidence in the things that you are doing right.

Changing the Importance of Your Expectations

When you can't change your *expectations* or your *behavior*, you can resort to the third method of coping with undesirable behavior. You can tell yourself that it is not important. This is easy for little things like those in the following situation:

> *William is never on time. He walks into church at the end of the opening song, and if he tells others he will pick them up at a certain time, they know he'll never be there when he says he will. He has good intentions. He's just never on time. He and his wife have talked about it, and he has tried to change, but he doesn't seem to be able to. They've given up in trying to change him, and she's adjusted her life to it. After thirty-five years of marriage, she'd still rather have him change, but he probably won't. She tells herself that it doesn't make much difference in the eternal scheme anyway. After all, "time only is measured unto men" (Alma 40:8).*

Your success in changing the importance of misbehavior will depend upon how closely it is tied to things you value. One wife, when faced with the continual frustration of having a husband who refused to become active in their church, decided that in order to relieve the weekly tension in the home she would decrease the amount of importance she placed on religion, and so she too became inactive. In doing so, she did not take into account her own conscience and guilt feelings, and she was unable to continue being inactive. A behavior problem in an area of great concern usually cannot be resolved by simply convincing oneself that it is no longer important.

Learn to Live with It Without Any Changes

When you can't change your *expectations*, your *behavior*, or your beliefs about the *importance* of a problem, you're stuck! You don't like the behavior, and you can't get rid of it. Does this happen, really? Unfortunately, the answer is yes. In fact, it happens to all couples. It happens to saints and sinners, the good and the bad, the rich and the poor, the smart and the less gifted.

It would be pleasant never to have this happen in *your* marriage, and you may even be so idealistic that you tell yourself, "That won't happen to *us*." Unfortunately, life is sufficiently complicated, and humans are sufficiently human, that it usually happens in a number of areas in a marriage.

What do you do when this happens?

Again, there are several strategies that can help. One of them is to use the old saying, "Keep your eyes wide open before marriage and half-shut afterwards." Keeping your eyes half-shut afterwards means that you need to ignore some things. It means that you keep those things in the attic of your mind. For example, if your spouse squeezes the toothpaste in the middle and it bothers you, you can buy two tubes at a time and never be reminded of your spouse's imperfection in this area.

A second strategy is to use a mechanism we have mentioned earlier, which psychologists call "compensation." Whenever you are bothered by undesirable behavior, you think about all the other positive things. If you are concerned about your own behavior, you can remind yourself that you have been doing pretty well in several other areas. If you are upset by the behavior of your spouse, you can think of all of his other virtues. This, at least, helps put the imperfection in a larger perspective and keeps you from being too distressed by one particular fault.

A third strategy is to use what sociologists call *relative deprivation*. This means looking at your situation relative to others' situations. If you can observe that others also have problems it can help you live with your own situation.

A final strategy in helping you learn to live happily with your limitations and those of your spouse is to memorize the inspiring and helpful lines of the following well-known poem:

> God, grant me the serenity
> To accept the things I cannot change,
> The courage to change the things I can,
> And the wisdom to know the difference.

SUMMARY

This chapter has discussed ways of coping with undesirable behavior. Some undesirable behavior in marriage occurs simply because the man and woman were raised in different families with different customs, traditions, and habits. Other undesirable behavior occurs because all of us are in a mortal and imperfect condition in this life. These two factors make it impossible to avoid undesirable behavior. Everyone will experience some undesirable behavior in his marriage—but he'd also have some if he didn't marry. The chapter points out that the first thing to do in coping with behavioral problems is to determine whether there are also disunity problems. If the situation also involves disunity, you need first to try to deal with it. (The skills and methods of creating unity are discussed in chapter 9.) After you have dealt with the unity issue, you have four main alternatives in coping with undesirable behavior. These are: (1) changing your expectations, (2) changing the behavior, (3) changing the beliefs about how important it is, (4) or learning to live with the situation—happily or unhappily. Several strategies for effecting each of these alternatives are then discussed.

SUPPLEMENTARY READINGS

Covey, Stephen R. *Spiritual Roots of Human Relations.* Salt Lake City: Deseret Book Co., 1972.

Dyer, William G. *Creating Closer Families: Principles of Positive Family Interaction.* Provo, Utah: Brigham Young University Press, 1975.

Kimball, Spencer W. *The Miracle of Forgiveness.* Salt Lake City: Bookcraft, Inc., 1969.

12

EFFECTIVE MONEY MANAGEMENT

And unto one he gave five talents,
to another two,
and to another one. . . .
For unto every one that hath shall be given,
and he shall have abundance:
but from him that hath not
shall be taken away even that which he hath.

—Matthew 25:15, 29

Research indicates that the financial area of marriage causes more arguments than any other area (Blood 1962), including in-laws relations, TV, religious differences, intimacy problems, recreation, or children. It is not the lack of money or the love of money that causes these problems, but simply the way couples *manage* their money. The problems arise when they don't plan wisely, don't spend wisely, don't keep track of what they do—or when they differ on what they want and can't find ways to agree. Too many are like the following couples:

"The more we make the worse off we are. There just isn't enough to go around. And then George bought those golf clubs last week. I was so upset! I told him that if this was the way he was going to act, I was going to go out and buy me a new dress. I need it a lot more than he needs those old clubs."

"But the loan company said that we could combine all of our payments into one, and it would be less than we are paying now. If we do that we might be able to buy the TV now."

"We just don't have enough to pay tithing now. It all goes for rent and food and the car payment and other necessities. We're just barely getting by; we're not making enough. Maybe if I took that other job we'd be getting enough that we could pay tithing."

THE MANAGEMENT CYCLE*

There is a cycle in the way you ought to manage money, and every couple repeatedly moves through it. They begin each week or month as they sit down with their bills and as they pay for their groceries. The cycle is the sequence of *planning, acting,* and *recording,* as shown below. The *way* you conduct this cycle makes a lot of difference in your life. If you pass through the cycle wisely, you will be able to accomplish economic goals that poor managers never reach.

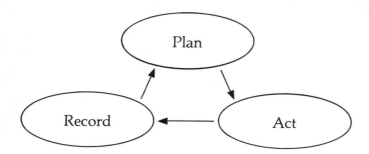

One fortunate aspect of this cycle is that there is more than one way to complete it. There is no standard "right" way to do it effectively. Some people are detailed planners. They like to make precise budgets and then stick to the budget by keeping accurate books. Others are impulsive and like a freer style of life. They enjoy doing things on the spur of the moment and having a lot of flexibility in their plans. Still others like to plan but prefer to keep their plans in their heads rather than on paper.

Is it possible for all of these couples
to use the management cycle wisely?

The answer is yes. It depends on *how they act* in the cycle. The cycle allows for flexibility if they understand what they are doing and do it well. This leads us to the question of how to be wise in each phase of the cycle.

Planning

This phase occurs as you decide where your money should go. It is important because if you don't decide beforehand where your money will go, you'll wonder later where it went.

An example of a lack of planning was provided by a young married couple known to the authors. They had set a preliminary financial goal to save a certain amount of money before their marriage. This they did, then they got married. What they did not do, how-

---

* The ideas in this part of the chapter were gleaned from Robert Bohn's *Budget Book,* Provo, Utah: BYU Press, 1976.

ever, was to plan precisely what it was they were going to do with the money they had saved. They had a general plan of using portions of it each month to supplement their part-time employment while they went to school, but they made no specific plans. They also knew they enjoyed pizza, particularly at a certain restaurant.

Five months into the school year, they discovered that their entire summer's savings were gone. Trying to reconstruct the disaster, they traced backwards in their checkbook and discovered that 80 percent of their savings had been spent on pizza. They had discovered they were pizzaholics and were in need of better planning and restraint.

Who should do the planning? It depends on the couple. Some couples want the husband and wife to sit down together to develop and revise their budget. Others want to divide the planning. Still others will want one person to do most of the work but get the partner's approval before the plan is implemented. *Flexibility is the rule.* It doesn't matter who does it, as long as the people (1) do a minimum amount of planning, and (2) work out a system that they both feel good about.

What type of budget should you have? Should it be a weekly budget, a monthly or annual budget, or all three? Again, this depends on the couple. Some couples work best with a weekly budget. Others will find that a monthly budget fits their needs best, and others will prefer a different system. This depends on when and how the breadwinner gets paid, and on the personal tastes of both the husband and wife.

How detailed should the budget be? This, too, depends on the couple. Some want a budget that has detailed categories. For example, when they are planning the part of their budget that deals with food, they want to specify the amounts for the milk bill, meat, fresh vegetables, and staples. Others are satisfied to lump all of the food costs into a total sum. You need to think about different systems and then choose or invent one that you feel good about.

> *The key is to find a system that both the
> husband and wife feel good about.*

This does not say that you should find a system of planning that only one of you thinks is wise. It also does not say that you are finished when you find a system that you both *think* is a good one. The key is in the emotional response you have. You need to find a budget that you both *feel* good about. A marriage is, more than anything else, an emotional relationship, and you need to deal with your emotions as you are refining your method of planning expenses.

Many couples make the mistake of thinking that planning about money is a rational process in which the most important criteria are accuracy, accountability, logic, and efficiency. These couples are planting the seeds of economic success—and marital failure. They need to realize that, as important as these criteria are, the most important criterion is the emotional reaction. The other criteria are intertwined in the sense that you need a certain amount of efficiency, logic, and accuracy in order to have positive emotional reactions to the economic part of your life. But you don't want to make the mistake of paying attention to the more rational criteria while ignoring the emotional ones. That

Terry and Patty Baker budget so they can tell their money where to go rather than ask where it went.

would be every bit as foolish as paying attention only to short-term emotional gratification and ignoring efficiency, logic, and accuracy. An example of this follows:

One husband had coldly and rationally decided there should be no money spent on Christmas and birthdays one year, since the money was needed elsewhere. From a logical and "wise" financial planning standpoint, the husband was probably correct, and he tried to stick with the plan. The wife, however, felt he should have been named "Scrooge," and she had such an emotional reaction to the plan that their arguing was not worth the savings.

How do you plan your budget? The budget is a plan for spending your income; therefore, the first step is to identify your probable income. For some this is very easy. If you have a salaried job, you can easily estimate your weekly, monthly, or annual income. Those who have irregular sources of income have more difficulty. For example, if you work in sales, your income may depend on commissions that may have wide seasonal variations. If you are a married student, you may have much more income during the summers but little coming in during the academic year. Whatever the case, you need to make some estimate of your probable income if you are to plan effectively. Activity 12:1 at the end of the chapter can help you make these estimates.

The next step in preparing a budget is to decide how much money should be spent in various areas. These projections can be fairly brief or they can be more detailed. Activity 12:1 at the end of the chapter shows one way of dividing these expenses.

The budget in Activity 12:1 is fairly detailed. It has the advantage of helping the couple know fairly closely where the money is to be spent—but it has the disadvantage of not being very flexible. There are many other ways of dividing expenses, and the two following examples illustrate ways that two families do it. The Smiths are a young couple with one infant, and the husband is still a student. The Jacobsens have a larger family, with elementary-school-age and teenage children. These two actual budgets should be viewed as examples, not as "ideal" ways to do things.

The Smiths

Usual monthly income after taxes $715

Savings:

Account for next baby	20
Regular savings account	25
Emergency savings account	20
Savings for tuition/books	40
	105

Fixed Expenses:

Tithing and fast offering	70
Rent	140
Utilities	60
Installment loan on furniture	40
Car payment	75
	385

Flexible Expenses:

Food	75
Medical expenses	15
Clothing	25
Automobile expenses	40
His personal money	5
Her personal money	5
Miscellaneous	60
	225

Monthly Total $715

The Jacobsens

Usual monthly income before taxes.................................... $2,500

Taxes:
Federal...	200
FICA	100
State..	44

Savings:
Regular account	100
Account for next automobile............................	75
Account for children's missions.........................	75
Account for food storage...............................	150
X-mas & vacation savings account	50
Retirement program	50

Fixed Expenses:
Tithing, fast offerings, etc..............................	275
House payment.......................................	300
Utilities	80
Milk bill...	35
Music lessons for children	45
Donation to grandparents	35
Telephone bill..	25
Donation to family organization.........................	50

Flexible Expenses:
Food, household items..................................	350
Monthly bills (charge accounts)	200
Miscellaneous (clothing, furn.)	250

These budgets are effective for the couples using them, and they illustrate the variation that is necessary in different life situations and personal preferences. The Smiths have a large percentage of their income going to educational needs. The Jacobsen family uses a strategy of having a number of savings accounts to prepare for expenses. The Jacobsens also make contributions to their elderly parents and to a family organization to promote genealogical and missionary work. They also tend to group larger amounts into lump sums. The point to ponder here is that couples need to determine their own needs and preferences and adjust their budgets as income and life circumstances change.

Remember, no plan is a plan—a plan for disaster.

The Acting Phase of the Cycle

This part of the management cycle is concerned with where you spend money for the things you need—where you actually put the money into savings accounts, pay bills, and make investments. In this step, *flexibility* is again the rule. Some families have found a joint checking account to be a useful system. Others have found it best for the husband to have his checking account and the wife to have hers. One family known to the authors has about eight checking accounts, each for different purposes. Some couples prefer the "bottles in the cupboard" or "envelopes" system. In these systems, the paycheck is cashed and the money is then put in the bottle or envelopes. When the husband or wife needs to buy something, they go to the envelopes or bottles for the funds. (In this system the source tends to dry up rapidly and unexpectedly unless a record is kept of withdrawals and balances. These systems are especially effective for many couples in the early months of marriage, when it is important to economize, when they have few categories of expenses, and when they want to work together.

Some couples find it effective for one partner to handle all the money while the other partner receives an "allowance." Other couples are so inept in handling money that they find it necessary to always work together to avoid making errors like forgetting to write something in the checkbook, writing down the wrong figures, adding or subtracting wrong figures, or forgetting certain bills. One couple known to the authors were so clumsy in this area that their checking account balanced only twice in the first fifteen years of their marriage. They relied on a "general impression" of how much money was in the bank. Their system was effective for them, but it was not accurate until one of the children became old enough to write the checks and balance the monthly statement.

Several skills can be helpful in this phase of the management cycle. For example, being aware of when different products are on sale can help save money. Knowing how to shop efficiently for food and clothing can also help. Comparing prices before buying can result in considerable savings on items such as clothing, tools, automobiles, insurance, appliances, furniture, etc. Most importantly, we can follow the counsel of our prophet by living within our means so that we don't need to pay the costs of interest on loans or finance charges. While it is difficult to go without while we are putting money away for something, in the long run we usually obtain what we desire and the financial savings are substantial as compared with going into debt for purchases.

The Recording Phase of the Cycle

There are many different ways to keep track of where your money is spent. Some couples prefer to keep a detailed set of books with journals and ledgers that help them know where everything is spent. One couple known to the authors keeps such books, and they know where every dollar in their entire marriage has gone. They enjoy their system and would be uncomfortable with less accountability. Other couples use other methods such as writing checks extensively and then using the returned checks to monitor how much is spent for various items. The checks are also useful as documentations of expenses in filling out deductions on income tax forms. Some couples save receipts to help them know where their money goes. A few couples rely on their memories and have an adequate system of knowing where their money is spent. While this works for some, for most it would be like recording in the sand.

Wise stewards develop a system of keeping track that assists them in periodically evaluating what they have been doing with their funds. Then they take these records into account in revising their budget plans and in knowing what they can and cannot afford. Those who are less wise, who don't want to take the extra few minutes to plan and record at all, have the benefit of freedom—they are free from the burdens of planning and recording. But unfortunately, this freedom is usually expensive, especially whenever financial resources don't go as far as they could. Without the help of any records, these people must then decide which things they will have and which they will go without.

WHAT ABOUT INDEBTEDNESS?

Some people think that credit is bad and that you should never buy anything on credit. That is like saying that fire is bad. Neither fire nor credit is inherently good or bad. It is what people do with them that is good or bad. You can do very effective things with fire, or you can be destroyed by it. It is the same with credit: If it is handled wisely it can be useful, but used unwisely, it can be destructive.

There are many different kinds of credit, but they can be grouped into two basic types, *open credit* and *installment credit.* In *open credit,* you receive a service or product and promise to pay for it at a later time; it does not cost you any more to pay later. This is the kind of credit offered by many professionals such as doctors and dentists. You receive a service and pay a bill at the end of the month. This is also the kind of credit used by utility companies such as the telephone and gas companies.

The biggest disadvantage of this type of credit is that some people cannot control their spending as easily when all they have to do is "charge it." The result is that many couples overspend. But this type of credit can be very useful because receipts are provided for each transaction and it is easy to document where the money is spent. It is also convenient because many couples learn to pay their bills in a monthly or weekly cycle. Another advantage of this type of credit is that it can be helpful in minor emergencies. For example, having a bank card or credit card can be useful in traveling when unexpected expenses like automobile repairs or medical expenses are incurred. Those families who do not have a card or two should carry cash or traveler's checks for these unexpected expenses.

With *installment credit* you purchase something on credit or get a loan and agree to pay a finance charge or interest for the privilege of paying the debt later. This is the type of credit you use in getting loans for major purchases such as automobiles, furniture, and a house. It is also the kind of credit you use when you charge more on a credit card than you can pay for when the bill arrives. This type of credit is very expensive, and the amount you pay for interest can be extremely high.

While a modest use of installment credit may be necessary, it is very easy to overuse it because there are so many enticements to buy, buy, buy. And advertising makes things so attractive that it is easy to succumb and buy more than you need. Advertisements are designed, of course, to appeal to emotions rather than to intellect, and those who are easily persuaded need to be especially wary. An additional complication is that the unfamiliar and sometimes lengthy wording in contracts may leave the uninitiated with only a confused idea of the actual finance costs.

Most couples need to use an installment system to purchase a house, because there is seldom another feasible way. Installment credit is also useful in business transactions, because it can help you gain access to larger blocks of money or goods; if you handle these wisely, you can pay the finance charge and still make money. Beyond these two uses, installment buying becomes very expensive. Many people think it is wise to get a loan whenever they need to buy a car or a major appliance, and occasionally it is. Much of the time, however, it is appropriate in the short run and foolish in the long run. When you realize that the couch is getting old or the washer is making funny noises, you would be wise to start putting some money away *before you need to make the purchase* so you can pay for it at the time of purchase. Occasionally it is necessary to buy something on time, but you will be ahead if you make this the exception rather than the rule.

The main point here is that it is tremendously expensive to use installment credit. With today's interest rates, you end up paying much more than the item is worth, at the same time keeping yourself financially strapped as you pay the debt.

There are many other reasons to avoid this type of debt. One is that research (Burgess and Cottrell 1939) has shown indebtedness to be correlated with marital miseries. Scientists are not sure whether indebtedness contributes to marital dissatisfaction or whether dissatisfaction contributes to installment buying. It is likely that the causality goes both ways. The important point is that they tend to go together, and this argues for avoiding indebtedness.

Another reason for avoiding installment buying is that the Church leaders have given very clear counsel regarding it. They have argued persuasively that Church members should avoid indebtedness except for the purchase of a house or for an emergency medical expense, etc. Typical of this advice are these admonitions:

> Elder Marvin J. Ashton: Avoid finance charges except for homes, education, and other vital investments. Buy consumer durables with cash. Avoid installment credit and be careful with your use of credit cards. (Ashton 1975.)

> Elder Ezra Taft Benson: If you must incur debt to meet the reasonable necessities of life—such as buying a house and furniture—then, I implore you, as you value your solvency and happiness, buy within your means.

> So use credit wisely—to acquire an education, a farm, to own a home. But resist the temptation to plunge into a property far more pretentious or spacious than you really need. (Benson 1962, p. 10.)

> President J. Reuben Clark, Jr.: It is a rule of our financial and economic life in all the world that interest is to be paid on borrowed money. May I say something about interest? Interest never sleeps nor sickens nor dies; it never goes to the hospital; it works on Sundays and holidays; it

never takes a vacation; it never visits nor travels; it takes no pleasure; it is never laid off work nor discharged from employment; it never works on reduced hours; it never has short crops nor droughts; it never pays taxes; it buys no food; it wears no clothes; it is unhoused and without home and so has no repairs, replacements, no shingling, plumbing, painting, or whitewashing; it has neither wife, children, father, mother, nor kinfolk to watch over and care for; it has no love, no sympathy; it is as hard and soulless as a granite cliff. Once in debt, interest is your companion every minute of the day and night; you cannot shun it or slip away from it; you cannot dismiss it; it yields neither to entreaties, demands, or orders; and whenever you get in its way or cross its course or fail to meet its demands, it crushes you. (Clark 1938, pp. 102-3.)

How Can You Avoid Debt?

You will likely agree that you should make every effort to avoid indebtedness, but you may still find yourself making some monthly payments on a loan or two . . . or three or four . . . or five or six. You believe, but somehow you aren't able to attain your ideal. There are several strategies that can help; four of them are described below:

Go slowly. You need to approach marriage with the expectation that it will take a few years to become established economically. You need to acquire your house and furniture and cars slowly. You may think you need to set up your house on the same economic level as your parents' home; after all, it is the style of life you are accustomed to. It is what you have known. You fail to realize that it took your parents twenty to twenty-five years to acquire what they have, and it ought also to take you a while. You need to realize that struggling together in the early years of married life can help build bonds and ties and love in a marital relationship. Working together for common causes and goals builds closeness. Obtaining your material possessions too rapidly by going into debt for them and then worrying about financial burdens has just the opposite effect. It is divisive and destructive. You are much better off getting by with an old clunker for a car and living with borrowed or used or handmade furniture while you save up to purchase your own. You are much worse off when you go into debt and start off "right," as you think, by getting all the things you want. Actually it is just the opposite—this is starting off dead wrong.

Many middle-aged couples look back on their first few struggling years as the happiest years of their marriage. They "got by" with little, helped each other, and did without. Then, after they became established economically and had less mutual effort, they became more complacent, and their relationship lost a certain cohesion, radiance, and beauty. It is very different to talk with couples in the first year or two of their marriage. Many of them are deeply in debt with car payments, furniture payments, house payments, loan payments, and have a nice house, nice car, nice furniture, and nice clothing. They have the illusion that their quickly acquired and easily acquired material possessions will help their marriage. Unfortunately, they also have depressing times paying their bills and arguing about finances, while secretly blaming each other or someone else for their troubles. They have the Midas touch: They have turned their lives into material success, and, *unknown to them,* it is destroying the things they care about the most.

The wise go slowly in obtaining material possessions.

Modern advertising makes it easy to spend more than we should.

As the scripture says in another context (D&C 10:4), you should not try to run faster or labor more than you have means to do.

Pay yourselves second. The first thing a Latter-day Saint couple should do with income is set aside ten percent as tithing. They should "pay the Lord first" and do so with a willing heart. Those who have the attitude of giving because they want to will receive many blessings. They will become more generous and kind and charitable. They will also feel better about themselves and thereby increase their self-esteem. The Lord has indicated that the windows of heaven will be opened to bless them. Your attitude toward your giving makes more difference than the giving, because when you give begrudgingly you deprive yourself of many of the blessings. In many ways, people would be better off not to give anything than to give unwillingly.

The next thing you should do in refining your financial posture is allocate money to a savings program. You ought to "pay yourself" second, and ten percent is a good figure to put aside in a savings program. It will allow you to build up and maintain enough savings that you can avoid installment credit, and many of you who are earning ordinary incomes can put part of the savings into an investment program that will gradually provide more and more income. If you can't take ten percent out at the time, you ought to take eight or five percent *but have a continuous substantial savings program.* If you take ten percent for tithing and ten percent for savings *first,* you then need to adjust your standard of living so that you can live on the remaining eighty percent. This is a very different strategy from thinking one hundred percent of your income is available to spend and then taking the tithing and savings last. Most people who do this find that they don't pay tithing or accumulate savings.

Most banks and credit unions have programs for automatically transferring money from a checking account to a savings account. These programs are effective because you don't have to go to the effort to take the money out each month. It is automatically done for you, and you never see the money.

Have specialized savings programs. Some couples find it useful to have different savings programs. For example, they have one account for investments such as stocks, bonds, land, or gold purchases. This can be used for income later or as part of a retirement program. They may also have an account for major expenses that occur infrequently, such as Christmas and vacations. It is also a good idea to have a savings account of five hundred to a thousand dollars that is for emergencies. Then, when the water heater goes out, the transmission needs rebuilding, or you need a new refrigerator, rug, washer, TV, or whatever, you can use your emergency account rather than take out a loan. This could save you ten to thirty percent on the major item you are purchasing. You need to remember then to bring the emergency account back up to normal as soon as possible after you take from it.

Some families also find it useful to start savings accounts for their children. These can be used for missions and college and at the same time can teach children early in life the process of saving rather than borrowing. The children can sign for deposits and keep the records themselves, and this adds excitement and interest, increasing the learning process.

Buy quality. When you are buying major items such as furniture, tools, appliances, and equipment, it is wise to purchase quality merchandise. Some couples learn this the hard way when they are first married. They see furniture stores' advertisements offering to "furnish" three rooms for five hundred dollars or get other "package" programs in which they seem to get a lot of items for the money. These packages usually have the lowest quality possible. The goods are made to look attractive while they are new, but they wear out or break very quickly. Most of the time the couple would have been better off to accumulate a few items of good quality at a time, and live a little longer in a furnished apartment or with borrowed or hand-me-down items. It takes a little longer to establish yourself this way, but in the long run you are much better off because the furniture or equipment that you get will last longer, need fewer repairs, be more serviceable, look better longer, and in the end be much more economical.

A good way to shop so that you know what you are getting is to talk with friends or relatives who have purchased similar items several years earlier. This will help you find out where the quality items are. Then it is wise to find out what the stripped-down models cost and determine how much is added for each package of extras or frills. For example, if you are buying a TV, you ought to find out what the basic model costs and then see what additional features such as the luxury cabinet, bigger speakers, remote control, and zoom features cost. You can then determine which of the various options you can really afford.

The same process should be followed for cars, appliances, furniture, draperies, and all of the other major things you buy.

SUMMARY

This chapter has discussed the importance of effective money management and a number of skills you can use in becoming an effective money manager. The cycle of management is discussed—the process of planning, acting, and recording, repeated again and again. Skills in consumership are also discussed, as are the wise and unwise uses of credit.

ACTIVITY 12:1
Your Income

Reserve Assets
    Savings account $_____
    Cash reserve   _____
    Stocks, bonds, etc.   _____
        TOTAL RESERVES: $_____

Monthly Income
    Husband's income   _____
    Wife's income   _____
    Bonuses, commissions   _____
    $$ from parents   _____
    V. A. benefits, pension   _____
    Social security benefits   _____
    Welfare benefits   _____
    State rehabilitation   _____
    Interest, dividends   _____
    Life insurance (loan value)   _____
    Real estate income   _____
    Loan payments received   _____
    Scholarship, grant, loan   _____
    Other   _____
        TOTAL RESOURCES/INCOME $_____

Your Expenses
Saving and Spending Plan

Uncontrollable Fixed Expenses
    Taxes and social security $_____
Controllable Fixed Expenses
    House payments (or rent)   _____

Donations (tithing, etc.)   _____
Food   _____
Utilities, phone   _____
Housing upkeep, furnishings   _____
Insurance (medical, life)   _____
Transportation
   Auto payments   _____
   Gas, oil   _____
   Maintenance   _____
Medical, dental expenses   _____
Clothing, laundry   _____
Education, books, etc.   _____
Grooming, clothes, etc.   _____
Other   _____
Other   _____
Variable Expenses
   Entertainment, movies, vacation _____
   Hobbies, snacks   _____
   Other   _____
     TOTAL EXPENSES $_____

SUPPLEMENTARY READINGS

Ashton, Marvin J. *One for the Money.* Salt Lake City: Deseret Book Co., 1975.
Bohn, Robert E. *A Budget Book and Much More.* Provo, Utah: Robert F. Bohn, 1974.
Wolf, Harold A. *Personal Finance.* 5th ed. Boston: Allyn and Bacon, Inc., 1978.
Tanner, N. Eldon. "Constancy Amid Change." *Ensign,* November 1979, pp. 80-82.

13

THE SOCIAL NETWORKS AROUND MARRIAGE

Therefore shall a man leave his father and his mother,
and shall cleave unto his wife.

—Genesis 2:24

And he shall turn the heart of the fathers to the children,
and the heart of the children to their fathers.

—Malachi 4:6

Your family does not exist in a vacuum. It is a delicate social system that is closely tied to a larger network of other systems. For example, you interact as a married couple with relatives, schools, hospitals, employment, neighborhoods, and churches. Each of these other systems has an influence on your family, and some have a great deal of influence. Inflation and in-laws can make a big difference, and your interaction with your employment determines what time you will arise from bed as well as retire, when you work, and when you play.

The accompanying diagram illustrates the complexity of the social network around a marriage and family. It shows that there are more systems than you may realize, and they make more difference than you might think.

It is important to realize that some parts of your network are unique to this life, and some will be with you eternally. Systems such as governments, hospitals, businesses, labor unions, and service clubs are, of course, unique to this life. Other parts of your network, such as your parents and grandparents, your married children and grandchildren, your brothers and sisters, and the patriarchal order, are part of your eternal network. These relationships begin in this life, but they can, if you are righteous, continue forever. It is also likely that you will have other systems that will be eternally with you. For example, you will doubtless have friends in the next life, and you will need to find ways to interact with them. You will also have people who will reside close to you, neighbors in neighborhoods, and you will need to interact with them. There will also be other systems in your post-mortal life that you don't have now. For example, those married couples who become gods will associate and work with networks of angels who will assist them, and will also have large families of spirit children with whom they will interact.

What does all of this complexity mean?
And what should we do about these networks?

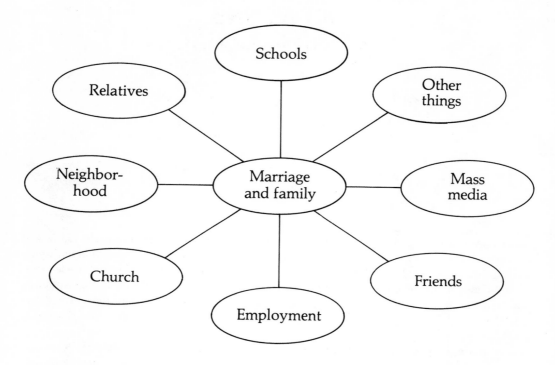

It is not possible to ignore these networks. We don't have the freedom to ignore them, and we wouldn't want to if we could. Our social networks provide essential services, and they help us attain our goals. *What you need to do is learn how these networks influence you and how you can interact with them effectively.* That's the goal of this chapter.

A GENERAL PRINCIPLE

There are no simple rules about interaction within the many systems in the social network. There is, however, one general principle that can help. The key idea in this principle was discovered by Aristotle about two thousand years ago. He suggested that one key to the good life is to avoid going to extremes. Too much or too little of certain things tends to be bad, and you are usually better off staying in the middle of the road. He called this idea the "golden mean." The *mean* is the average or middle of something. Aristotle suggested that finding the mean or middle usually leads to the greatest happiness or joy.

The principle that uses this idea is:

11. The Golden Mean: Finding moderation by avoiding extremes generally leads to the most desirable results.

It is obvious that people should not seek the golden mean in every area of life. There are some areas in which the more you have of something, the better. One example is honesty. You wouldn't want to settle for a moderate amount of honesty by avoiding too little or too much of it. You wouldn't want to be honest some of the time, but be careful to not overdo it. With honesty and other values and behaviors that are purely moral, the more the better.

This raises the question, "When is finding moderation truly a 'golden' idea?" The authors think the best answer is that whenever something involves an investment of *time, effort, energy,* or *emphasis,* Artistotle is right, and we ought to seek moderation. Too much or too little will be unwise. The degree to which you interact with friends is an example. It takes time and energy to interact with friends, and moderation is wise. You can interact too little with them, and when you do this you feel lonely, isolated, and out of circulation. On the other hand, you can spend so much time with them that you create different problems. You don't accomplish other things and your life is lopsided.

It is the same with employment. If you work too little, you lack the necessities of life such as food, shelter, clothes, and medicines. But if you moonlight on several jobs, put in a lot of overtime, or stay at the office too much, things won't go well at home. There is a moderate level of time, effort, energy, and involvement that you ought to seek in your work, and you need to determine what it is and maintain it.

The golden mean is very useful in your learning how to interact with the social networks around you. The general rule is that though you need to be involved with each of the areas of your complex network, you need to determine the optimal amount and not become too involved with one or two areas. You should be involved with some systems more than others, and these will change as you move from one stage of life to another. For example, when you retire you will become less involved with employment, but during the years when your children are between six and eighteen you will be highly involved with education. You need to continually evaluate each of the separate parts of your social network to determine whether you are involved too little or too much.

Interaction with Relatives

The scriptures provide a few guidelines as to how you ought to relate to your relatives. At the beginning of marriage the partners should leave their fathers and mothers and set up a separate home of their own. President Spencer W. Kimball has elaborated on this teaching:

> Sometimes in marriage there are other cleavings, in spite of the fact that the Lord said, "Thou shalt love thy wife with all thy heart, and shalt cleave unto her and none else" (D&C 42:22). This means just as completely that "thou shalt love thy husband with all thy heart and shall cleave unto him and none else." Frequently, people continue to cleave unto their mothers and their fathers and their friends. Sometimes mothers will not relinquish the hold they have had upon their children, and husbands as well as wives return to their mothers and fathers for advice and

Close ties with relatives adds richness to the lives of all.

counsel and to confide; whereas cleaving should be to the wife or husband in the most things, and all intimacies should be kept in great secrecy and privacy from others. Couples do well to immediately find their own home, separate and apart from that of the in-laws on either side. The home may be very modest and unpretentious but still it is an independent domicile. Their married life should become independent of her folks and his folks. The couple love their parents more than ever; they cherish their counsel; they appreciate their association; but they must live their own lives, being governed by their own prayerful considerations after they have received the counsel from those who should give it. To cleave does not mean merely to occupy the same home; it means to adhere closely, to stick together. (1976, pp. 24-25.)

The intricate balance suggested here is beautiful. You ought to leave your parents, and be independent from them—to stand on your own four feet as a couple—but it is not wise to become *too* independent. The principles of the patriarchal order still operate. You ought to seek counsel by asking your parents what they think about some of the major decisions you face in life. You ought to have the freedom to go against the advice if you wish, but their views should be taken into account as you make decisions.

Again, as with most things, you can operate at differing levels of perfection. At the highest level, a couple will feel a deep love and respect for their parents, and the parents will do the kinds of things that deserve this love and respect. The father is a patriarch for all of his posterity, and the mother is an important person who gives wise counsel and love to her children, grandchildren, and great-grandchildren. The patriarch who is a grandfather still presides over his posterity, and he has an interest in the welfare of his married children and their children whenever and however he and his children feel comfortable. He gently shares his wisdom by giving counsel, blessings, and advice. As the younger generations reach maturity, they become responsible for their own lives, and they therefore have the freedom to accept, modify, or reject the advice of their parents. In short, the role of the patriarch who presides over grown children is that of a counselor and advisor rather than a director or controller. The patriarch should not resent it when his children or grandchildren choose to do things differently than he would, since they have agency over their lives. He needs to accept the fact that they have the responsibility and freedom to make their own decisions. They will learn by their wise choices and by their mistakes, and they need love and acceptance after making both.

As Malachi taught (Malachi 4:6), the hearts of fathers and mothers should be turned to their children and the hearts of the children turned to their fathers and mothers. This means that there should be strong bonds of affection and love that will last through the eternities. It means that parents and children should interact, visit, and do things together in ways that will promote good feelings and love and harmony. It does not mean that married couples need to spend all of their time with their relatives. It means that an optimal involvement is *some* interaction, *some* concern, and *some* attention, but not so much that it interferes with the other aspects of life that also compete for attention, effort, and energy.

Some people are not able to interact with their relatives at this high level. In their less-than-perfect condition, they don't have the patience, tact, and interpersonal skill that this ideal interaction demands. For example, a person's parents may be so conditioned in the traditions of the world that their attempts at giving him advice and counsel would be more like commands or bribes—they may be manipulative ploys with strings attached. In these less-than-ideal conditions, some people cannot go to their parents for advice and counsel. And some do not have feelings of love, respect, and admiration for their parents or other relatives.

When relatives operate at a terrestrial or telestial level in this part of their lives, they ought to keep the ideals in mind as something to ultimately strive for, and then make the best of their situation as it is. This may mean that when you visit your parents you restrict the topics of discussion so that you don't delve into issues that divide you. It may be that in some families only one person will have a continuing relationship with one of the sets of parents. If this is the best you can do at the present time, you ought to rejoice in the good that does exist in the situation, be as positive and pleasant as possible, and be satisfied with the blessings you have. At the same time, you can do everything possible to gradually improve this aspect of life. You need to recognize, however, that you have little control over the way others behave, and you may live your entire life with a less-than-ideal relationship with your kin.

Sometimes it is not relatives that prevent you from having a desirable type of interaction. The problem may be with yourself or your spouse. For example, one person may find it very difficult to cut the apron strings. He may go home regularly, depend on the opinions of his parents, or rely on them for affection and love. When problems such as these occur, you need to recognize that you have trouble and use the skills discussed in chapters 8 and 9 to grow and progress by dealing creatively with those problems. Different solutions work for different couples. For example, it may be that one individual remains overly dependent on his or her parents because the spouse does not meet important needs of affection, security, or tenderness. In other situations, it is merely a matter of forcing yourself to take the last step in growing up. A good way to do this would be to move a long distance away from the parents, to correct the problem. Couples need to determine where they are in this dimension of their lives, what they need to do, and what will help them progress and grow.

The World of Work

Since very few people inherit enough wealth that they can go through life without an occupation, each marriage needs someone to provide economic necessities. The traditional pattern is for the husband to be the provider, but you need to be careful not to underestimate the ways in which the wife has also been traditionally involved in providing economic necessities. A century ago the wife worked long hours to help with these necessities—spinning, canning, baking, tanning leathers, caring for animals such as chickens and cows to provide eggs and milk. She spent many hours each week washing and ironing clothes, sewing, mending, curing meats, tending gardens, and preparing meals for the hired help as well as for the family. Most pioneer girls and women also found themselves in the fields helping with the work, especially in the planting and harvesting seasons.

Hence the traditional pattern was for the husband to be the main provider but for the wife to assist in many, many ways. This complemented the other division of labor wherein the wife had the primary responsibility for rearing the children and the husband assisted in that task in many, many ways.

As today's society has become industrialized and urbanized and has developed an advanced technology, there have been many important changes. The provider roles used to be carried out at home or close to the home, but now the home and the work place are generally separate. One leaves home to go to work, and the work world and home life seldom mix. This means that the typical father is away from the wife and children most of the time. Also, many of the things that used to be done in the home can now be done much more efficiently elsewhere. For example, home baking, quilting, canning, and sewing are fast becoming more expensive and inefficient than their commercial counterparts (though quality and nutrition may still be the determinants in some cases). This means such home activities may well become luxuries or hobbies that could actually drain economic resources rather than add to them. Such a situation makes it much more difficult for the wife to make significant economic contributions while also staying home where she can care for the children. (Despite such trends, the need for the skills in an emergency of course requires that they be acquired in normal times.)

The golden mean can help couples find a balance in work and play.

What do all these changes mean?

What are their implications for your modern role?

*How can husbands and wives effectively team
up to provide the economic necessities,
while they are also doing their most
important task of rearing a
family wisely?*

The following five suggestions are offered:

1. *Keep your priorities straight.* Whatever you do in providing your economic necessities, you need to remember that there are several different roles that marriage partners must perform, and they must perform all these roles at what is at least a minimal level of adequacy. They cannot work so hard at one or two that the others are inadequately dealt with. Some *essential* roles are these: (1) You need to seek first your *exaltation* in the kingdom of God as an individual. (2) You need to maintain a harmonious, loving, pleasant relationship in your *marriage.* (3) You need to rear your *children* so they will become good

saints and citizens—able to love others, provide a livelihood, and assume the responsibilities of adulthood. (4) You need to provide *service* to others by being adequately involved in Church programs such as missionary, genealogical, and welfare work, and at the same time provide service in your neighborhood and community. (5) You need to provide the minimal *economic necessities* for your family. This does not mean that you have to "keep up with the Joneses." *Necessities* include modest housing, comfortable clothing, nutritious food, adequate education, essential medical care, etc. They do not include luxuries such as fine carpets, TVs, stereos, newer cars, boats, campers, vacations, symphonies, etc. Luxuries such as these are fine, but you should worry about them only when the five essential roles are performed adequately.

Those who spend so much time in their provider roles that the others are inadequately performed need to *rearrange their priorities.* The father who works two or three jobs to provide things that are really luxuries is probably not adequately performing his husband or father role, since these other roles take a great deal of time, energy, commitment, and interaction. The father involved in a profession such as medicine, business, management, law, or teaching who works long hours or is away from home a great deal may be very successful financially, but he may discover years later that he was a failure in several other areas that ultimately count more.

If you keep your priorities in order, many of the following suggestions will take care of themselves.

2. *Avoid spending too much or too little time on the job.* Few people can provide for their families if they work less than full time—forty hours a week. You should therefore get and keep a full-time job. On the other hand, few people can do everything else they need to if they are working more than fifty or sixty hours a week. Sometimes you may need to work long hours for short periods of time. For example, if you were to start your own business you might need to spend long hours in the beginning. Or if you are both a student and a spouse, you may need to work at these roles more hours than you would like. If you can make sure that it is only a temporary pattern, it will probably do little harm. Many people, however, kid themselves. They tell themselves that they will only temporarily work at that pace, while at the same time they develop a habit of working too hard, and they never break the habit. You need, therefore, to be very careful in the first several years of your marriage to not establish destructive patterns that unwittingly continue and become your undoing.

3. *Be creative in the way the wife assists in the provider role.* You need to be creative in evaluating your abilities, needs, personalities, and preferences and then work out the arrangement best for your family. In most homes, the best arrangement is to have the husband be the main provider and have the wife assist him, while she has the primary responsibility for the children, assisted by him.

How, though, should the wife assist?

Some wives assist in inappropriate ways. For example, the wife may spend a lot of time shopping to find the best bargains. She may spend three dollars' worth of gasoline and two hours to save thirty-five cents on some green beans and sixty-five cents on fifty pounds of flour. Or she may spend a lot of time baking bread when the same bread could be bought less expensively at a store. Or the wife may can fruits and vegetables or make homemade quilts, when the economic gain might be as small as fifteen to twenty-five cents per hour for her work. *These would not be wise ways* to have the wife assist in the provider role. In other situations, these same behaviors might be economically wise, and you would be ahead by having the wife bake and sew and can. The answer is that you ought to examine these various activities rather than simply assume them to be natural roles for women. You need to examine them in terms of their economic value and the woman's personal interests, abilities, and tastes, and then decide together which roles are appropriate in your given circumstance.

In some homes, the best arrangement may be for the husband to become more involved in the housekeeping chores and for the wife to run a small business in the home. In other situations, the temperament and abilities of the couple are such that the husband should concentrate on being the provider and the wife should use the time she doesn't need in her homemaker, wife, and mother roles, in service activities that may or may not provide financial gain. In still other situations, the wife may make a financial contribution by the sale of literature or music she writes at home. Some couples may find it useful to have the wife work at a part-time job when the husband can be at home caring for the children. Some couples can work out arrangements in which the wife can be highly involved in the provider role. For example, the husband and wife may each have a Ph.D. degree and the two of them may occupy one professorial position in a university. They can then arrange their roles so both teach and do research and both are involved in the parenting and house-keeping roles.

How creative are you? What innovations can you make?

We are limited only by ourselves.
The sky is the limit!

What you need to do is *keep your priorities in a proper order,* and then kick off the fetters of traditions that were appropriate for earlier and different times but are inappropriate for you. You can then be creative and innovative in arranging your unique patterns of providing for yourselves.

It is challenging to think of the innovative minds of the pioneer and early Church leaders. Joseph Smith inaugurated a women's organization in 1842. Brigham Young organized cities with wide and straight streets. The early Saints rebelled against some of the religious traditions of the time by promoting singing and dancing. The Saints in Utah were the first in the United States to give women the right to vote. They were not afraid to innovate. They were creative and bold and faced their challenges with a willingness to "do things differently."

Even so, while you are being creative, you need to continually remember to keep your priorities straight. Your top priority should be your personal growth toward godhood, and your second should be to adequately perform your spousal and parental responsibilities.

Your creativity in arranging your provider roles should be directed toward helping you meet these needs.

4. *Have a back-up plan.* It is wise to have some well-designed plans for what to do if unusual emergencies were to arise. For example, what would you do if the husband were to become physically disabled, so that he couldn't provide a living? What would you do if the husband were to pass away? What would you do if sickness or accident were to keep the wife from making the financial contribution that you expect?

Women are encouraged to become educated and trained. This is wise, because then a wife will have an occupational skill she can fall back on if something happens to her husband. The advice fits in well with several other truths. Social scientists have discovered that marriages are usually better if the partners wait until they are well into their twenties before they marry. This gives both the man and the woman time to spend the first few years out of high school preparing for meaningful and rewarding occupational roles. The wife may not be active in this role while there are small children in the home, but she has the capability of doing it if needed.

5. *Be willing to rearrange your provider roles at different stages of the life cycle.* You have different needs at different stages of your life. Most people have a great need for financial resources when they are initially setting up a home and are raising their children. Needs are fewer after the children are gone. These changes provide the opportunity for you to have unusual methods of providing for yourself. For example, you may want to have the husband and wife both work for several years after the children are reared, and save the extra money. You may then both quit work for a period of time and do something different, such as travel, study, develop artistic skills, or go on a mission. Young couples may want to have both the husband and wife work for the first few months of their marriage to acquire the resources for furniture or a down payment on a house. In this, however, there is a danger if you become accustomed to two incomes but need to cut back to one income after a child is born—you may find the cut very difficult. One way to avoid this problem is to have the second income earmarked exclusively for major purchases such as cars, housing, or furniture so you don't get used to "living on" the two incomes. Another possibility is to make provisions so that the wife can work inside the home after the child comes, if she desires.

Church Activity

The Church is another part of the social network, and it is imperative that you become involved and active in it. We are commanded to "meet together often" (D&C 20:75) to "instruct and edify each other" (D&C 43:8). In practical terms this means that families have several meetings on Sunday—priesthood meeting, Relief Society, Mutual, Primary, Sunday School, and sacrament meeting. In addition, one evening during the week may be set aside to attend other meetings. These include presidency meetings, planning meetings, Scout meetings, home teaching, visiting teaching, etc. If you are "seeking first the kingdom of God," you also become involved in a number of other religious activities. You involve yourself in missionary work, genealogical research, temple work, the welfare program, and firesides. You also study the scriptures regularly and "pray continually."

Is it possible that the "golden mean" should operate in the religious part of life too?

Can you become too involved or too uninvolved in Church activities?

In a sense we can say that the golden mean is involved in this area of married life, but there is a difference. We cannot plan service in the kingdom merely on a basis of preference or convenience, for example, as we can in the case of purely social activities. The Lord has indicated that we ought all to be "anxiously engaged in a good cause" (D&C 58:27). Some persons never become anxious or engaged enough, while others may be too anxious and too engaged to provide religious balance, at least in some areas. You need to exercise moderation, wisdom, and good judgment in continually monitoring how much you are and ought to be doing. This is one reason why Church members are being reoriented to spending more time and effort with their families.

Prior to the 1980 change in meeting schedules, many ward and stake leaders had the best intentions in leaving home early Sunday morning to be involved in Church activities all day. Unfortunately, many who did this were seriously abusing the Lord's instructions that his day is to be a day of rest. Some of the same people were then away from their homes so much during the week that they neglected their other responsibilities. Too often, a few years of excessive Church service drove a wedge between a husband and wife or between parents and children, and they were never able to recover. Unfortunately, it was usually family life that paid the highest prices when a person became too involved in Church activities. The husband-wife relationship withered, and the wife was left with more than her share of parental responsibilities.

If this pattern involved merely an occasional individual who got carried away, it could be mentioned in passing and few would need to be concerned. Unfortunately, however, it has become a common theme among Latter-day Saints—so common, for example, that jokes about the incorrigible "bishop's kids" are a common part of our humor. The General Authorities have become so concerned about this that in 1978 they issued a number of directives to local leaders asking them to curtail the number of meetings held and to be more efficient in the ones that are held so that leaders will be able to fulfill their family and other responsibilities.

Later, in early 1980, a new meeting schedule was announced by the Church. The new schedule is designed to resolve some of the conflicting demands on members' time, and it is now easier to be more responsible for one's own stewardship of time, and be better able to handle Church callings as well as family and other duties. It is still possible to be over-committed, however, and precautions are still necessary.

So . . . What can you do about it?

Here are several suggestions:

1. *Evaluate.* When you have evaluation and planning sessions for your marriage and family life (annual, monthly, or whatever), you ought to devote some time to this topic. You ought to determine how much you are involved in the various aspects of the Church and see whether you are too involved or too uninvolved in specific things. For example, you may be overly busy in genealogy work or some other activity and not enough in something else. You ought also to look at the overall picture of your religious activity to determine if it is a desirable amount—whether it is too much or too little in the light of your family situation and other needs.

2. *Listen to others.* Sometimes you can get carried away without realizing it. Sometimes you can keep yourself more balanced if you ask for and then listen to someone else's opinion about how you are doing. Your spouse, your friends, and sometimes your children will see patterns that you don't, and if you are open to their suggestions, they may help.

3. *Learn to sacrifice without overdoing it.* Involvement in Church activities is different from employment. In the latter you spend time so that you can *receive* something—money; you get as well as give. But in religious activity, you can simply give without concerning yourself with getting. It is important that you lose yourself in the service of others, that you extend yourself, that you give (even until it hurts a little), that you sacrifice. Your sacrificing, however, needs to be monitored so that you don't neglect other important things such as your marriage or children. This is a delicate balance that requires fairly frequent attention. In some ways, it is like watching a speedometer or fuel gauge when driving a car. It is only one part of the complex process, but you must keep your eye on it.

4. *Share information with presiding officials.* Sometimes presiding officials such as bishops or stake presidents talk with you about additional Church callings. The usual pattern is for the presiding officer, before extending a call, to ask you how you would feel about a particular calling. Such moments are very important in the management of this part of your life. The presiding official is earnestly seeking information about how you feel, what you think, what is going on in your home and life. If your response conceals crucial information, he may extend a call that is not good for you. For example, you may say things like, "Oh, things are going pretty well," or "I feel good about the jobs I have now"; while the truth of the matter is that things are pretty hectic in the home and you are struggling to get everything done. This is unfair to your leader and is unwise management of the stewardship you have over your own life. You ought to explain how you really feel and what you really think, and if you think your marriage or family life is suffering from the demands you already have, you ought to say so. When you do share this information, it helps the presiding official make wise decisions about his stewardship, and he may or may not extend a call.

5. *What if you don't agree with a call?* Sometimes you hear that you should never say no to a Church call. It is interesting that this myth persists in the Latter-day Saint culture even though it never appears in official Church publications and the General Authorities counsel against it. The counsel of the Brethren is that you ought to fast and pray about these decisions yourself and receive your *own answer* from the Lord about callings rather

than always automatically accepting a call. Fortunately, most of the time your feelings will be the same as those of the presiding official, and you will learn from your prayers that the call is what the Lord wants you to do. In some situations, however, for a variety of reasons, your answer may be different from that of your presiding authority. When this happens you ought to discuss your feelings with him and then perhaps fast and pray together, sharing your feelings honestly and openly. Most of the time your differences can be reconciled, and you will both feel good about the outcome. Only rarely will a difference persist. When it does, you are the one responsible for your own life. Your life is *your* stewardship. It is not your leader's, and you ought to decide in accordance with the dictates of your conscience.

In summary, it is important that you manage the religious activity in your life. You need to monitor what you are doing and compare it with your beliefs as to what you ought to do. You should listen to the counsel of your loved ones to help you decide what to do, and you should be "anxiously" involved in building up the kingdom of God. Therefore you should do your part by being involved in considerable activity, but not so much that other legitimate concerns suffer.

Volunteer Organizations

There are many volunteer organizations that compete for your time, money, and participation. The following list identifies some of them:
—Service clubs (Lions, Sertoma, Rotary, Kiwanis, Elks, etc.)
—Labor unions
—The Red Cross
—Professional associations
—Political parties
—Boy Scouts and Girl Scouts
—YMCA and YWCA
—Leisure clubs like hiking, skiing, swimming, backpacking
—United Fund drive or specialized drives such as cancer or heart
—PTA
—Racquetball clubs
—Country clubs
—Missionary reunions
—Family organizations
—Little League
—Hobbies such as model building, model trains
—Jogging clubs
—Health spas
—Fraternities or sororities
As in all other parts of the social network around marriage, it is easy to become too involved in some of these volunteer organizations. Sometimes you begin with a little

activity in one of them and soon find yourself committing more and more of your time. You are elected to office and are then responsible for some of what occurs. Typically, the office demands more time and energy than you thought it would, but you realize that it is important to a number of other people. Gradually, you are swept into more and more involvement, until one day you realize that you are more involved than you really ought to be. You then cut back, painfully. Many go through this cycle over and over again by adjusting their activities, gradually becoming too involved again, and having to readjust to cutting back.

Others have a different challenge. They don't ever get involved in these organizations, but remain on the sidelines, isolated, lonely, and alienated. They need to become involved in some of these associations as part of being good citizens who are making contributions to others. This is a secondary benefit from the consolidated Church meeting schedule. Members are now more free to participate in community involvement.

> *The key: Establish an optimal amount of involvement in these activities*
> *—not too much, not too little; enough that you are involved in a helpful way,*
> *but not so much that it interferes with other important parts of your life.*

Friendships

Most people have a network of close friends, and it is important to spend some time with them. Some are "couple" friendships, while others are men that the husband likes to associate with and women the wife enjoys as separate friends.

Research on friendship networks has discovered several facts, one of which is consistent with the golden mean principle: You can have too many *or* too few friends. If you have too few, you tend to be lonely, and if you have too many you tend to be strained and uncomfortable. You feel that you "can't get everything done" that you have to do.

The optimal number of friends is also related to the kind of relationship you have with your spouse. If you have a companionate marital relationship in which your spouse is a close "friend," the optimal number of same-sex friends is lower than if you have less companionship with your spouse. It is as though there is a certain amount of *sociability* (Nelson 1966) that all people need, and you can meet your socializing needs in several different ways.

Those who have a lot of companionate interaction in marriage don't need as much interaction with friends. In fact, having a lot of friends would be a problem because they wouldn't have enough hours in the day to interact with both spouse and friends. Those who have less companionate interaction with their spouses usually feel a need to find someone outside of the marriage to be close to as a friend. They tend to find some friends of their own sex and enjoy visiting, playing games, and working with them.

There is some evidence that these patterns change at different stages of the life cycle (Rodgers 1973). Typically, newly married couples have highly companionate marriages. They spend a lot of time with each other, and friends tend to take a back seat in the relationship. Later, after a couple has several children and the marriage is stabilized, many

Friendships, as shown by Margaret Yorgason and Patty Baker, can provide a resource that complements marriage.

couples have less companionate interaction with each other. Those who compensate for these changes by interacting more with friends remain happy with their marriage and their life situations in general. Those who do not seek out other ways of meeting their friendship needs tend to be less satisfied with their marriages and their lives.

This illustrates that the golden mean applies to more than just the social networks outside of marriage. You need to evaluate how much energy, time, and interaction you have in your marital relationship and in your parental relationship as well as in the networks outside your family. Then, when you have a feeling for your total interests and demands, you can determine whether you are at the optimal mean for you.

THE GOLDEN MEAN IN YOUR LIFE . . . NOW

All of this discussion about the golden mean and social networks is useful, but so far it has been all discussion and no action.

How can you use this information
right now in your life?

There are three things you can do: First, you can identify some specific situations in which the golden mean can help you solve problems in your life. Second, you can evaluate your social networks right now to determine how they are influencing you and how satisfied you are with them. Third, if you aren't completely satisfied with the way things are going, you can do something to change your networks.

Situations in Which the Golden Mean Helps Solve Problems

There are a number of ways in which the golden mean can help you solve problems. It can help you cope with a marital situation in which one person is dissatisfied with a marriage because the spouse is not as friendly as the person wants him to be. The principle suggests that there are several different ways the two can handle this problem. One obvious way is for the less companionate spouse to change his or her behavior; a second is for the dissatisfied spouse to change his or her expectations. Most people learn, however, that changing this type of behavior is quite difficult, frequently impossible, even when they want to change. A more realistic solution suggested by the golden mean is for the lonely spouse to solve his or her dissatisfaction by becoming more involved in nonmarital relationships that provide friendship and companionship. The wife has such options as joining service organizations or increasing her involvement in neighborhood study groups, morning breaks with neighbors, or recreational groups. The husband can foster friendships with co-workers or join service, social, or sports clubs. When a person prefers that his companionate activity be with his spouse these substitutes may be less desirable, but they may be the more desirable solutions when it is not possible to change other aspects of the marital situation. Research (Nelson 1966) shows that these nonmarital substitutes can genuinely improve marital satisfaction.

The golden mean is also relevant for student marriages. In many student marriages the schedule of the student spouse is extremely demanding, especially when he or she works part-time or full-time while finishing up his or her schooling. This intensely demanding period also occurs right after the wedding, when most couples are accustomed to having considerable companionship with each other and want to maintain this high level of interaction. It isn't uncommon for the nonstudent spouse (usually the wife) to develop frustrations over playing "second fiddle" to the books. She may feel that she is less important to him than she was before the marriage, and the husband may have so many demands that he feels overwhelmed. According to the golden mean principle, the wife is having too little sociability and the husband too much.

There are several ways to cope with such situations. One is for the couple to make the demands less intense by taking longer to finish their schooling. Another is for the nonstudent spouse to acquire nonmarital forms of involvement during this period and to terminate them when the couple leaves the "married student" status. The nonstudent spouse could achieve an appropriate balance of involvement through a variety of activities: artistic creativity, employment, continuing his or her own education, Church service, or friendships. Employment is a choice many young couples opt for, partly because it has the added benefit of enabling the student spouse to be less burdened with providing income.

The golden mean is also relevant in other situations, such as (1) when the children leave home and there are fewer parental responsibilities, (2) when the husband or the wife returns to work or retires, and (3) when the couple moves away from or back to areas where they have relatives with whom they are expected to interact. In each of these situations, they can use the principle to reestablish a desirable equilibrium in their informal involvements with each other and with acquaintances outside their marriage.

Evaluating Your Social Network

The second way you can use the golden mean is to evaluate your social network *right now*. In doing this you need to determine what systems you interact with in your network, how these systems influence you, how you influence them, and how satisfied you are with the way things are going now. You may discover several things. You may find that you have been aware of what has been going on in your social networks and don't want to make any adjustments. On the other hand, you may discover that a few things (or many things) have been going on that you haven't been aware of, and your life would be better if you made a few adjustments. Activity 13:1 at the end of this chapter can help you do this, and it may be well worth the effort.

Making Changes in Networks

The third step in using the golden mean is to *do something* about the evaluation you have just completed. The first thing to do is to think about things that are going well in your social network. These things should provide you with an inner feeling of pride and peace and joy. You should try to "tune in" on these feelings, and then keep and savor them.

If you think it would be wise to make some changes in your network, you should develop some plans and begin making the changes, and Activity 13:2 at the end of the chapter can help you accomplish this.

SUMMARY

This chapter has discussed the many ways your social network influences your marriage. The golden mean, a concept originally developed by Aristotle, is identified, and several ways of using it are discussed. The main points in the chapter are that you need to monitor your interaction with the many systems in your social network to determine how they are influencing you and how you are influencing them. Periodically you need to make adjustments by becoming more or less involved with various parts of your total social environment. Your network can help you attain your goals, but it can also get in the way when you don't manage it wisely.

ACTIVITY 13:1
Evaluating Your Social Network

Goal: To determine what is happening in your social network and how satisfied you are with it.

1. First of all, identify how much time you spend in an average week in each of the different parts of your social network. Do this alone, and write the hours down. Do it on a separate piece of paper.

Average number of hours spent
with system each week

_____ a. Interacting with relatives. (If you live away from home, include parents as relatives.)

_____ b. In Church activities. (Include preparation time; don't include genealogy work.)

_____ c. In employment. (Include travel to and from work.)

_____ d. In school work—studies, classes, assignments, etc.

_____ e. Visiting with friends.

_____ f. Participating in sports. (This includes leagues, backyard football, etc.)

_____ g. Watching sports. (This includes watching sports on TV, going to games, etc.)

_____ h. Watching nonsports programs on TV.

_____ i. Attending meetings of clubs, lodges, social groups, service groups, etc.

_____ j. Shopping. (Include grocery, clothing, window shopping, etc.)

_____ k. Working at personal interests such as genealogy, hobbies, letter writing, etc. (Include time practicing musical instruments.)

_____ l. (Other) _____

_____ m. (Other) _____

2. Next, go back over the above list and evaluate each part according to how much it controls your life. How much are your activities or schedule determined by that particular system? How much does it "push you around?" Some things are very powerful, and that's all right. Other things may be very powerful without your realizing it. For

example, your parents or friends or the TV may be influencing your life more than you've realized, and you don't like it. Rate each system with the following schedule:

> 3 = Very large influence.
> 2 = Substantial influence, but not great.
> 1 = A little influence, but not much.
> 0 = No influence, or almost none.

3. After you've completed steps 1 and 2, find a time when you can discuss your evaluations with someone close to you. Someone such as a spouse, roommate, parent, sibling, or close friend would be best. See how much the other person agrees and disagrees with your evaluation of where you spend your time and how much the different parts of your network influence you.

4. As part of this discussion, determine how satisfied you are with the way things are going in your social network. Even those who would like to make major changes have some parts of their social networks that are functioning well.

If you think it would be wise to make some changes in your network, write them down.

ACTIVITY 13:2
Changing Your Network

Goal: To determine how to change part of your social network, and then to make the changes.

Getting ready: An important part of this exercise is thinking up new ideas; an effective way to do it is to use a discussion group in a class or get together with one or two other couples. In the group discussion, identify which individual or couple you are trying to help. (If you try to help everyone at the same time, there will probably be more chaos than help.)

1. Write down the goals on a piece of paper. Be brief and specific.

2. Of the five steps in this exercise, the hardest step is this second one. It is to *identify a realistic set of alternatives.* These are things you can do to attain your goal. First, select one person to write down the suggestions, and then classify them according to whether they involve a possible change (1) in the person or spouse or (2) in a person or group outside the marriage. Try to list at least three or four suggestions in each category.

3. The third step is to tentatively select *one alternative* as the one to try. You may find it useful to modify the alternative or add to it.

4. After an alternative has been selected, *identify a plan of action* that describes how to

accomplish the alternative selected. A group can be useful in helping think up a plan and keeping it realistic, but this is the last place a group can help.

5. Implement the plan.

6. After the plan has been implemented long enough for some changes to have occurred, evaluate how effective the plan was. If it was effective, repeat Activity 13:1, "Evaluating Your Social Network." If the plan was not effective and you still want to expend the energy it will take to change this aspect of your life, look over the list of alternatives you acquired in step 2 of this exercise. If one of them looks like a good possibility, select it and go on to step 4. If none of them look realistic, try to get some help from others, such as friends, religious leaders, or a marriage counselor, to get a better list of alternatives.

SUPPLEMENTARY READINGS

Bott, Elizabeth. *Family and Social Network.* New York: The Free Press, 1971.

Maxwell, Neal A. *That My Family Should Partake.* Salt Lake City: Deseret Book Co., 1974.

Stapleton, Jean, and Richard Bright. *Equal Marriage: A Solid Alternative to the Extremes of Open Marriage and Total Woman.* New York: Harper and Row, 1976.

Wells, J. Gipson. *Current Issues in Marriage and the Family.* New York: MacMillan Publishing Co., Inc., 1975.

Young, M., and P. Willmott. *Family and Kinship in East London.* New York: The Free Press, 1957.

14

BONDS
IN
MARRIAGE

As one string upon another builds a
rope to anchor the mightiest ship,
One loving act upon another builds
ties that bind beyond the grave.

The term *bond* in the social sciences refers to the ties that keep two or more people together. A number of other words in the English language have almost the same meaning. Some of them are: cohesion, attachment, connectedness, solidarity, interdependence, and attraction. The word *bond* is used here because it has been the most widely employed in recent literature (Turner 1970) and has fewer other meanings. In more figurative terminology, the bonds in a relationship are the glue or magnetism that keep a couple together.

There are several reasons why you should study the bonding process in dating and marriage. First, you probably desire strong bonds in your marriage. You want to be close to your spouse, to feel like you are a part of each other. This does not mean that all couples want the same degree of bondedness. Some want extremely intense bonds, while others, such as the O'Neills (1972), are satisfied with weaker ties. These differences are illustrated by the two following comments:

Jay and I find most of our satisfaction in life in the things we do as individuals rather than as a couple. We want to be married and to have a family, but it is our own individual interests that really keep us lively and enthusiastic about life. We are pretty independent people.

We want to be a close-knit couple—to be very much involved with each other—to feel like a team instead of just two people who are married. We'd be lost without each other.

The first couple want to have some bonds in their marriage, but they don't want the extremely strong bonds that the second couple seek.

A second reason for studying bonds is that all people get in situations in which they want to *decrease* their bonds. For example, all marriages are disrupted by death or divorce, and when this occurs you need to decrease your interdependence with the other person.

Research evidence suggests that recovery from the disruptive effects of death or divorce is influenced by how well one is able to reduce or break his bonds with the other person (Goode 1956). There may also be times when you may want to become slightly less tied to each other, and at such times it is important to know how to slightly increase or decrease bonds.

The main goal in this chapter is, therefore, to discuss principles that you can use to strengthen or weaken your bonds in marriage.

THE MEANING OF THE TERM "BOND"

Bondedness was briefly defined earlier as the ties that keep two or more people together, and several synonyms were identified. We need to say more about the meaning of the term because it is easily confused with several closely related terms such as love, harmony, and marital satisfaction.

Bonds are not the same thing as love. Love frequently arises from or accompanies bonds, but the two are different. One author has clarified the difference by stating that "love is a feeling or experience that reflects the presence of bonds between people more than it is a bond in itself" (Turner 1970, p. 47). Another way of looking at this difference is to view love as a feeling, sentiment, or emotion that you have, while bonds are characteristic of a relationship. Another reason why bonds and love are different is that it is possible to have bonds with people you do not love. In fact, you may even have strong bonds with people you dislike. Love is a barometer of how much you like someone, while bonds are the extent to which you are tied to someone.

Bondedness is also different from satisfaction with the marital relationship. Marital satisfaction is a subjective evaluation of the quality of a marriage, whereas bonds are the interpersonal ties or interconnectedness of the relationship. When we are thinking about a couple's bonds, we are thinking about how interdependent they are or how tied they are to each other, not how satisfied they are with their marriage. It would be possible for a couple to have very intense bonds and not be satisfied with their marriage at all. This often happens to couples going through a divorce. Conversely, couples may have very low bonds and yet be very satisfied with their marital situation. If a couple were to want a certain amount of cohesion in their marriage, their marital satisfaction would undoubtedly be affected by whether or not they were as cohesive as they wanted to be, but the cohesion and the satisfaction are two different things.

Harmony and *consensus* are two other concepts sometimes equated with cohesion, but they are also different. Turner (1970) defines harmony as lack of conflict. It is the degree to which people agree or disagree, or the amount they support rather than detract from one another's identities. High bondedness can exist when there is high harmony, but it is also possible to have high harmony and low bondedness. It is also possible to have low harmony and either high or low bondedness. The distinction between bondedness and consensus was also made by Durkheim (1933) when he pointed out that bonds can be created by either consensus or a division of labor.

> Bonds in marriage are like two porcupines on a cold night. If the porcupines get too close to each other . . . it's uncomfortable. But, if they get too far away from each other, it is cold and lonely. The solution is to find just the right amount: close enough to feel the warmth and security with the other and not so close that it is uncomfortable.

It is also important to understand that bondedness is a variable, as shown on the accompanying scale. The lowest point on the variable is no bonds, and occurs when there is indifference or a lack of attachment. It is a condition in which there is no involvement between the persons, no interdependence, no indication that the other person matters. The low point of bondedness is not the same as having negative feelings about the other person, because sentiment is a different phenomenon from bondedness. It is also not true that a divorce implies an absence of bonds. As the following comment illustrates, many kinds of ties can remain after a marriage is dissolved:

Strength
of bonds   None   Low   Moderate   High   Very High

I see now that there's not much of me that isn't Joe's wife. Even though I've been eager to have this divorce finalized and to begin a different life, there are so many ways I'm still connected to him—even silly things like counting on him to tease me back when I start to tease him about his weight. I miss that, in spite of myself.

Brown has described the experience of high bondedness as "a feeling of union with someone else, a feeling that the self has grown beyond its skin" (1965, p. 82). High bondedness is also illustrated by the husband who tells a friend, "We're pregnant!" or the wife who says, "We have a new job." Low bondedness is illustrated by, "He did ask me out three weeks ago, but he doesn't stop and talk when we meet on campus, and he hasn't called me again. I guess he's just not interested."

Ideal Level of Bonds

Several Church leaders have suggested that bonds are important in marriage. David O. McKay, for example, says: "The family tie is an eternal one; it is not one of experiment; it is not one of satisfying passion; it is an eternal union between husband and wife, between parents and children. That eternal bond is one that must be held sacred by the man as well as by the woman." (1953, p. 480.)

PRINCIPLES CONCERNING BONDS

The following six principles identify variables that influence the bonds in a relationship.

Shared activities build bonds.

It is hoped that a knowledge of these principles, when coupled with the skills to implement them, will increase your ability to create the degree of cohesion you want in your dating, your marriage, and your other interpersonal relationships. This should not be interpreted to mean that very strong bonds are necessarily an optimum goal. The amount of cohesion that is optimal in some relationships may be fairly low, while the optimal amount in other relationships may be high. It is your value system that determines the strength of the bonds you desire in your relationships, and the following principles are vehicles you can use to help you attain your goals.

Shared Experience

Turner (1970, pp. 81-83) has suggested that the amount of shared experience influences bonds. *Shared experience* refers to the extent to which two individuals have common experiences, either by doing something together or by talking about something in enough detail to genuinely share it. One kind of shared experience occurs when people interact with each other, as in dating or in working together. Another kind occurs when people learn that they have had a similar experience, even though no interaction between them was involved (for example, both saw the same TV show; both worked in the same political campaign; both were reared in large families). A single person's experience can become a shared experience when two people discuss it. The amount of shared experience is a continuous variable ranging from none (as with a girl who likes a boy who "doesn't even know she's alive") to a very high amount. The principle that ties shared experiences and bondedness together is:

12. The Shared Experience Principle: The more you experience with a person, the stronger your bonds.*

One reason a relationship exists between shared experience and bondedness is that when two individuals experience the same things and then discuss what has happened, as well as how each feels about the experience, they begin to have similar conceptions of reality and similar attitudes. This provides a validation for each person, and gives him confidence in his ideas. Sharing thus provides a more stable basis for action than one person alone would have. Sharing also provides a basis for interaction, and as shared experiences accumulate over time, both partners become more interdependent. Another reason why shared experiences probably foster cohesion is that when partners interact "alone together," outsiders consider them to be a unit and treat them as such. This tends to make the couple think of themselves as connected with each other (Bolton 1961).

The implications of this principle are many. Suppose, for example, you want to increase the cohesion between yourself and a person you are dating. The principle suggests that the two of you should do a lot of things together. One way you could do this would be to continue dating, and build up a backlog of shared experiences. You could also deliberately spend time talking about each other's past and present experiences, thus transforming non-shared experiences into shared ones. In addition, the more you explain your own attitudes, perceptions, and feelings, the more you are sharing each other.

In situations where couples, whether married or not, are separated from each other by such things as the military, missions, or schooling, an understanding of this principle is essential. Two of the authors were able to observe firsthand the effects of separation on married couples during the Vietnam War. It quickly became apparent that those servicemen and women who took the time to share experiences with their loved ones were having fewer marriage problems than those who didn't.

Soldier after soldier would come in for counseling, heartbroken about a letter he had just received and couldn't understand. In the letters of over one hundred wives of servicemen, a

---

* Turner (1970, pp. 81-83) has extracted this principle from the symbolic interaction literature. As with most ideas in symbolic interaction, the idea is an integrated part of a very complex description of human interaction, but empirical tests of the ideas have not yet been made. Turner ties the idea to other analytic essays, such as Halbwachs (1950, pp. 1-34) and Berger and Kellner (1964), and this makes the idea fairly plausible. This principle is thus rationally derived and a part of a complex theory, but it has not been thoroughly tested by rigorous empirical data. Those who limit their thinking to empirically tested ideas will thus perhaps be skeptical of this principle, but those who have more confidence in social science as an analytic, interpretive, rational process will have considerable confidence in it. Readers may want to give credence to both the empirical and the analytic approaches, and accept, tentatively, ideas from either.

similar pattern emerged in nearly all of them. Most of the "good-bye" letters came after several months of separation. They had all been preceded by long periods of no communication on either side—or if a communication had been made, it was usually a short letter that described only trivial things. It was also interesting to note that nearly half of these short letters ended with the words, "Well, I just can't think of anything else to say." This is a sign of not caring or not thinking about the relationship as much, and of weakening the bonds that had once been there.

On the positive side, there were many soldiers in that war who took advantage of the free mail system and kept the bonds of their relationships strong by daily communication. Phone calls could be made inexpensively through a variety of sources, and cassette tapes could be sent free of postage. One serviceman increased bondedness by reading onto tapes from the illustrated *Book of Mormon Stories* and then sending the tapes and books back for use in family home evenings. Through the use of tapes, he was able to conduct all family councils and home evenings, send special birthday messages, and so on. In return, the family would send back tapes of these same meetings.

The point is that relationships, like cars and airplanes, need constant maintenance and upkeep. They can go only so long being neglected before damage is done. The shared experience principle is one way to keep your relationships strong.

This principle can also be used by a couple who have been married for several years, even if they are not physically separated. Couples frequently go through a stage in which a gradual decrease in shared experience is brought about by such responsibilities as child care and community activities. This happens because often these responsibilities involve long working hours, large distances between work and home, the segregation of occupational and family life, fatigue, mistrust, vocabulary-language barriers, educational differences, role differentiation, and periods of separation. The result is often an undesired decrease in the couple's bonds. When this occurs, it is possible to develop new ways to share, such as providing a time for talking, establishing regular family rituals and traditions, making plans for being together, engaging in joint recreation or education, and writing notes and letters. The net effect will be an increase in bonds in the relationship.

It is usually quite easy to see the effects of shared experience when relationships have low bondedness. Thus, in a relationship in which two individuals are just getting acquainted and the bonds are still fairly low, a marked increase or decrease in the amount of shared experience usually has a visible effect on bondedness.

Changes in shared experience can also have an effect on a relationship that has become so routine, taken for granted, and "everydayish" that many of the bonds have gradually withered away. In such a relationship, a substantial change in the amount of shared experience can very quickly have an effect on the bonds. It is considerably more difficult to observe the effects of changes in shared experience when a relationship has fairly strong bonds because the bonds are so complex that it takes time to change them.

Activities 14:1 and 14:2 at the end of the chapter can help couples increase or decrease their bonds by changing their shared experiences. Try them!

Incomplete Action

13. The Incomplete Action Principle: The more incomplete action in a relationship, the stronger the bonds.*

Incomplete action occurs when a couple invests time, energy, thought, or planning in something that requires both of them for its completion. You have few things that are incomplete when you are dating, but as you start planning a future together, you experience a lot of incomplete action.

You can use this principle in your dating and marital relationships because the amount of incomplete action in these relationships can easily be increased or decreased. When couples want to use this idea to enhance bonds they can plan things to do together in the immediate future, such as take a vacation or remodel their home. They can also plan retirement. Probably one of the reasons that children provide additional bonds between a couple is that so much of the parental role includes the expectation of guiding and rearing the children.

This principle can also be used to reduce bonds in such situations as breaking an engagement, terminating a relationship with someone other than your spouse, or adjusting to the death of a loved one. The principle suggests that the fewer the incomplete joint activities, the weaker the bonds. The way to use this principle to decrease bonds is to decrease these uncompleted activities by completing them or by changing plans. For example, a clear-cut break with daily routines and rituals, rearranging the furniture, or moving to a new house can disrupt the expected interaction patterns with someone, and such changes seem to help in coping with bereavement.

Activity 14:3 at the end of the chapter shows one way of implementing this principle, and it can be done by married couples or in relationships that are transient, such as those of classmates in a marriage course.

The Amount of Reserve

Another of the principles developed by Turner (1970, pp. 85-87) has to do with the amount of "reserve" in relationships. Turner points out that most "communication is hedged about by a certain amount of reserve—some concern about how freely one ought to speak on certain subjects, how best to state the matter to avoid misunderstanding, or what kind of reaction to anticipate from the other person" (1970, pp. 85-86). Usually when you decrease this reserve with someone, it is a very gradual process, and you do it by selecting one or two areas at a time in which you can relax your ordinary defenses and become less

---

* This idea is implicit in Mead's (1934, 1938) social philosophy and is more thoroughly developed in Faris's (1937) analysis of human nature. Turner (1970, pp. 80-81), however, made the principle explicit. The principle has not been tested with quantified empirical data, but it is probably defensible to tentatively accept it as valid because it is an integral part of symbolic interactionist thought and because it seems to be consistent with everyday reality.

inhibited. As the reserve decreases, a sense of privacy develops in that particular relationship, and the bonds between the individuals become stronger. The principle is:

14. The Reserve Principle: The less the reserve in a relationship, the greater the strength of the bonds in that relationship.*

Low reserve is illustrated with the following lines: "Oh, the comfort, the inexpressible comfort, of feeling safe with a person, having neither to weigh thoughts nor measure words, but pouring them all right out—just as they are, chaff and grain together . . . Take and sift them, Keep what is worth keeping, and with the breath of kindness blow the rest away. . . ." (Dinah Maria Mulock.)

There is probably an optimum amount of reserve in all relationships, and you can gradually discover the amount you are comfortable with in different relationships. For some there will be very few areas of reserve, but others may be comfortable in relationships with more reserve. For example, people usually want to be tactful, considerate of others' feelings, and polite most of the time. Such restrictions are forms of reservedness. Other people are comfortable with even more formal relationships in which much of their private lives and selves are "reserved."

The reserve principle can be used to either increase or decrease bonds. During courtship and the early stages of marriage, most couples want to increase their bonds, and the principle provides a method for doing this—decreasing the reserve in the relationship. The "Decreasing Reserve" activity (14:4) at the end of the chapter is designed to help you learn ways to accomplish this.

At other stages of life you may want to decrease the strength of your bonds, and there are many ways in which this, too, can be accomplished. The communication may be changed so that it is more formal, more guarded, and less spontaneous. If the principle is correct, this will decrease bonds and probably prevent other bonds from appearing that might have otherwise developed. When couples are terminating a marriage, this strategy is frequently used. The individuals restrict their areas of communication, talk only at certain times, and on occasion talk to each other only through a third person, such as a lawyer. The conversations usually become businesslike, to the point, and unemotional, and this very quickly builds reserve and decreases bonds. The "Increasing Reserve" activity (14:5) at the end of the chapter is designed to help you accomplish this.

The Interdependence of Roles

As people become involved with one another, their living patterns become intermeshed, and their roles become interlocked. Some of this interlocking is due to their taking com-

---

* Turner does not analyze empirical data in developing this principle, as it is apparently derived from the symbolic interaction school of thought. The idea is thus rationally rather than empirically derived. The idea also seems to be intuitively reasonable, but at present it should not be viewed as a very thoroughly proven scientific principle.

plementary roles in the division of the tasks that must be done. Some, however, is due to interdependence in more emotional and personal matters, such as a wife learning to depend on her husband for humor in a tight spot, or a husband learning to depend on his wife for intellectual stimulation. The following example from the wife of a well-known evangelist illustrates the interlocking of roles and the effect this has on bonds:

> When I was first married, I had no real experience or deep interest in church affairs. I knew nothing of board meetings or committee functions. I certainly could not see myself presiding over one. But it soon became apparent that this was an area where I could be of great use to Norman. Studying him made me realize that this sort of activity was not one of his strong points. Organizational work left him impatient and restless. He was at his best when he was preaching or writing, or dealing with the emotional difficulties of individuals. I began to see that if I could take some of the organizational work off his back, go to the committee meetings, report back, summarize, simplify, help Norman make the big decisions and spare him from having to make the little ones, I would be making an enormous contribution—one that would make me even more indispensable to him (Peale 1971, p. 35).

The interdependence of roles is a continuous variable. It is possible to have very little interdependence, as in a marriage between two very independent people in which each relinquishes few tasks to the other, and each satisfies many needs by himself or with others outside the relationship. But it is also possible to have a great deal of interdependence, as in a marriage wherein the partners' personal needs are fulfilled largely by each other. The generalization is:

15. The Interdependence of Roles Principle: The degree to which the roles in a relationship are interdependent influences the strength of the bonds in the relationship.*

One way in which you can employ this principle in everyday life is to learn ways to increase or decrease the amount that your roles interlock. There are many ways this can be accomplished. You can increase the meshing of your roles by (1) having one member of the couple be primarily responsible for handling the finances for both; (2) turning to each other rather than to parents or friends for support in times of difficulty; (3) having one member do such things as type up the other's papers; (4) having one member assume responsibility for the maintenance of the other's car; (5) helping each other with occupational problems; or (6) dividing up household jobs so that each member becomes dependent on the other for getting things done. A side effect of some of these activities may be to decrease shared experience, and so you may not want to go too far.

At certain times you may want also to use this principle to decrease bonds. To do this you can (1) seek companionship outside the relationship; (2) have such jobs as ironing clothes or repairing household gadgets done by persons other than the partner; or (3) turn

---

* Waller and Hill (1951, pp. 328-33) described ways in which interdependence is important in marital relationships. The variables involved, however, were not clearly described until Turner's (1970, p. 83) analysis of the effects of interdependence on bonds. The principle is based on qualitative analysis of what goes on in relationships rather than on quantified, empirical data, and hence it should be accepted with an appropriate tentativeness.

to friends or relatives rather than to your partner for companionate and/or supportive experiences.

If you want to alter the strength of bonds by changing the interdependence of your roles, you can use the "action plan" outline on pages 42-43. It is fairly easy to devise a brief action plan that will make a big difference in bondedness in a premarital relationship. After you have been married for a while, your bonds become so complex that they change more slowly. Even then, however, an action plan can make a major difference in bondedness; it just takes longer. Those who are just starting a relationship or whose bonds have virtually disappeared can expect a short-term action plan to make substantial changes in bonds by changing the degree to which roles are interlocked.

Support

Another principle mentioned by Turner (1970) can be termed the support principle. The independent variable in this principle is the extent to which you help the other person when he is depressed, show him you care in difficult moments, enhance his self-esteem when he needs it, and "be there" when you're needed.* High supportiveness occurs when a person does a great deal that enhances the other person's self-esteem. Low supportiveness exists when the net effect of a person's behavior is to decrease the other person's self-esteem. Supportiveness occurs when a person's behavior shows he likes to be around the other, indicates admiration or affection, or demonstrates concern and caring. Supportive communication says, "You are important to me"; "You are what you want to be, and it is okay"; "You are worthwhile." You have undoubtedly noticed the different ways you feel about yourself in the presence of different responses. When a person looks directly at you, rather than away or down at his work, when he acknowledges your thinking by relevant comments, or when he shows delight in being around you, you are experiencing supportiveness, and you usually feel pleasant. Supportiveness is a continuous variable, and can be stated as a principle, as follows:

16. The Support Principle: The more you support each other in a relationship, the stronger the bonds in that relationship.

It is likely that with all of the independent variables dealt with in this chapter, this is the most easily manipulated. If this is true, it is very likely the variable that gives you the greatest control over bonds in your dating and marital relationship. You can learn to increase or decrease your supportiveness quite easily, and you can do this in such a wide variety of situations that it can make a substantial difference.

Activity 14:6 at the end of the chapter is designed to help you increase your ability to be supportive. No exercises are provided to help you learn how to decrease supportiveness,

---

* A number of different terms could be used instead of supportiveness. Turner, for example, uses the term responsiveness (1970, p. 65). Another term that has wide usage is warmth (Sears, Maccoby, and Levin 1957). The term support is used here because it seems to these authors to be the best term in prior literature (Straus 1964; Becker 1964; Rollins and Thomas 1979).

Being supportive takes care . . . and it builds bonds.

because that skill is so pervasive in today's society that most people are already adept at it. Supportive behavior usually takes effort or energy, and if you found yourself in situations in which you wanted to decrease bonds, you could just stop behaving supportively.

Identification with the Other Person

We often hear the expressions "I can identify with that," or "I identify with her." What does it mean to *identify*?

To identify is to connect yourself with something or someone. It occurs when you are so connected to someone that you feel embarrassed if you know that person is in an embarrassing spot (if, for example, he approaches the cafeteria cashier with a full tray and finds he has no money with him). To identify is to feel proud if someone is in a prestigious position (if, for example, he is on the city council or he is the obvious leader at a group meeting). You identify with such people as other members of your race, other members of your student body, other members of your religion, other members of your family, and other members of your friendship group. This can be noticed even on casual dates. For example, you may feel proud if your partner is polite to someone who seems to have taken your seats at a ball game, or you may feel proud if you are introduced to someone who obviously admires your date.

Turner (1970, pp. 65-72) points out that a person's self-esteem may be enhanced or damaged through identification, and the independent variable in this principle is the extent to which identification enhances self-esteem. This is a continuous variable, and its highest point is a condition in which a person's self-esteem is greatly enhanced by identification with another person. Its lowest point is a condition in which identification damages self-esteem. The idea that relates the two variables is:

17. The Identification Principle: When identification with someone helps your self-esteem, this increases the bonds in the relationship.

This principle has many implications for everyday life. Popular advice encouraging teenage girls to cultivate their talents, improve their appearance, and involve themselves in worthwhile activities is at least partly aimed at helping them increase the possibility that a boyfriend's self-esteem will be enhanced through association with them, and thus make cohesion more likely. When a woman or a man hunts for a job that the partner will feel proud of, one effect may be that the self-esteem of the woman or the man will be enhanced through the connection, and thus the cohesion of the couple may be enhanced. The person who plans his or her hairstyle and wardrobe to have "the look of success" is also probably increasing the possibility of cohesion with the spouse.

SUMMARY

This chapter deals with factors that influence bonds in dating and marital relationships. Six generalizations are identified, and various ways to apply these hypotheses are discussed. The first principle discussed is the *shared experience principle,* which asserts that a positive relationship exists between the common experiences of two individuals and their bondedness. The second principle discussed is the *incomplete action principle,* which asserts that the greater the amount of investment someone has in activities that are not yet completed and that involve someone else, the greater the bonds with the other person. The *reserve principle* asserts that the less the need to behave in controlled, careful ways in a relationship, the stronger the bonds in the relationship. The *interdependence of roles principle* suggests that the more two individuals rely on or need each other to perform various activities, the stronger the bonds, and conversely, the more independent they are of each other, the weaker the bonds. The *support principle* states that the more two individuals engage in supportive or warm behaviors with each other, the greater the bonds. The *identification principle,* the last principle discussed, asserts that when identification with someone else enhances one's self-esteem, this tends to increase the bondedness in the relationship. On the other hand, when identification detracts from one's self-esteem, this tends to decrease the bondedness.

ACTIVITY 14:1
Increasing Shared Experience

Goal: To increase the bonds in a relationship by increasing the amount of shared experience.

1. Identify a relationship in which you want to increase the strength of the bonds.

2. Each day for a week deliberately plan to do one of the following two things:

   a. Engage in some pleasant activity that you have not previously done together. Do it as a pair only—no one else with you. This can involve such ordinary things as visiting a neighbor, one helping the other with some school work, engaging in a new leisure activity such as miniature golf or billiards, visiting a museum, etc.

   b. Discuss some previous experience in your life or lives that you have not talked about before. Try to select something that is or was fairly important, and remember that the object is for the other person, in a sense, to share the experience.

3. At the end of the week both of you try to identify whether there are differences in the bonds in your relationship.

ACTIVITY 14:2
Decreasing Shared Experience

Goal: To decrease the bonds in a relationship by decreasing the amount of shared experience.

1. Select a relationship in which you want to decrease the bonds permanently or in which a temporary reduction in the bonds would not be a problem in the relationship.

2. Carry with you a notebook or a piece of paper for one week.

3. During the week try to identify experiences you are now having or have had in the past that you have not and will not let the other person know about, become involved in, or in any other way share with you. Number these experiences and describe them briefly in writing. (Experiences with this exercise indicate that if you are doing this only as an experiment and plan to share these things with the other person after the week, you may not experience a discernible decrease in the bonds. The more you plan to eventually share these things with the other person, the less likely it is that this exercise will decrease the bonds you feel.)

4. At the end of the week, review the list of experiences and evaluate how much this exercise has increased your independence from the other person.

ACTIVITY 14:3
Increasing Incomplete Action

Goal: To increase bonds by increasing the amount of incomplete action in a relationship.

1. Select a relationship in which you want to increase the bonds between you and the other person.

2. Think up several things to do that (a) cannot be done unless both members of the couple are involved in them, and (b) will take a relatively long period of time. These could include such diverse activities as joining a bridge or dance club; playing musical duets; working on a committee; collaborating on something, such as writing or decorating; planning now what to do on next year's vacation; starting a new tradition, such as going out on a certain date each month or having breakfast in bed every rainy Saturday; or assuming a parent-surrogate role in a rehabilitation or prison system in which both a husband and wife are needed. Be creative in thinking up novel or exotic things.

3. Select one of the ideas in step 2 and implement it. After you have become involved in it enough to have really invested yourself in the experience, take some time to evaluate whether you have experienced any change in the bondedness in the relationship. (Theoretically, you're supposed to.)

ACTIVITY 14:4
Decreasing Reserve

Goal: To increase the strength of the bonds in a relationship by decreasing the reserve in the interaction.

1. Identify a relationship in which (a) you want to increase the strength of the bonds, and (b) you can spend several hours more time visiting with a person in the next week or so than you have in the recent past.

2. Most of the time you interact with other people in certain "roles," and you have to be proper and conform to the expectations that you and others have for yourself in those roles. Some of these fairly "ceremonial" roles are being a spectator at a concert or a sporting event; being a dancing partner for an evening; being a parent, where you have all kinds of responsibilities that have to be carried out in a "proper" or "right" manner; and going hunting. What you are to do in this exercise is spend some time (several hours if possible) with the other person during which you mostly just talk and visit with him or her as a person—as a person in a whole or total sense rather than as someone who is supposed to be doing something or going someplace with you. This is a good time to

talk about such things as wants, wishes, aspirations, memories, tender moments, goals, and especially, how you and the other person feel about these things. The more you can get away from things that have to be done and the more informal you can be during these hours, the better.

Most of the time you feel you need to be "doing" something with someone in some role (often people use these roles as a sort of crutch so that they don't have to relate to the person as a person), and so you may be a little uncomfortable at first. To help overcome this, you may want to spend only a little while together on the first few occasions, and then gradually spend more and more time together.

3. At the end of a week or so, has your tendency to be reserved with the other person decreased? Does the exercise seem to have had any effect on the bonds of your relationship? If not, you may be able to devise some ways of your own to decrease the reserve in your relationship.

ACTIVITY 14:5
Increasing Reserve in a Relationship

Goal: To decrease the bonds in a relationship by increasing the reserve in the interaction.

1. Select a relationship in which you want to decrease the strength of the bonds. (If you do not have such a relationship, do not do this exercise.)

2. Change your method of communicating with the other person for a period of time by doing as many of the four following things as you can.

   a. Limit your interaction with the other person so that it is confined to things that need to be done or accomplished.

   b. When you do interact with the other person, confine your interaction (talking, spending time together, etc.) to a narrow aspect of life, such as a certain role or a specific activity. Be businesslike in your manner by being precise, formal, clear, and efficient.

   c. Avoid talking about how you feel about things or letting your actions reveal your emotions.

   d. Be suspicious about the other person's motives.

3. After a period of time, evaluate the amount of reserve in the relationship and whether or not there has been a change in the bonds.

ACTIVITY 14:6
Evaluating and Increasing Support

Goal: To identify situations in which supportiveness occurred and did not occur in a relationship, and to increase supportiveness.

1. In a long-term relationship, such as one with a spouse, fiance(e), friend, or sibling, find the time for a thirty-minute discussion about supportiveness in the relationship.

2. Identify five recent situations in which you were supportive. List these on a piece of paper. If you are interested in increasing the supportiveness of the other person, also complete steps 2, 3, and 4 for that person. Some situations in which supportiveness may have occurred are:

   a. When one person did something to make the other feel better about herself or himself.

   b. When one person was feeling low or discouraged and needed someone to turn to.

   c. When one person encouraged the other.

   d. When one person showed confidence in the other.

   e. When one person did something that showed he or she cared about the other.

3. Identify three situations in which you could have been more supportive than you were. List these on a piece of paper.

4. Select one way in which you could be more supportive, and develop an action plan. (See pages 42-43 for the outline of action plans.) You may want to select one of the behaviors mentioned in step 3, or choose some other behavior.

SUPPLEMENTARY READING

Turner, Ralph. *Family Interaction.* New York: John Wiley & Company, 1970.

SUMMARY OF PRINCIPLES

1. *The Love Principle:* The more spouses act in loving ways, the better the marriage and family life.

2. *Deutsch's Law:* The more you act in a certain way, the more others around you also tend to act in that same way.

3. *The Self-Esteem Principle:* Changes in your self-esteem influence many aspects of your life, including your ability to be a loving person, the quality of your communication, the quality of your problem solving, your striving behaviors, and your feelings of liking or disliking those who influence your esteem.

4. *The Communication Principle:* The more effective the communication, the better the marriage and family life.

5. *The Emotionality Principle:* When emotions become intense, they decrease self-control.

6. *The Consistency Principle:* The greater the consistency in communication, the better the communication.

7. *The Problem-Solving Principle:* The better you can solve problems, the better your marriage and family life.

8. *The Unity Principle:* The greater the unity between marriage partners, the greater the happiness in the marriage.

9. *The Congruence Principle:* The greater the perceived congruence between role expectations and role behavior, the higher the marital and family satisfaction (especially with important expectations).

10. *The Success Principle:* The more often a person's activity is rewarded, the more likely he is to perform the activity.

11. *The Golden Mean:* Finding moderation by avoiding extremes generally leads to the most desirable results.

12. *The Shared Experience Principle:* The more you experience with a person, the stronger your bonds.

13. *The Incomplete Action Principle:* The more incomplete action in a relationship, the stronger the bonds.

14. *The Reserve Principle:* The less the reserve in a relationship, the greater the strength of the bonds in that relationship.

15. *The Interdependence of Roles Principle:* The degree to which the roles in a relationship are interdependent influences the strength of the bonds in the relationship.

16. *The Support Principle:* The more you support each other in a relationship, the stronger the bonds in that relationship.

17. *The Identification Principle:* When identification with someone helps your self-esteem, this increases the bonds in the relationship.

REFERENCES

Ackerman, Charles. "Affiliations: Structural Determinants of Differential Divorce Rates." *American Journal of Sociology,* 69, July 1963.

Aldous, Joan. "A Framework for the Analysis of Family Problem Solving." In Joan Aldous et al. (eds.), *Family Problem Solving.* Chicago: Dryden Press, 1971.

Allport, G. W. *Pattern and Growth in Personality.* New York: Holt, Rinehart and Winston, 1961.

Arnold, Magda B. *Emotion and Personality.* New York: Columbia University Press, 1960.

Ashton, Marvin J. *One for the Money.* Salt Lake City: Corporation of the President of The Church of Jesus Christ of Latter-day Saints, 1975.

Bales, Robert F., and Fred L. Strodtbeck. "Phases in Group Problem Solving." *Journal of Abnormal and Social Psychology,* 46:485-95, 1951.

Balswick, J. O., and C. W. Peak. "The Inexpressive Male: A Tragedy of American Society." *The Family Coordinator,* 20:363-68, 1971.

Bateson, G., D. D. Jackson, J. Haley, and J. H. Weakland. "Toward a Theory of Schizophrenia." *Behavioral Science,* 1:251-64, 1956.

Bavelas, Alex. "Communication Patterns in Task-oriented Groups." *Journal of Acoustical Society of America,* 22:725-30, 1950.

Becker, W. C. "Consequences of Different Kinds of Parental Discipline." In M. C. Hoffman and L. W. Hoffman (eds.), *Review of Child Development Research,* Vol. 1. New York: Russel Sage Foundation, 1964.

Becvar, R. J. *Skills for Effective Communication: A Guide to Building Relationships.* New York: Wiley, 1974.

Benson, Ezra Taft. *Speeches of the Year.* Provo, Utah: Brigham Young University Press, 1962.

Berger, Peter, and Hansfried Kellner. "Marriage and the Construction of Reality." *Diogenes,* 46:1-24, Summer 1964.

Bernard, Jessie. "Factors in the Distribution of Success in Marriage." *American Journal of Sociology,* 40:49-60, 1934.

Bernard, Jessie. "The Adjustments of Married Mates." Ch. 17 in Harold C. Christensen (ed.), *Handbook of Marriage and the Family.* Chicago: Rand McNally, 1964.

Bienvenu, J., Sr. "Measurement of Marital Communication." *Family Coordinator,* 19:26-31, 1970.

Blau, Peter M., and W. Richard Scott. *Formal Organizations.* San Francisco: Changler Publication Co., 1962.

Blood, Robert O. *Marriage.* New York: The Free Press, 1969.

Blood, Robert O., Jr., and Donald M. Wolfe. *Husbands and Wives: The Dynamics of Married Living.* Glencoe, Illinois: The Free Press, 1960.

Bolton, Charles D. "Mate Selection as the Development of a Relationship." *Marriage and Family Living,* 23:234-40, 1961.

Bossard, James H. S., and Eleanor S. Boll. *The Large Family System.* Philadelphia: University of Pennsylvania Press, 1956.

Brinley, D. E. "Role Competence and Marital Satisfaction." Unpublished Ph.D. dissertation, Brigham Young University, 1975.

Broderick, Carlfred B., and Harvey Pulliam-Krager. "Family Process and Child Outcomes," In W. R. Burr, R. Hill, F. I. Nye, and I. L. Reiss (eds.), *Contemporary Theories About the Family*, Vol. 1. New York: The Free Press, 1979.

Bronfenbrenner, Urie. *Two Worlds of Childhood: the U.S. and USSR.* New York: Russell Sage, 1970.

Brown, Roger. *Social Psychology.* New York: The Free Press, 1965.

Burgess, E. W., and H. J. Locke. *The Family: From Institution to Companionship.* New York: American Book, 1953.

Burgess, Ernest W., and Leonard S. Cottrell, Jr. *Predicting Success or Failure in Marriage.* Englewood Cliffs, New Jersey: Prentice-Hall, 1939.

Burgess, Ernest W., Harvey J. Locke, and Mary Margaret Thomas. *The Family.* 3rd ed. New York: American, 1963.

Burgess, Ernest W., and Paul Wallin. *Engagement and Marriage.* Philadelphia: Lippincott, 1953.

Burr, Wesley R. "An Expansion and Test of a Role Theory of Marital Satisfaction." *Journal of Marriage and the Family*, 33:368-72, 1971.

Burr, Wesley R. *Theory Construction and the Sociology of the Family.* New York: Wiley, 1973.

Burr, Wesley R., Brenton G. Yorgason, and Terry R. Baker. *Creating a Celestial Marriage.* Salt Lake City: Bookcraft, Inc., 1982.

Cameron, Norman, and Ann Margaret. *Behavior Pathology.* Boston: Houghton Mifflin, 1951.

Casler, Lawrence. *Is Marriage Necessary?* New York: Human Sciences Press, 1974.

Clark, J. Reuben. *Conference Report.* Salt Lake City: The Church of Jesus Christ of Latter-day Saints, pp. 102-3, 1938.

Coopersmith, S. *The Antecedents of Self-Esteem.* San Francisco: Freeman, 1967.

Corrales, Ramon G. "Power and Satisfaction in Early Marriage." In R. E. Cromwell and D. H. Olson (eds.), *Power in Families.* New York: Wiley, 1975.

Crook, John H., "Sexual Selection in the Primates." In B. Campbell (ed.), *Sexual Selection and the Descent of Man.* Oxford: Clarendon Press, 1972.

Davitz, Joel R. *The Language of Emotion.* New York: Academic Press, 1969.

Deutsch, Morton. *The Resolution of Conflict.* New Haven: Yale University Press, 1973.

Dittman, Allen T. *Interpersonal Messages of Emotion.* New York: Springer, 1972.

Durkheim, Emile. *The Division of Labor in Society.* New York: The Free Press, 1933. (First published in French in 1893.)

Duvall, Evelyn Mills. *Marriage and Family Development.* Philadelphia: J. B. Lippincott, 1977.

Engels, Friedrich. *The Origin of the Family, Private Property, and the State.* Chicago: Charles H. Kerr and Co., 1902. (Originally published in 1894.)

Faris, Ellsworth. *The Nature of Human Nature.* New York: Harper, 1937.

Feldman, Julian, and Herschel E. Kantor. "Organizational Decision Making." In James G. Marsh (ed.), *Handbook of Organizations.* Chicago: Rand McNally, 1965.

Freud, Sigmund, and Joseph Breuer. *On the Psychical Mechanisms of Hysterical Phenomena.* 1893.

Fromm, Erich. *The Art of Loving.* New York: Harper, 1956.

Geiger, Kent. *The Family in the Soviet Union.* Cambridge, Mass.: Harvard University Press, 1968.

Goode, William J. *After Divorce.* Glencoe, Illinois: The Free Press, 1956.

Gordon, Thomas. *Parent Effectiveness Training.* New York: Wyden, 1970.

Gouldner, A. W. "The Norm of Reciprocity: A Preliminary Statement." *American Sociological Review,* 1960.

Guerney, B. G. *Relationship Enhancement.* San Francisco: Jossey-Bass, 1978.

Guetzkow, H., and W. R. Dill. "Factors in Organizational Development of Task-Oriented Groups." *Sociometry,* 20:175-204, 1957.

Guetzkow, H., and H. A. Simon. "The Impact of Certain Communication Nets upon Organization and Performance in Task-oriented Groups." *Management Science* 1:233-50, 1955.

Halbwachs, Maurice. *La Memoire Collective.* Paris, France: Presses Universitaires de France, 1950.

Haley, Jay. *Strategies of Psychotherapy.* New York: Grune and Stratton, 1963.

Harper, Robert A. "Communication Problems in Marriage and Marriage Counseling." *Marriage and Family Living,* 20:107-12, 1958.

Hartman, Carl G. *Science and the Safe Period.* Baltimore: The Williams & Wilkins Company, 1962.

Hawkins, James L., and Kathryn Johnson. "Perception of Behavioral Conformity, Imputation of Consensus, and Marital Satisfaction." *Journal of Marriage and the Family,* 31:507-11, 1969.

Hoffman, M. L. "Moral Development." In P. H. Mussen (ed.), *Carmichael's Manual of Child Psychology,* 3rd ed., vol. 2. New York: Wiley, 1970.

Holman, Thomas B. *A Path Analysis Test of a Model of Early Marital Quality.* Unpublished Ph.D. Dissertation, Brigham Young University, 1981.

Homans, George C. "Fundamental Social Processes." In N. J. Smelser (ed.), *Sociology: An Introduction.* New York: Wiley, 1967.

Johnson, David W. *Reaching Out.* Englewood Cliffs, New Jersey: Prentice-Hall, 1972.

Jourard, Sidney. *The Transparent Self.* New York: Van Nostrand Reinhold, 1971.

Kahn, M. "Non-verbal Communication and Marital Satisfaction." *Family Process,* 9:449-56, 1970.

Keltner, J. W. *Elements of Interpersonal Communication.* Belmont, California: Wadsworth, 1971.

Kimball, Spencer W. *Conference Report.* Salt Lake City: The Church of Jesus Christ of Latter-day Saints, Apr. 1975.

————. *Conference Report.* Salt Lake City: The Church of Jesus Christ of Latter-day Saints, Apr. 1975a, p. 8.

————. "The Lord's Plan for Men and Women." *Ensign,* Oct. 1975b.

————. *The Miracle of Forgiveness.* Salt Lake City: Bookcraft, Inc., 1964.

————. *Marriage and Divorce.* Salt Lake City: Deseret Book Co., 1976.

Kirkpatrick, Clifford. *The Family Process and Institution,* 2nd ed. New York: Ronald Press, 1963.

Klein, David M., and Reuben Hill. "Determinants of Family Problem-solving Effectiveness." In W. R. Burr, R. Hill, F. I. Nye, and I. L. Reiss (eds.), *Contemporary Theories About the Family.* New York: The Free Press, 1979.

Kolers, P. A. "Sublimational Stimulation in Problem Solving." *American Journal of Psychology,* 70:437-41, 1957.

Kotlar, Sally L. "Middle Class Roles . . . Ideal and Perceived in Relation to Adjustment in Marriage." Unpublished Ph.D. dissertation, University of Southern California at Los Angeles, 1961.

Leavitt, Harold J. "Some Effects of Certain Communication Patterns on Group Performance." *Journal of Abnormal and Social Psychology,* 46:38-50, 1951.

Lederer, William J., and Don D. Jackson. *The Mirages of Marriage.* New York: Norton, 1968.

Locke, Harvey J. *Predicting Adjustment in Marriage: A Comparison of a Divorced and a Happily Married Group.* New York: Holt, 1951.

Luckey, Eleanore B. "Marital Satisfaction and Its Association with Congruence of Perception." *Marriage and Family Living,* 22:49-54, 1960.

Magoun, F. Alexander. *Love and Marriage.* New York: Harper, 1956.

Mangus, A. R. "Role Theory and Marriage Counseling." *Social Forces,* 35 (March):209-20, 1957.

Manville, W. H. "The Locker Room Boys." *Cosmopolitan,* 166:110-15, 1969.

McConkie, Bruce R. *Doctrinal New Testament Commentary.* Salt Lake City: Bookcraft, Inc., 1973.

McKay, David O. *Gospel Ideals.* Salt Lake City: Deseret News Press, 1953.

Mead, George H. *Mind, Self, and Society.* Chicago: University of Chicago Press, 1934.

————. *The Philosophy of the Act.* Chicago: University of Chicago Press, 1938.

Miller, Sherod, Elam W. Nunnally, and Daniel B. Wackman. *Alive and Aware.* Minneapolis: Interpersonal Communication Programs, Inc., 1975.

Murphy, Donald C., and Lloyd A. Mendelson. "Use of the Observational Method in the Study of Live Marital Communication." *Journal of Marriage and the Family,* 35:256-63, 1973.

Murstein, D. I., M. Cerreto, and H. G. McDonald. "A Theory and Investigation of the Effects of Exchange Orientation on Marriage and Friendship." *Journal of Marriage and the Family,* 39:543-48, 1977.

Navran, L. "Communication and Adjustment in Marriage." *Family Process,* 6:173-84, 1967.

Nelson, Joel I. "Clique Contacts and Family Orientations." *American Sociological Review,* 2:663-72, 1966.

O'Neill, Nena, and George C. *Open Marriage.* New York: Avon Books, 1972.

Ort, Robert S. "A Study of Role-Conflicts as Related to Happiness in Marriage," *Journal of Abnormal and Social Psychology,* 45:691-99, 1950.

Packer, Boyd K. "Eternal Love." *1970 Speeches of the Year.* Provo, Utah: Brigham Young University Press, 1970.

———. "The Equal Rights Amendment." *Ensign,* Mar. 1977, p. 6.

Parson, Talcott. *The Social System.* New York: The Free Press, 1951.

Peale, R. S. *The Adventure of Being a Wife.* Englewood Cliffs, N. J.: Prentice-Hall, 1971.

Pincus, Gregory. *The Control of Fertility.* New York: Academic Press, 1965.

Powell, J. J. *Why Am I Afraid to Love?* London: Fontana/Collins, 1974.

Pratt, Parley P. *Key to the Science of Theology.* Salt Lake City: Deseret Book, 1855, p. 173.

O'Neill, George C., and Nena O'Neill. "Patterns in Group Sexual Activity." *Journal of Sex Research,* 6:101-12, 1970.

Raush, Harold L., Ann C. Greif, and Jane Nugent. "Communication in Couples and Families." In W. R. Burr, R. Hill, F. I. Nye, and I. L. Reiss (eds.), *Contemporary Theories About the Family.* New York: The Free Press, 1979.

Raush, Harold L., William A. Barry, Richard K. Hertel, and Mary Ann Sawin. *Communication, Conflict and Marriage.* San Francisco: Jossey-Bass Publishers, 1974.

Reymert, Martin L. *Feelings and Emotions.* New York: McGraw-Hill, 1950.

Rodgers, Roy H. *Family Interaction and Transaction.* Englewood Cliffs, N. J.: Prentice-Hall, 1973.

Rogers, Carl R. *Client-Centered Therapy.* Boston: Houghton-Mifflin, 1951.

Rollins, Boyd C. "Value Consensus on Cohesion in the Husband-Wife Dyad." Unpublished Ph.D. dissertation, Cornell University, 1961.

Rollins, Boyd C., and Darwin L. Thomas. "Parental Support, Power, and Control Techniques in the Socialization of Children." In W. R. Burr, R. Hill, F. I. Nye, and I. L. Reiss (eds.), *Contemporary Theories About the Family.* New York: The Free Press, 1979.

Romney, Marion G. "In the Image of God." *Ensign,* Mar. 1978, pp. 2-4.

———. "Guidance of the Holy Spirit." *Ensign,* Jan. 1980, pp. 2-5.

Scoresby, A. Lynn. *The Marriage Dialogue.* Reading, Massachusetts: Addison Wesley, 1977.

Scoresby, A. Lynn, Franklin J. Apolonio, and Gary Hatch. "Action Plans: An Approach to Behavior Change in Marriage Education." *Family Coordinator,* 23:343-48, 1974.

Sears, Robert R., Eleanor E. Maccoby, and Harry Levin. *Patterns of Child Rearing.* Evanston, Illinois: Row, Peterson, 1957.

Shibutani, Tomotsu. *Society and Personality.* Englewood Cliffs, N. J.: Prentice-Hall, 1961.

Smith, Joseph Fielding (comp.) *Teachings of the Prophet Joseph Smith.* Salt Lake City: The Deseret News Press, 1938.

Spiegel, John P. "The Resolution of Role Conflict Within the Family." In Norman A. Bell and Ezra F. Vogel (eds.), *The Family*. Glencoe: The Free Press, 1957, pp. 545-64.

Spiro, Melford E. *Kibbutz: Venture in Utopia*. Cambridge, Mass.: Harvard University Press, 1956.

Straus, Murray A. "Power and Support Structure of the Family in Relation to Socialization." *Journal of Marriage and the Family*, 26:318-26, 1964.

———. "Leveling, Civility, and Violence." *Journal of Marriage and the Family*, 36:13-20, 1974.

Tallman, Irving. "The Family as a Small Problem Solving Group." *Journal of Marriage and the Family*, 32:94-104, 1970.

Terman, Lewis M. *Psychological Factors in Marital Happiness*. New York: McGraw-Hill, 1938.

Thomas, Lewis M. *Marital Communication and Decision Making: Analysis Assessment and Change*. New York: The Free Press, 1977.

Turner, Ralph H. *Family Interaction*. New York: Wiley, 1970.

Wallen, J. L. *Behavior Description*. Portland: Northwest Regional Educational Laboratory, July 1968 (mimeo).

Waller, Willard, and R. L. Hill. *The Family: A Dynamic Interpretation*, Rev. ed. New York: Dryden, 1951.

Watzlawick, Paul, Janet Lemick Beaven, and Don D. Jackson. *Pragmatics of Human Communication*. New York: Norton, 1967.

Widtsoe, John A. *A Rational Theology*, 7th ed. Salt Lake City: Deseret Book Co., 1965.

———. *Priesthood and Church Government*. Salt Lake City: Deseret Book, 1954, p. 83.

Wilie, Ruth C. *The Self Concept*, vol. 2. Lincoln, Neb.: University of Nebraska Press, 1979.

Wirth, L. "Consensus and Mass Communication." *American Sociological Review*, 13:1-15, 1948.

Yorgason, Brenton G., Terry R. Baker, and Wesley R. Burr. *From This Day Forth*. Salt Lake City: Bookcraft, Inc., 1982.

Young, Brigham. *Discourses of Brigham Young*. Selected by John A. Widtsoe. Salt Lake City: Deseret Book Co., 1941.

———. *Journal of Discourses*, vol. 1. Liverpool: Richards and Islington, 1854.

INDEX